In Praise of Negotiating the

"Chelsea Wakefield's work is a major contribution to our field and *Negotiating the Inner Peace Treaty* is a real gift to anyone interested in finding out more about the many selves that make up our Inner Cast of Characters. It's a great read! Clear, thoughtful, and lyrical, it guides the reader along the fascinating journey of self-discovery with a "four-step process for living", providing support and practical suggestions along the way."

Hal Stone, Ph.D. & Sidra Stone, Ph.D.
Creators of Voice Dialogue, the Aware Ego Process, and the
Psychology of the Selves and authors of *Embracing Our Selves;
Embracing Your Inner Critic; Partnering;* and *The Shadow King.*

"In this creative work, Chelsea Wakefield presents a lucid, practical set of tools for those not formally trained in Jungian psychology, who seek to come to peace with the inner turmoil that fragments our lives. Her personal and clinical experiences give a depth and uniqueness to the soul nature of her work. Her clear presentation of shadow and dream work are very helpful. Most unique is her reminding us of how to work with our Inner Cast in the process of peace seeking and Individuation. I highly recommend it!"

Keith Parker, Ph. D.
Jungian Analyst, author of *Seven Cherokee Myths.*

"*Negotiating the Inner Peace Treaty* inevitably leads to greater peace and productivity in the outer world as well. The exercises and insights offered here are profound, clear and attainable for anyone. I am particularly impressed with how this book presents a view of Jung's "archetypes" that is lucid, moving and transformative."

Jeremy Taylor, D.Min.
Unitarian Minister and author of *Dream Work* and
Where People Fly and Water Runs Uphill.

"Chelsea Wakefield brings a rare intelligence and wit to her depth of clinical training and practical savvy. In *Negotiating the Inner Peace Treaty* she leads us to explore the extraordinary drama of our lives, from everyday scripts to realms of mystery and shadow—moving us beyond wounds and archetypes of the past toward ways to open our minds, resolve our conflicts, expand our potential for love and intimacy. The result is a guide that is both visionary and integrative. I will recommend it widely to colleagues and clients."

Gina Ogden, PhD, LMFT
Author of *The Heart and Soul of Sex* and *The Return of Desire.*

"Chelsea brilliantly approaches dream work in the most natural effective way by actively engaging our "Inner Cast of Characters" the way the dream does. She places us in the middle of the dream, actively engaging the various part of who we are in a negotiation and dialogue which not only provides us with an understanding of our dream but permits us to actively bring about a new understanding and acceptance of our whole selves."

Robert Hoss, MS
Author of *Dream Language*, Past President of IASD, Haden Institute faculty and director of the Dream Science Foundation.

"A great work! Chelsea gets rave reviews every time she gives a presentation on *Negotiating the Inner Peace Treaty* to The Haden Institute Training and Conferences!"

Bob Haden, M.Div. MA
Episcopal priest, pastoral counselor, founder and director of the Haden Institute and author of *Unopened Letters from God.*

NEGOTIATING THE INNER PEACE TREATY

Becoming The Person You Were Born To Be

by

CHELSEA WAKEFIELD, LCSW

BALBOA
PRESS
A DIVISION OF HAY HOUSE

Balboa Press books may be ordered through booksellers or by contacting:

Balboa Press
A Division of Hay House
1663 Liberty Drive
Bloomington, IN 47403
www.balboapress.com
1-(877) 407-4847

ISBN: 978-1-4525-4404-5 (sc)
ISBN: 978-1-4525-4405-2 (hc)
ISBN: 978-1-4525-4403-8 (e)

Library of Congress Control Number: 2012900377

Printed in the United States of America

Balboa Press rev. date: 02/10/2012

To Tom—
#1 Supporter, Wonderful Husband, Sage Father,
Border Collie, Safe Harbor and Soul Mate.
I love your Inner Cast!
Thank you for loving mine.

INTRODUCTION

You are about to undertake a wondrous journey. It is a journey of self-discovery that will change your life. It does not require a passport or an airline ticket. It only requires the courage and willingness to look inward and to engage yourself in all your amazing complexity. It is a fascinating, inspiring and occasionally surprising journey, for we are many faceted creatures.

For some of you, this may be the first time that you have dared to explore your inner world. Others of you are seasoned travelers. All of you will find some new tools for navigating the psyche, and a means of "charting" your discoveries. You will discover new possibilities and unearth buried treasure. Finally, you will make peace with ALL of who you are.

The book includes some theory, some stories, and lots of ways of exploring the mystery that is you. I have found the method to be complementary with a wide variety of therapy methods and spiritual perspectives.

Chapter One will introduce you to the central metaphor of the book, the *Inner Theatre of Our Lives*. It will outline some basic ideas and describe the four-step process of working with your *Inner Cast of Characters*: *Naming, Knowing, Negotiating* and *Integrating. Part One* will introduce you to Patricia and Dominic and show how they used the process to resolve some difficult struggles. You will learn a technique for gathering *Inner Characters* who are in conflict around an *Inner Round Table* to negotiate creative solutions for life's perplexing problems.

Part Two talks about the places where our inner *Negotiations* get stuck. It will cover the unconscious *Scripts* we live, and introduce you to two important *Inner Characters* that have more influence on how we live than we generally realize, the *Innocent* and the *Orphan*. *Part Two* will also help you to identify and deal with your *Not So Supporting Cast*. These include the *Inner Critic* and the *Voices of Pressure* and *Warning* that undermine your peace and interfere with your capacity to move forward.

Part Three is about *Integrating* what you need to become whole. In this section you will learn to use *Shadow Work* and *Dream Work* as tools for illumination, healing and transformation. You will learn how to access the deep resources of your *Soul Print* and develop potentials you never knew existed.

The entire journey is ultimately about *Individuation*, a Jungian term that means living increasingly from your most essential *Self,* that which I call the *Soul Print*. When you make peace with ALL of who you are, and open yourself to the purposeful creativity that is ever seeking to express itself through you, your life will change in amazing ways.

The most important outcome of this work is the development of a deepening sense of peace and trust in the unfolding process of life, the establishment of a quiet center that will hold. From this *Calm Core*, you can live confidently and consciously, even as you weather the storms of living.

I'd like to give you permission to engage this book in a variety of ways. You can read straight through or you can hop around and read what interests you most. You can read one chapter a night curled up in bed and sleep on it, or you can go away for a quiet weekend and really dive deep. You can answer every exploratory question, or you can answer just the ones that speak to you at this time. You might consider gathering some fellow travellers and forming a book study group or a dream group. Whatever you do, see if you can incorporate this perspective in an ongoing way of looking at yourself and your life.

As I finish writing this, I am aware that we are living in increasingly conflicted times. Many people are fearful because the bastions of safety that we once relied upon seem to be eroding. Our culture encourages us to look for answers and meaning outside of ourselves, to look to others for hope. We are disconnected from our deep resources. It is my hope that through this work you will discover new sources of wisdom and replenishment as you make peace with yourself, your life, and ultimately with others. As the old song said, "Let there be peace on earth, and let it begin with me."

Making peace is no easy task, but it becomes more crucial to our world every day. It begins with each of us doing our own inner work. This book will give you some good tools for doing that. Here is a list of outcomes that others have experienced as they have *Negotiated* their own *Inner Peace Treaties*.

Understand yourself better
Make peace with yourself and your past
Transcend your self-limiting scripts and develop new potentials
Heal old emotional wounds and reduce your reactivity
Improve your relationships
Make better life choices and become more confident
Become more discerning and less judgmental
Develop your creativity
Experience a greater sense of personal empowerment
Learn to use Dream Work as a tool for personal transformation
Transform your relationship with your dark side through Shadow Work
Discover the meaning and purpose of your life

It is my hope that as you engage this process you can increasingly claim these outcomes. As you clear the path to your core essence, your *Soul Print*, you can bring your gifts to the world. When you do this, your life will be increasingly meaningful, fulfilling, and joyful. This is how each of us can do our part to heal the world.

I would love to hear your stories, how you creatively apply this work and how it changes your life.

Deep peace to you,
Chelsea Wakefield, LCSW
2012

ORIGINS OF THIS WORK

My Story

I was 23 years old when I was first introduced to the concept that I had a variety of *Inner Selves* living in me. Bob and Mary Goulding had created a new approach called *Redecision Therapy*, which blended *Gestalt Therapy* with *Transactional Analysis*. I attended a workshop they gave in Santa Cruz, California and they asked for a volunteer. I raised my hand.

Bob asked me what I wanted to work on, and I began to talk about the discouragement and self condemnation I felt that I had not accomplished certain professional milestones in my life. He smiled and asked me how I had come to this distressing conclusion and we identified an *Inner Voice* that he called the *Accountant*. Bob asked me to move over into an empty chair and had me speak from the perspective of the *Accountant*, who seemed to be a highly critical, male voice. The *Accountant* detailed expectations and standards that no human being at 23 years of age could hope to achieve. I was amazed when I heard the list out loud. Bob asked me if I'd like to fire this overbearing *Accountant* and release myself from the relentless pressure that he was putting on me. Yes, I did!

As I fired the *Accountant*, I immediately felt the release of internal pressure and an influx of new energy for my life. In his place I enrolled a very creative, relaxed, earthy *Wise Woman* who could encourage me. She reassured me that I didn't have to be in such a hurry and that all my goals would come to fruition in their perfect time. This was my first experience of separating out from an *Inner Voice* and working with an inner set of "people" to change my experience of living. True to the words of that earthy *Wise Woman*, I set out in my life and began to accomplish a great many things in my life. I still encountered than mean old *Accountant* periodically, but now I knew how to deal with him.

When I became a mother, I began to grapple with a new set of competing agendas. There were aspects of myself that were fading into the past, crowded out by new responsibilities. I loved my new life, but I missed my old one. Who was I now? How was I going to reconcile my ambitious self with her professional goals with this surprising desire to quit everything and devote my life to making a home and raising my son? How would I express my artistic side? Different *Inner Selves* were in conflict.

Around that same time, my seventy-three-year old mother experienced a significant personal crisis. I was overtaken by guilt. I felt that I should have been able to prevent this situation if I had been paying closer attention to her. I blamed myself and in the weeks to come, I was overtaken by a dark mood and a sense of foreboding and hopelessness that I had not experienced since childhood. The world suddenly seemed uncertain, and feelings from long ago came forward to haunt me.

I had been in therapy years before and I realized I needed to go back. So I got a referral for a therapist who had a good reputation for working with depression and anxiety. He was cognitively oriented, and we began to look at my thought distortions, including the irrational belief that I should have, or could have somehow prevented my mother's loss. Identifying irrational beliefs and releasing myself from them was very helpful and I began to feel better, but I still had the uneasy feeling that there was something deeper that needed to be addressed.

I kept thinking about the dark mood that had overtaken me. It was as if some primordial creature from the bottom of a deep lake had surfaced. I had the sense that "she" was still in the background, observing this therapy, but not participating in it. She had receded in the light of all this "talk therapy," but I feared that she might return again someday and overtake me, should I ever face some serious life challenge.

One afternoon, I sat down and began to journal about my process. I decided to write about my various parts of self, to look at the conflicts between them. I decided to think of them as "characters." They represented different moods and aspects of my personality, different jobs I had held and different chapters of my life. I came up with a group of *Inner Characters* that I called *The Committee*. Some were male, some were female, some were young, some were old. I named them all and described their characteristics and what area of my life they were active in.

The model intrigued my therapist. He assured me that I did *not* have a "multiple personality." I knew that, but I still didn't know how one goes about resolving the conflict between the irrational parts of oneself, all the competing wishes and longings and fears and agendas inside. How would my *Inner Professor*, the *Lady of the Manor*, the *Social Justice Crusader* and the *Devoted Mother* ever get along? Where did the *Brooding Creature* from the lake fit in? My therapist assured me that my "rational, functional selves" were in control now and that they could handle any problems I would face in the future. I still had misgivings, but I liked him, and didn't want to undermine the pleasure he felt at my "cure." We finished our work together shortly after that.

On my own, I continued to explore my metaphor of a system of "sub-selves" that lived in me. I began to journal and observe how my *Inner Characters* operated in different situations. I found an old acting book that had "character development" exercises in it and used it to flesh them out. I added some new characters to the list. I developed a system of journaling that allowed me to consult with my *Inner Committee* to solve problems, handle difficult situations, and make decisions about my life. What was once an anxious cacophony of voices inside me became a resource, rather than an annoyance.

When I felt overcome by strong emotions, I began to check in and ask "who" was upset within me and what their problem was. When I asked them what their needs and concerns were, I found that I could address them. My anxiety dissipated. I became less needy and emotional. I began to feel more centered, present, and peaceful.

As I continue to dialogue and journal, patterns in my life began to become evident. I became aware that there was a theme that laced throughout my life having to do with being a *Compassionate Counselor* and an *Advocate*. I had grown up reading biographies of strong women who had made a difference in the world. Several times, during the years I worked in business, bosses sat me down and said, "Chelsea, this is not social work." One had kiddingly dubbed me "the girl most likely to join the Peace Corps."

My *Inner Committee* was sorting out the next chapter of my life. As I reviewed my life, it was very clear that I had been drawn for years to the study of human potential, both spiritual and psychological. It was also evident that the archetype of the *Social Worker* was strong in my *Soul Print*. So, with the full support of my *Inner Committee*, I entered graduate school to train as a clinical social worker and psychotherapist. It was there that I encountered the work of Carl Jung for the first time.

The reference was only brief, but I was thrilled by Jung's understanding that there was an important intersection between the realms of psychology and spirituality. He believed that the work of our lives was to discovery our unique "destiny" rather than conform to theories and models of living defined by others. When we began to tune in and follow the information coming from our soul, our lives became whole.

After graduate school, I continued to study Jungian Psychology and began Jungian analysis. I soon discovered that the kind of engaged dialogue practice I had begun doing was something that Jung himself practiced and referred to as *Active Imagination*. Jungian analysis opened up *Dream Work* and introduced me to my

Shadow Material. I began to engage the deep nonverbal aspects of my being. In doing so, I began to respect rather than fear the dark creatures within me. I continued to dialogue with my sub-personalities, identifying their archetypal energies, working with my *Inner Characters* that carried my wounding and caused me difficulty (my complexes), untangling the threads of my life. I began to use my system of inner work with clients and teach it in workshops. Everyone found it helpful and many Jungians described it as an accessible map of the journey of *Individuation*.

In 2005, Susan Sims Smith introduced me to the work of Hal and Sidra Stone, whose work dovetailed beautifully with mine. I began to study with them and to learn a new technique called *Voice Dialogue*. The introduction of *Voice Dialogue* into my *Inner Peace Treaty* process took my interview process off the pages of a journal into an actual interviewing process. It also taught me that archetypes are not categories. You can experience them. They are systems of energy.

The theoretical underpinning of *Negotiating the Inner Peace Treaty* has developed from many years of study in psychological theory that includes *Ego Psychology, Transactional Analysis Scriptwork, Re-decision Therapy, Gestalt* dialogue methods, *Pesso-Boyden Psychomotor* work, *Transpersonal,* and *Jungian Psychology* with its understanding of archetypes, complexes, shadow and dream work.

Other famous theorists in addition to Jung, who have worked with the model of *Inner Selves* are Roberto Assagioli (*Psychosynthesis*) and Virginia Satir (*Family Systems*), who referred to them as "sub-personalities." Eric Berne explored the world of internalized scripts and began to analyze how different ego states (Parent, Adult and Child) affect how we interpret life, react and interact with others. Fritz Perls (*Gestalt Therapy*) developed a technique of creating insight by moving people back and forth between two chairs as they externalized the voices in their heads. John Bradshaw had begun to work extensively with shame and the *Inner Child.*

Joseph Moreno blended theatre concepts with an externalization of our inner psychological processes to create *Psychodrama*. Ira Progoff developed a method for exploring our depths through inner dialogues and journal writing in the *Intensive Journal Process*.

Hal and Sidra Stone, two important teachers in my life, developed a technique called *Voice Dialogue*, which was built on a Jungian foundation. The Stones emphasize interviewing each *Inner Self* and getting to know them individually. Each has a distinct feel, viewpoint, and set of qualities. As you dialogue with each one and separate out from their energies, awareness increases. The development of an *Aware Ego* means that you still "house" all of these inner energies, but you have separated out from them. Thus, they no longer lead you around unconsciously. You are now the conductor of a wonderful *Inner Orchestra*. As you expand your awareness, you can make space for new energies to be developed and incorporated into your *Inner Self System*.

To this list of theorists, I add my own metaphors, perspectives, and the exploratory methods outlined in this book.

TABLE OF CONTENTS

PART 3-INTEGRATION—SHADOW WORK DREAM
WORK WHAT PEOPLE NEED TO BE WHOLE

NEGOTIATING THE INNER PEACE TREATY

PART ONE

NAMING, KNOWING AND NEGOTIATING
IN THE THEATRE OF OUR LIVES

CHAPTER 1

THE THEATRE OF OUR LIVES

*"All the world's a stage, and all the men
and women merely players. They have their
exits and their entrances and one man, in his
time, plays many parts"*
Shakespeare

Human beings are not simple creatures. Shakespeare said that
we play many parts during our time on earth. Underneath the
surface of our lives, forces compel us to play particular roles. We
live out underlying scripts, but sometimes we mystify ourselves by
behaving in ways that are "out of character." *Inner Peace Treaty*
work is about exploring these hidden forces, and learning to direct
them in creative ways so that we can fulfill our greatest potential.

I have found the metaphors of the theatre useful in describing
the workings of people's inner lives. If we view our impulses,
thoughts, moods, reactions and behavior patterns, as if they were
coming from an *Inner Cast of Characters,* this framework opens
up a whole set of possibilities. If we name our *Inner Characters,*
we can dialogue with them, and begin to recognize when they are
active on the stage of our lives. How do they operate, to influence
us for good or ill? We can learn their histories, who wrote their
scripts, and what their needs and agendas are.

Our *Inner Characters* play out the different roles and chapters of
our lives. They enter and exit the stage and interact with each other.
Each *Inner Character* generates a recognizable set of perspectives,
energies and body sensations that influence us to act in particular
ways.

We are often unaware of these underlying dynamics, even though they drive us constantly and cause us to be at war with ourselves. With awareness, we can transform our internal conflict into an alliance for living an integrated, purpose filled life. A life that springs from our deepest essence is an adventure to be lived with passion and curiosity rather than a series of problems to be solved.

The Inner Cast of Characters

People don't usually think about how multi-faceted they are and the problems this creates. I am not talking about having a "multiple personality disorder," which requires serious clinical intervention. I am talking about how normal people have conversations with themselves and will say things like, "a part of me wants to do this and another part of me wants to do that."

The process outlined in this book is for healthy people who want to become more integrated and anchored in a centered awareness, directing the potential of the sub-personalities within them. Our feelings do not always agree with our thoughts. Our practical and spiritual lives often seem at odds with each other. Our impulses sometimes do not agree with our values. These inner arguments go on under the surface of our awareness, creating much unrest, which manifests itself as a low-grade anxiety or irritation. We find it difficult to settle into a sense of peaceful well-being. How we manage these internal tensions really determines our success and our happiness.

Negotiating the Inner Peace Treaty is about learning to live with clarity and a core sense of peace amidst the diverse agendas and dynamic tensions of your *Inner Self System*. In gathering your differing aspects of self at an *Inner Round Table*, you will learn to resolve inner conflicts, negotiate dynamic alliances, and discover new possibilities for creative and purposeful living.

In the following pages, we will explore the premise that we are multidimensional people. We are beings of tremendous complexity. Although we each have characteristics that we think of as "who we are", there is a lot more going on under the surface. That is why we surprise ourselves and sometimes act in ways that we do not understand. This unexpected behavior can cause us regret and embarrassment. Sometimes we demonstrate acts of profound courage that seem to spring from some unknown place. The fact that we can act in ways beyond our current self-definition shows us that we can move beyond the limits of past history and live into new possibilities.

As we begin to observe our inner dynamics, things that were once a mystery begin to make sense. When we begin to understand our *Inner Cast of Characters*, we can direct their energies. We can discover their scripts and even rewrite them, introducing new story lines and cast members that will result in profound changes.

Most of our *Inner Characters* are there to help us, but they differ in their views of how to accomplish this. Allowing one *Inner Character* to dominate our life, while the needs of other *Inner Characters* are neglected, leads to imbalances and problems. Some *Inner Characters* try to protect us by watching and warning of possible dangers on the horizon. Some criticize our every thought, word and deed, trying to keep us from coloring outside the lines. Some *Inner Characters* comfort, encourage and guide us, like good parents. Some solve problems, analyze situations and formulate plans. Some are childlike, playful, and full of wonder. Some are driven by instinct, with no regard for rules or consequences. Some *Inner Characters* carry the longings of the heart and help us to connect to what is meaningful in human relationships. Some are quiet and monastic and seek soulful communion.

Carl Jung, Archetypes, and Individuation

Carl Jung, the founder of Analytical Psychology, recognized that human beings play many parts and have many inner patterns of being. These patterns spring from a realm called the collective unconscious and are recognizable throughout history and found in all cultures. He called them *Archetypes.*

Archetypal patterns are the basis for all characters and story lines in myths and fairy tales, as well as the story of *our* lives. There is a particular energy and expression at the core of every archetype. Examples of these are the G*ood Mother, the Wise King, the Innocent, the Orphan, the Stern Father, or the Hero.*

Jung also described how "our personal unconscious, as well as the collective unconscious, consists of an indefinite . . . number of complexes or fragmentary personalities." In this book, we will refer to these complexes and fragmentary personalities that take on a life of their own as *Inner Characters.*

Becoming aware of our unconscious patterns and drives, integrating them into the conscious personality, and living ever more deeply into our destiny, Jung called the process of *Individuation.*

How the Inner Self System Develops

Where do these *Inner Characters* come from and why does each person have a different "cast?" Psychologists Hal and Sidra Stone explain this process beautifully in their book, *Embracing Our Selves.* The *Inner Self System* develops from the time we are born. As little children, we are vulnerable and depend on the people around us to take care of us. We learn what kinds of behaviors and personality characteristics will be rewarded and which will be punished. We develop the *Selves* that will protect our vulnerability and help us get our needs met. This author refers to them as our *Inner Cast of Characters.* The aspects of our personality that we disown descend into the unconscious shadow lands of our lives.

When I was introduced to Hal and Sidra Stone's work, I was reminded of the explorations I did in acting classes years ago, where we entered deeply into each character's world to study and understand them. What was reality like for them? How did they come to see it in this way? How did they move and gesture? Each character had a distinct feeling. "Getting into character" meant leaving our own personality behind, becoming someone entirely different, and then returning to our original identity after the play was over. I began to reflect on how fluid identity could be, and how we each have an *Inner Cast of Characters* that play out the roles in our lives. One of Hal and Sidra's greatest contributions to my understanding of the *Inner Self System* is their emphasis on how our *Inner Selves* or *Characters* carry distinct and differing energies which can be identified and understood through a dialogue process.

The Theatre of Our Lives

Many people come into my office with the question of "who am I . . . *really?*" They have a sense that they are more than the face or persona they show to the world. Returning to the metaphors of the theatre, we discover that they are often living a script written by others. This disturbing discovery breaks a spell of unconsciousness and starts them on the journey to discover their essential *Self,* the path of *Individuation.*

Most of us don't think about what motivates us to do the things we do, let alone *who* is driving us. We are engaged in the flow of life. Each of us has a unique *Inner Cast of Characters.* Our foundational "cast" develops in childhood. The experiences we have, the roles we play, our relationships, the work we do, and the challenges we face influence our *Inner Cast* over the course of our life. At one time or another certain *Inner Characters* may have larger or smaller roles. Some of our *Inner Cast* get written out of the script, left behind in the mists of the past. New *Inner Cast* members are added as we develop or as the need arises. *Shadow Selves* may emerge unexpectedly, bringing upheaval or the invitation to grow into greater wholeness.

Most of us have a set of *Inner Characters* that operate consistently in the world. This is how people gain a sense of our "character". It is a good thing to have a stable, consistent ego identity, but this identity is only one of many possibilities within us.

YOUR INNER CAST OF CHARACTERS

Here are some ways of thinking about your *Inner Cast of Characters:*

Main Players

All of us have aspects of self that clearly define us. I call these *Main Players*, because they have starring roles, occupy the stage most of the time and motivate the primary actions of our lives. We have *Main Players* in each of the domains of our lives. They develop out of our roles in family and work life, achievement and reputation, traits and abilities, wounds and struggles, personal and cultural history, values and beliefs, body and health, sexuality, group affiliations and spiritual life. *Main Players* in different domains of our lives, such as work and home, may have significant conflicts with one another.

Supporting Cast

Our *Supporting Cast* is not as visible as our *Main Players* because they operate behind the scenes. They watch over us, attending to our needs, providing inner nurture, structure, encouragement and protection. They help us plan and problem solve, set limits and remind us of our values. Some people have an inadequate internal support system. *Inner Supporting Cast* members can be invited in and integrated through *Inner Peace Treaty* work.

Not So Supporting Cast

The *Not So Supporting Cast,* includes such characters as the *Inner Critic,* who harasses us and tears us down. The *Voice of Pressure* will not let us rest. The *Script Monitor* and the *Rule Keeper* constrain us, and the *Voices of Warning* frighten or shame us, reminding us of painful events or secrets.

Inner Children

Behind our more powerful *Inner Characters* you will find vulnerable *Inner Children.* We try to forget about them, but they are still with us and can influence us significantly. I call these parts of self the *Kids Behind the Curtain* because they often hide behind the masks we show the world.

Retired Selves

Our *Inner Cast* changes over time. Each of us has a set of *Retired Selves* who carry important pieces of our personal history. When life becomes a litany of dull work routines and family responsibilities, the aging football star remembers the glory days of adoring girls and cheering crowds. The harried mother of teenage children may reminisce about the days when her beauty and charm captivated the heart of the midlife man who now sits absorbed in the television set. These longed-for "days gone by" are remembered by our *Retired Selves.*

Sometimes people get stuck in life because they hang onto an *Inner Character* that needs to be retired. I see this in *Empty Nest Mothers* who must now redefine their purpose, and write a new chapter of life once their children are grown. *Corporate Executives* retire and must find a new identity apart from their profession. *Veterans* and *War Heros* sit at the VFW bar, reminiscing about the supercharged days when death was a constant companion and their buddies had their backs.

Shadow Players

Finally, locked away in trunks, closets, and the basement of the internal theatre, dwell our *Shadow Players,* the disowned parts of self we banished because they were unacceptable or dangerous to our survival. Here is where our most troublesome material resides; all the impulses, instincts, longings, trauma and anything that makes us frightened or uncomfortable about ourselves.

It is important to understand that everyone has shadow material, even those who live quiet, idyllic lives. Good, moral people, and those that exemplify our highest societal virtues have *Shadow Selves. Pleasers* often have a *Shadow Rebel. High Achievers* can have *Shadow Slackers.*

Shadow Characters can hijack the system with sudden unexplained actions or overwhelming emotion. This is why we need to get to know them. They often appear on the stage of our night time dreams as terrible, frightening characters or cataclysmic events.

Uncovering shadow material can sometimes be frightening and disturbing, but it is also the arena where some of our greatest potential lies. It helps to travel this terrain with an experienced guide, who can hold a safe space for dark and instinctual material. Dark shadow, once surfaced and consciously integrated, often becomes the raw material of our greatest gifts to the world.

It is also important to understand that not all shadow is dark. We tend to think of our shadow material as that which is negative or shameful, but many of us banish that which is most bright and beautiful about us. We do not want to stand out too much.

We do not want others to envy or resent us for being gifted or "special".

The Mystery That We Are

You can see that there is a lot going on inside of us. This is why we are often such a mystery to ourselves. Even when we are trying to be real and authentic, the question remains, "which *me* is the real *me?*"

Each situation in life requires something different from us. The *Inner Characters* that operate at work are different from the *Inner Characters* that operate at home. The face we show in public, our *Persona*, is not the same face that we show in our most private moments. When we return to our childhood home, we often find ourselves feeling and behaving like the person we were when we were kids. Without defining the *Inner Cast* and who is behind the scenes, a lot remains hidden or unknown.

Sharon's Story

My client, Sharon, went home for the holidays. Seated around the table after the meal, the topic turned to the economy and current politics. Sharon was forty two years old, and a successful trial attorney, who was able to formulate powerful closing arguments in the face of tough opponents. She was well informed about politics and began to offer her own well considered opinion. After about six words, her older brother, John, cut in and began to quote a popular television news commentator. The whole family immediately turned away from Sharon and began to listen attentively to what John was saying.

Sharon was suddenly overcome by the same feelings of helpless outrage that she had felt as a teenager, when her brother constantly interrupted and ridiculed her ideas. She tried to reassert her opinion, after her brother's disrespectful interruption, but when she began to speak, she heard an odd little voice come out of her mouth. She sounded young and unsure of herself, completely unlike her typical courtroom voice. She suddenly couldn't remember what she was going to say. Her brother gave her a disdainful look and continued to expound opinions that Sharon considered simplistic and uninformed.

Sharon had been shut down just like when they were kids. She sat at the table, overcome and wanting to cry. In the midst of old family dynamics, she had been driven back into the thirteen year old self they used to call *Little Sis.* The confident, articulate *Attorney* she had become vanished into thin air.

Sitting in my office the following week, she reviewed the experience with some dismay. "How does this happen? It was like I was in a time warp. I guess to my parents and my brother, I'll always just be *Little Sis.*"

Sharon was struggling with one of the important issues of life. Will we allow ourselves to be defined by others? Are we at the mercy of old plot lines or can we move beyond these constraining scripts?

As Sharon and I worked together, she began to develop a stronger *Inner Supporting Cast,* and she was able to hold her own on subsequent trips home.

Who Do You Think You Are?... Your "Soul Print"

"Who am I . . . . *really?*" is one of the fundamental questions of all time. We share common human experiences, but our individual essence, our *Soul Print*, is as unique as our fingerprint.

My use of the term *Soul Print* parallels what the Jungian psychology refers to as the *Self.* It is hard to maintain contact with our essential *Soul Print* as we go through the process of growing up and becoming socialized. So much of our *Soul Print* gets layered over by pressures to achieve, to please and fulfill our parent's expectations, then our spouse's and employer's. Before you know it, our life script gets written by others. All of this makes the question, "who do you think you are?" more difficult to answer.

How We Define Ourselves — Our Ego Identity

There are many ways in which we define ourselves:

- ***Roles and Relationships***: We are all someone to somebody, a son or daughter, sister or brother, mother or father, partner, wife, husband, widow, friend, caretaker, teacher, employee, etc. We are different people in different places depending on the roles and relationships.
- ***Achievements and Reputation***: Our successes and failures, our resumes, education, awards, titles, lost opportunities and roads not taken all define us.
- ***Group Affiliations:*** We belong to and identify with various groups: cultural, religious, political, philosophical, and recreational. We are Democrats, Republicans, Christians, Buddhists, Environmentalists, Harley Davidson Bikers, Runners, Artists, Foodies, etc. We have learned that we are often judged by the company we keep.
- ***Health/Body:*** Our appearance defines us, as well as our health and how we relate to our bodies. People who are diabetic, disabled, or mentally ill can struggle with being limited by these labels.
- ***Natural Abilities, Gifts and Traits***: This includes our talents, personality traits, strengths, weaknesses, habits and quirks. People who have an Astrological Chart done, or take certain personality tests, such as the Myers Briggs, may identify strongly with their typology.

Not immediately visible to others, but still operating in our inner world are:

- ***Personal and Cultural Histories***: We each have pivotal life events that shape our sense of self and our world view. Our family and cultural history also have a significant influence on our values and how we view life.
- ***Values and Beliefs:*** These are generally learned from our culture and upbringing although they can change as we grow up and re-evaluate our lives. We see everything through the lens of our beliefs and focus on what we value.
- ***Wounds, Fears and Vulnerabilities:*** These are all part of our personal history, but can become a major part of our ongoing identity. They must be addressed in order for us to move forward.
- ***Goals, Dreams and Longings:*** These are things that really matter to us, but they are deeply personal and not always known by others, including experiences we long for, and fantasies that play in our heads.
- ***Life Skills***: The life skills we gather shape our identity because they affect how we interact with others. These skills are learned and include: communication and relationship skills, conflict resolution, time and money management, organization and life planning skills, and the capacity to manage intense emotions, like fear, anger, grief, frustration, despair, sexual arousal, and anxiety.
- ***Sexuality***: Our early sexual experiences, sexual identity, values, longings and practices all define us. Anyone who falls outside the box of "accepted mainstream sexuality" knows how significantly their sexuality can affect how others view them and how they feel about themselves.

- *Spiritual Life*: This domain can include religious practices, dream work, and any other method we use to contemplate the Holy, or listen to the voice of Soul.

Uncovering Our Unique Essence — The Soul Print

Even if you were to go through this whole list and write down "who you are" in each of these areas of life, it still would not capture the totality or essence of who you are.

Uncovering your deepest essence often becomes something akin to an archeological dig. People tell the story of their lives based on their current frames of reference. Our stories are too small to contain the vastness of our souls. Over the course of this book you will brush away the sediment and uncover the underground secrets of who you are, your true essence, your *Soul Print*.

Our essential *Soul Print* calls us to a particular pathway in life. Each person's destiny is different. The more a person is aligned with their essential *Soul Print*, the more meaningful their life will become.

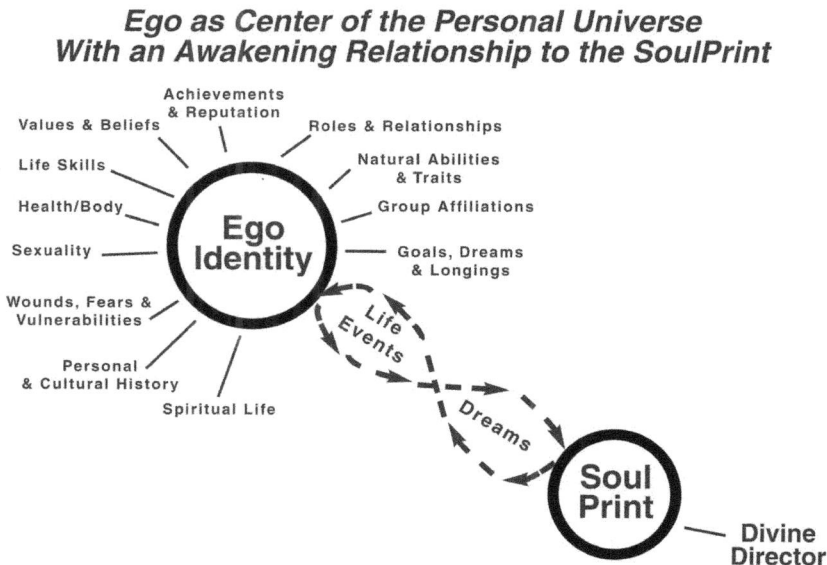

Ego as Center of the Personal Universe With an Awakening Relationship to the SoulPrint

Achievements & Reputation

Values & Beliefs

Roles & Relationships

Life Skills

Natural Abilities & Traits

Health/Body

Group Affiliations

Ego Identity

Sexuality

Goals, Dreams & Longings

Wounds, Fears & Vulnerabilities

Life Events

Personal & Cultural History

Spiritual Life

Dreams

Soul Print

Divine Director

The Observing Self

One of the most important and natural outcomes of doing *Inner Peace Treaty* work is the development of what psychiatrist Arthur Deikman called the *Observing Self.* You may also be familiar with the Buddhist reference to the *Witness State.* In this state, we experience separating out from our internal processes, and moving to a place of neutral observation.

This is hard to grasp until you begin to experience it. We are generally swept up in our internal dialogues, thinking about events in the past or anticipating events in the future. We are rarely ever in the present moment. We rarely slow down enough to observe our own internal process or think about our thinking.

If all of the things we use to identify ourselves were stripped away, there would still be someone there, quietly watching. In this quiet place is profound peace and clarity, a place without agenda.

"Emotions, thoughts, impulse, images, and sensations
are contents of consciousness: we witness them; we are
aware of their existence. Likewise, the body, the
self image, and the self concept are all constructs that we observe.
But our core sense of personal existence, the "I"
is located in awareness itself, not in its content."
Arthur Deikman

Consciousness or awareness is a process, not an achievement. In *Inner Peace Treaty Work* we become aware by defining our *Inner Cast of Characters,* beginning to observe them, and realizing that while we play out the events of our lives, we are more than the events. In *Inner Peace Treaty* work, we are not seeking to get rid of anything in ourselves. We are seeking to have a new relationship with it, to direct our inner energies in ways that are creative and life giving. In this process of unfolding growth we will also expand and integrate new potentials that have been hidden or undeveloped.

As you begin to separate out from the story that others have given you, and the limiting ways in which you have defined yourself, you will begin to experience yourself as something far greater than the contents of your life. Your own unique *Essential Self* will begin to glimmer, and you will experience a great sense of calm amidst the sea of changes. You will begin to understand that you are both participant and observer of an awesome unfolding process, the mystery of your life.

You will have an increasing sense of confidence that you can dance with the flow of life, and respond creatively to what comes your way. This is living in a state of grace, from a *Calm Core*, owning all of who you are, and all of who you can become. It is the foundation of profound peace, power and potential.

THE INNER PEACE TREATY PROCESS

STEP ONE: NAMING

In this step, you will identify and *Name* the *Inner Cast of Characters* that play on the inner stage of your life.

Who are the *Main Players,* who are on stage most of the time, living out the central roles of your life? Who is in the *Supporting Cast,* helping you structure your life, attending to underlying needs, warning you of potential dangers, reminding you of values and priorities? Who is running the show, the *Director, Author* or *Orchestrator* of the dramas, romances and comedies of your life? Who is in the *Not So Supporting Cast,* the inner voices that undermine, criticize, frighten, and constrain you?

STEP TWO: KNOWING

You can now get into conversation with your *Inner Characters*, ask exploratory questions, dialogue and come to understand their wants, needs and agendas. What are they concerned about? What is their history and what is at stake for them? Look behind the scenes to see if there are hidden characters that are influential players. Understanding creates a foundation for the next step, *Negotiating*. Just as in the outer world, *Inner Characters* whose concerns are taken seriously are more likely to cooperate and work towards mutually agreeable solutions.

In the process of naming and dialoguing with your *Inner Characters*, you will begin to have the experience of separating out from the drama. This is the beginning of the experience of the *Observing Self*. In Buddhism, this non-judgmental place in the psyche is called the *Witness State*. Notice what it feels like to be able to observe and reflect on the process of life without being caught up in it. This separation lays the groundwork for *Negotiation,* and the exploration of new creative options.

STEP THREE: NEGOTIATING

Understanding opens the door for new ways of relating. This applies to those in your outer life as well as your inner life. Once you understand what drives your *Inner Characters,* you can address their concerns and do collective bargaining around an *Inner Round Table*.

The Inner Round Table is a metaphor for gathering the parts of you that have a vested interest in some outcome in your life. When you are negotiating at the *Inner Round Table*, you will shift into the stance of an *Inner Moderator,* directing and mediating the conversation. This way, all parties have a say and vulnerable or quieter selves are honored as much as powerful players. At the *Inner Round Table* you can mediate between warring selves, find mutual concerns, create cooperation, and resolve long-standing conflicts.

The Inner Round Table allows us to hold inner tensions, waiting for new perspectives and possibilities to emerge. New *Inner Characters* can be invited to the table. Marginalized *Inner Characters* can be heard. *Banished* or *Disowned Selves* can be reclaimed. *Negotiating* an *Inner Peace Treaty* recaptures inner resources previously wasted in conflict and directs them into more purposeful endeavors.

STEP FOUR: INTEGRATING

This is an ongoing process that will continue for your whole life. It includes *Shadow Work, Dream Work*, and answering the invitations that life brings you to grow and change. As your life continues to evolve, you will *Integrate* more and more of the possible spectrum of archetypal energies and add new players to your *Inner Cast of Characters*.

Shadow Work

We draw the concept of *Shadow* from Jungian psychology. Shadow material is always unconscious. It is revealed to us in our strong emotional reactions to people and situations in life. Strong attractions or repulsions, admiration or judgments are indications that we need to do some integration work. Shadow material also comes to us as disturbing characters and dark plotlines in our nighttime dreams. The cutting edge of our personal growth lies in surfacing and integrating shadow material.

Dream Work

Dream work can play a significant role in expanding our *Inner Cast of Characters*. Each night a deep change process is going on as we sleep. Our conscious mind is off line and we are in communication with the depths of our unconscious world.

New archetypal energies and alternative realities filter into our experience as we dream. We can incorporate these new energies and perspectives into our daily lives. Our dream characters teach us new ways of being and relating. Dreams change our perspectives, shift our energy, and expand our definitions of self.

Incorporating New Inner Characters

No one had a perfect childhood. Even with the best parents, there are parts of our story where we didn't get what we really needed. Our parents may have been too tired, busy or distressed by their own problems to provide us with comfort, protection or support. They may have found some of our personality traits frightening and tried to shut them down. Some parents suffer from addiction and mental illness, which can cause them to neglect or abuse their children.

As we get to know our *Inner Cast of Characters* better and learn about their histories, it becomes evident what they need. Incorporating new *Inner Cast* members can fill these needs. We can re-write our scripts and heal the wounds of childhood. We can draw *Possible Selves* from examples in our waking life, but also from our dream life and the archetypal realm. When you ask the negotiation question "what is needed in this situation?" you may find that you don't currently possess these qualities. That does not mean that they cannot be developed.

Everything is available to you in the depths of your *Archetypal Seedbed*. Imagine an ideal someone who possesses these qualities. Then imagine creating an *Inner Character* that possesses these qualities and add them to your *Inner Round Table*. Include them in future conversations and allow their potential to grow in you as they contribute their healing presence.

CHAPTER 2

YOUR INNER CAST OF CHARACTERS—
Naming the Voices

"You have but to know an object by its proper name
for it to lose its dangerous magic."
Elias Canetti

"To become a totality,
we must acknowledge in thought and in detail
all of our parts."
Strephon Kaplan Williams

We all talk to ourselves. It doesn't mean we're crazy. In fact, most of the time, we have a constant stream of inner conversation going on right beneath the surface of our awareness. If you think you don't talk to yourself, tune in sometime when you are getting dressed in the morning, notice how an internal voice is going over the list of tasks you have yet to finish, in order to get out the door on time. Perhaps you are harassing yourself for gaining weight as you try to button a tightening waistband. As you are pulling on your coat, you might be reminding yourself that you haven't called your mother in a long time, and you need to do it soon. On the way to work, you may be rehearsing for a meeting that will happen later that day, or remembering a conversation from yesterday, wishing you had said something different.

One of the benefits of *Inner Peace Treaty* work is having a method to resolve the inner conflicts that plague you. Any time you notice that you are feeling anxious or agitated, you have an inner argument going on. If you tune in, you will hear it. If you follow each side of the conflict back along the thread, you will find an *Inner Character* at the end that has needs and wants, and a distinct world view.

As you trace your inner arguments and learn more about what is behind them, you will discover that most of your *Inner Characters* are trying to help you. There is usually some need or vulnerability that has gotten stirred up that you failed to notice. An inner voice is trying to warn you. If you ignore the voice, that particular *Inner Character* may escalate its attempts to get your attention. Now you may be experiencing a fluttery sensation in your stomach, a headache, or a tight jaw.

For example, if you ignore an *Inner Character* that tells you of a need for quiet time, you might suddenly find yourself in a "bad mood" that seems to come out of nowhere. If you continue to ignore your need for rest and replenishment, your body might begin to communicate to you by getting sick.

Ignoring messages from within does not silence the messengers, it only serves to escalate them. Often we are encouraged to ignore our inner chatter, or worse, tell it to shut up. What I am encouraging you to do instead, is to *tune in* and begin to understand what is going on underneath the chatter. What is driving these inner energies and their voices? In the following explorations, we will ask purposeful questions, gain understanding and address needs rather than ignoring them. You have been talking to yourself your whole life, now it's time to really listen.

"Who's Upset?" versus "What's Wrong?"

Before I began to think about my *Inner Self System*, if I felt anxious or sad, I would wonder, "What's wrong?" Now, I think in terms of my *Inner Characters* and ask myself, "Who is upset?" This shift in perspective made an enormous difference in how I related to myself! When I discovered "who" in my *Inner Cast of Characters* was upset. I then conducted a dialogue with them to discover what they needed to be OK. I found that often their needs could be easily known and addressed. They were things like reassurance, comfort, quiet time, sleep, information, organization, healthy food, a good movie, the beauty of nature, affection, stimulating conversation, a meal with friends, laughter, play, movement, and occasionally chocolate.

How did I know "someone" in me had needs or was upset? I could feel it in my body. I began to tune into the state of my body throughout the day. Did I feel a sense of well-being, calm at my core, or was I stirred up, heavy or nervous? Emotions are always felt somewhere in the body, that is how we come to recognize them. Being stirred up signaled that I was feeling vulnerable in some way. I could address the need when I tuned in, identified "who" was upset in me and began to dialogue with them. I noticed that there were patterns in the ways I got stirred up in certain situations. So I begin to imagine these patterns as sub-personalities or *Inner Characters*.

I took some character development exercises from an old theatre class and used them to explore these sub-personalities further, picturing them as having an age, a gender, a history and other characteristics. I began a journaling process where I fleshed them out, creating an *Inner Cast of Characters*. In the next chapter on *Knowing*, we will outline a series of questions, in which you can explore the many aspects of each *Inner Character*.

I noticed that in the process of writing down my inner dialogues, I was able to separate the voices more easily. Getting these inner voices out onto paper helped me to clarify both thinking and feeling. Writing out the dialogue gave me a sense of perspective and breathing room, apart from the emotions and dynamics going on inside of me. It was like taking the fast train to the source of the upset and quickly learning what the real issues were. I began to sort out and resolve conflicts that were once confusing and overwhelming.

The shift from "what's wrong?" to "who's upset?" has made a huge difference in the lives of those who have tried it. Free floating anxiety is always related to an un-addressed internal conflict. We have many *Inner Characters* and they certainly do not always get along, but we can move towards cooperation if we understand which *Inner Self* is upset and why.

Let's look at how one client used this process to resolve a common human dilemma, the struggle to eat right and maintain a healthy weight.

Patricia

When Patricia came to me, she was confused and frustrated with herself. She had been trying to lose forty pounds for several years with little success. It wasn't just her appearance that bothered her. She came from a family with a history of diabetes and heart disease and she was concerned about her health. Patricia already knew what to do, but she couldn't make herself stick with it.

She explained how every morning she would pack an un-inspiring, healthy lunch and head off to work. If a friend called and asked her out for lunch, Patricia felt compelled to say yes. She would leave that boring bag lunch in the office and out she would go. Lunch was about connecting, catching up and being supportive, the pleasures of tasty food, and everyone knows you can't really celebrate life without dessert! Patricia sighed heavily when she came to the part about dessert.

As I listened to her, I noted the changes in her voice, facial expressions, body postures, energy and the gestures she used as she expressed different aspects of the situation. Each provided clues about the *Inner Characters* at play.

When she talked about how much she valued her friendships, her face brightened and her voice took on a warm resonance. She sat back in her chair, looking confident and attractive, regardless of her weight.

Then, her brow would furrow, and she began to look sullen and drawn. Her voice was tighter and thinner. She sat forward and earnestly explained that her doctor had given her a stern warning during her last medical checkup. Her cholesterol was up and blood work indicated that she was borderline diabetic. She was going to have to make some significant life changes if she expected to remain healthy. She looked anxious and uncertain of herself as she talked about being a woman alone, with no family nearby. Who would care for her if she became ill?

I noted that we already had several *Inner Characters* at odds here, and I mentioned some of my observations. I introduced Patricia to the idea that she had a collection of sub-personalities that were in conflict about her health and weight. We talked about the *Inner Self System,* and how viewing the internal world as a theatre, where life dramas are played out, helps us approach problems differently.

As in any good story, conflict occurs between *Inner Characters* that have differing agendas. Sometimes they work it out, sometimes they go to war with each other. When this happens, we end up in a power struggle with one foot on the gas and one foot on the brakes. Before we could really understand who was sabotaging Patricia's attempt to get healthy, we needed to get to know her *Inner Cast of Characters* and what their agendas were.

Patricia had never paid much attention to the internal arguments over her desire for health, the need to stay connected to friends, and the many meanings of food in her life. We began to work through the *Inner Peace Treaty* process separating out the tangled threads of this problem. There is power in naming and we began to name the *Main Players* in her cast. Her *Inner Cast of Characters* began to take shape as we tracked the inner voices and identified the different energies. I then began to ask each character questions about the situation.

Patricia's Inner Cast of Characters

As Patricia worked through this exercise she identified the following *Main Players*, the *Inner Characters* with a starring role in her situation.

Voice #1—The Dedicated Dieter

This was the *Inner Character* that had brought Patricia into my office. The *Dedicated Dieter* worried about Patricia's health. She had attempted to follow all the major diet trends for the past five years and failed at every one. She could recite the dieting pitfalls and strategies for success. She knew how many minutes of workout would be required for every diet transgression. *The Dedicated Dieter* felt sad and overrun by other forces in Patricia. She had a pale, drawn quality about her and was increasingly resigned that Patricia had little hope for a healthy future.

Voice #2—The Social Butterfly

Patricia named this *Inner Character* the *Social Butterfly* because she loved to make friends, gather people together and introduce them to one another. This part of her was vibrant and engaging. Patricia's entire demeanor took on a special glow when she was in this energy. The *Social Butterfly* had helped Patricia develop a large, interesting, and influential network of friends. This delightful *Inner Character* loved to celebrate and no celebration could be complete without good food and something sweet.

Every Story has a "Heavyweight"

Voice #3 — Coach Stern

In the process of naming the *Dedicated Dieter,* and the *Social Butterfly,* Patricia became aware of a third voice in the background that really drove the *Dedicated Dieter* into deep bouts of self condemnation and hopelessness. Every person alive has an *Inner*

26

Critic. Some people have a whole team, with a different critic for every area of their life. *Inner Critics* fall into the category of the *Not So Supporting Cast.*

As Patricia closed her eyes and tuned into this condemning energy inside, a memory floated forward. She began to talk about a high school athletics coach who had humiliated her every day. Patricia was one of those hapless kids who was not very athletic and had to suffer through mandatory PE classes. She could picture this coach standing with her hands on her boxy hips, glowering and sarcastic. As hard as Patricia tried to perform, she was continually berated for being lazy and undisciplined. Patricia remembered how she left that class so beaten down and then comforted herself with a snack cake. So Patricia named her *Inner Critic, Coach Stern. Coach Stern's* job was to "stay on her back and whip her into shape."

In the process of naming and getting familiar with *Coach Stern,* Patricia had the realization that this harsh inner voice came at her whenever she was alone. *Coach Stern* criticized her for everything she had done wrong that day. Feeling beaten down and hopeless, Patricia needed comfort and headed for the kitchen. Comfort, when she was alone, meant ice cream. She found this very enlightening.

Harsh *Inner Critics* don't really help us achieve excellence; they only tear us down. The strong emotions they evoke often lead to compulsive choices based on relieving the anguish and feeling better in the moment. *Inner Critics* can be part of the *Main Players* in your cast, or they might be offstage lobbing in little zingers from the wings. We will talk more about the *Inner Critic* in chapter nine.

NAMING YOUR INNER CHARACTERS

Real mastery in life begins with becoming aware of what is going on inside. So, tune in to your inner process and begin to identify "who" is talking, pushing, warning, comforting, harassing, etc. Separating out and *Naming the Inner Voices* is the first step of putting you in the director's chair of your life.

Make an investment in yourself. Carve out some quiet time for self exploration. You may need to deal with an inner *Voice of Pressure* that says, "You don't have time for this. You have more important things to do." You can conduct your first inner negotiation right here by assuring this *Inner Voice* that the time you invest will pay off greatly when you are less "at war" with yourself. Perhaps you have a *Voice of Warning* that says, "Spending time on yourself is selfish." Or, "It's better not to think too much about the past. Let sleeping dogs lie." Try negotiating with these *Inner Voices* by reassuring them that the time will be well spent. Being clear, centered, and more at peace is good for everyone.

To begin this process, pick a situation, goal or problem that you are currently experiencing in your life. It can be as simple as "what am I going to do this weekend?" or as complex as "should I marry this person?"

STEP ONE
NAMING

1. Quiet and center yourself in whatever way works best for you. Some people like to light a candle to signal the psyche that they are doing something important. Some like to do an entrance meditation to calm the mind and body. Get some paper or a special journal that you can use just for your *Inner Peace Treaty* explorations. You also have the option of talking into a tape recorder as you work through the exercises and then listening to your responses later.

2. Begin to think about a situation, problem or question in your life. Tune into the individual thought streams and follow the inner voices. You will notice that your internal

voices tend to interrupt and talk over one another. Begin to separate out the tangle and stay with one stream of thought. Write down what this voice has to say. Each time you hear an opposing opinion, it's a new voice. Put the interrupting voices on hold until you finish writing down what the previous voice has to say. Now follow the next one. Write down what that voice has to say.

3. As you listen to each train of thought and write things down, close your eyes and imagine what the person speaking these words might look like. You are forming a picture of this *Inner Character*. Each will have a different feel, and a different set of qualities. They may be young or old. They may feel masculine or feminine (we have both within us). They might look like someone from your own past history or perhaps a character from a book or movie. You may be able to imagine a tone of voice, facial expression, attitude, style, gestures and body language. Sometimes *Inner Characters* take the form of an animal or a force of nature. You may experience them as a panther, an owl, a puppy dog, a whirlwind, a deep blue pond, or a luminous pearl. Sometimes clients describe inanimate objects like a lighthouse, a doormat, or a rock. These all have specific qualities that describe inner energies that drive thoughts, feelings and impulses. Write down the main characteristics of these sub-personalities. You are discovering your *Inner Cast of Characters*.

4. If you were going to give a name to this *Inner Character*, what would it be? You might want to use a category like *Pleaser, Perfectionist, Responsible Person, Playful Child, or Caregiver*. Or you could give this *Inner Character* a more personalized description. Consider people in your childhood, or characters from fairy tales, stories and movies.

Naming something begins to define it. It begins to shape your awareness of it and helps you to recognize the energy when it is activated in you. It gives you a starting point for dialoguing and getting into relationship.

5. Notice as you are doing all of this that "someone" is observing the process and naming the players. This is your *Observing Self,* the still, aware part of you that witnesses your internal dynamics without getting caught up in them. Notice what it feels like to separate out from these internal conversations and observe them. Notice what it feels like to be aware that you have *Inner Characters* in conflict and experiment with just observing, without having to solve anything or resolve anything. If you can't do it right now, over time you will development this capacity to observe from a centered, neutral place. This will be the foundation of a growing sense of peace and empowerment. I like to call this the *Calm Core.* When you are centered in your *Calm Core,* you can direct an amazing life.

Creative Naming and Personal Archetypes

Over the years I have enjoyed the wide variety of creative names people give their *Inner Characters.* Remember that an *Inner Character* can be male, female, animal, object, or a person from a movie, book or history. Each carries an archetypal energy.

Archetypes that carry negative energy might be: the *Devouring Mother,* the *Prodigal Son,* the *Jealous Shrew,* the *Tyrant,* the *Witch,* or the *Whore.* Positive examples might include: the *Good Mother,* the *Protective Father,* the *Caregiver,* the *Devoted Daughter,* the *Innocent Maiden,* or the *Hero.* Remember the list of possible archetypes is endless and your particular variation will be unique to you.

In this work, people get very creative naming their *Inner Characters*. I had a client years ago, who needed to cultivate the ability to stand up for herself and set better limits. One day, she discovered an *Inner Character* she named *Boundary Girl*. She pictured this *Inner Character* as a female *Super Hero* who would fly in, cape and all, and stand between her and whoever was trying to pressure or intimidate her. As she developed her relationship with *Boundary Girl*, she could call up this energy when she needed support to say "no" and to stand up for herself.

You can put your own personal stamp on an archetypal energy to capture its distinctive feel. For example, although there are recognizable qualities in the archetype of the *Good Mother*, your own representation will have a particular flavor. She might look like your own mother, but if you didn't have a good mother, she may look like the mother of a childhood friend. She might be embodied in the television character of *Donna Reed*, or *Mrs. Walton*, or the beloved mother in some childhood story.

You will find a list of potential *Inner Characters* in the Appendix to get your creative juices flowing. These are just categories, so don't limit yourself to this list. Create unique names of your own. Try asking your *Inner Characters* what they would like to be called. Over the years, I have met the *Queen of England, Clair of Assisi, Eve, Peter Pan, Cleopatra, Erin Brockovich, the Wicked Witch of the West, Joan of Arc, James Bond, the Terminator,* the *Star* and more. I have also met a *Rock of Gibraltar, a Swampland,* and a *Steel Rod*. Each captured the essence of a particular energy in the *Inner Self System*.

CHAPTER 3

GETTING TO KNOW YOU—
Dialogues and Explorations

"Know Thyself"
Socrates

"The sincere examination of the individual human life
is one of our fundamental religious acts."
Ira Progoff

The first step of *Negotiating the Inner Peace Treaty* was *Naming* your *Inner Characters*. Once you have *Named* them you can begin to get to *Know* them more deeply by dialoguing with them. This chapter will give you approaches you can use to understand how they influence you: your perspectives, your reactions, your choices.

Getting It Out Of Your Head

The best way to do these inner explorations is by writing them down or typing them out. You may want to get a special journal, just for this purpose. You can also use a tape recorder and answer the questions out loud, listening back later. If you are a creative person, you could use art to explore your *Inner Characters*. You can create collages, clipping out magazine images that capture their essence and interests. You can even go into your closet and wonder which *Inner Characters* bought these clothes, scarves and jewelry and which ones wear them! Think about your *Inner Self System* for a minute. *Who* in you selected your car, decorated your house, chose your friends, your job, your hobbies, or your life partner?

The important thing is to begin to get the jumble of internal dialogue out of your head and begin to separate the threads. You have been living with these tangled inner conversations for years. You know how it goes. One voice talks over the other, and it becomes impossible to follow one line of thought to its conclusion before an opposing voice jumps in. Putting your thoughts onto paper will help you distinguish among the voices, prevent you from being carried off on tangents or being dominated by one strong voice.

Active Imagination

We are going to enter into conversation with your *Inner Characters,* asking them questions and getting to know them. In the Jungian world, these imaginary dialogues are referred to as *Active Imagination.* This approach is most often used to dialogue with dream characters. We will do some of that in a later chapter. The Gestalt community calls this dialogue process the *Two-Chair Technique.* In the *Inner Peace Treaty* process, you'll need more than two chairs.

Dialoguing with your *Inner Characters* through *Active Imagination* may seem simple on the surface, but it can move you deeply into your interior world. It is a powerful tool for self-understanding and will change how you experience yourself. Sometimes these explorations will stir up old memories and emotions, and it is a good idea to have someone with whom you can process what arises. Always begin and end these explorations by doing something that reorients you in present time and grounds you fully in your body.

STEP TWO
KNOWING

In any *Voice Dialogue* session I conduct with an *Inner Character*, I always open with *"Tell me about yourself."* Their entire story may unfold with that one inquiry. Another way of getting to know an *Inner Character* is by exploring the thoughts, feelings and body sensations you feel when they are activated within you.

Basic Explorations: Thoughts, Feelings and Sensations

A basic exploration of thoughts, feelings and sensations is an excellent way to begin to understand how your *Inner Voices/ Characters* influence you. Some *Inner Characters* are *Thinkers*. To them, rules and the facts of a situation are all important. Others are *Feelers,* swept along by anger, fear, love and longing, concerned about whether they are pleasing or perfect enough. Every *Inner Character* generates a recognizable set of body sensations.

How the Body Speaks To Us

We don't often think of the body as having a voice, but the body speaks to us in a variety of ways. It speaks to us through heaviness, agitation, flutters, tingles, tight muscles, headaches, dizziness, arousal, digestive problems, and pain. Our modern, civilized culture is a thinking oriented culture, and we are quite out of touch with how the body communicates. The body has a lot of wisdom. Just learning to tune in to the *Voice of the Body* and letting it speak has produced profound insights for many people.

When clients are talking to me about their feelings, I often ask them "where do you feel that in your body?" Often, they will stare at me blankly. We don't make it a practice to tune in to the sensations that accompany our thoughts and emotions, even though every emotion is accompanied by a set of body sensations.

All emotions are felt in the body. These sensations signal us that we are feeling sadness, fear or happiness or anger.

Each of your *Inner Characters* generates a different set of body sensations. After a while, you can actually trace *who* is activated by scanning the sensations in your body. You might become aware that when your shoulders get really tight, you are experiencing a *Voice of Pressure*. This *Inner Self* is always creating internal pressure, driving us, saying things like, "Hurry up, do more, achieve more, get going, you can do better than that!" Hal and Sidra Stone call this voice the *Pusher*. What kinds of sensations do *you* feel when this intense energy gets going in you?

Perhaps your stomach starts to flutter when you speak to your boss. This may indicate that a *Vulnerable Child* in you feels fearful and intimated and needs support. You might experience tension in your lower arms when someone mistreats you, as your *Inner Rebel* gets ready to haul off and hit somebody. Meanwhile, another *Inner Self* might hold you back and constrain this energy. It might be an *Enlightened One,* who is above anger or a *Well Behaved One* that knows this would get you in trouble. The body will tighten in the midst of this inner argument. Our *Inner Characters* are constantly speaking through our bodies, if we pay attention.

Exploring an Inner Character: Thoughts, Feelings and Sensations

This exploration is something that you can do quickly, anytime, anywhere, to help you gain insight into what is driving you. You can use this exercise as a quick check in, to make wiser and more conscious choices.

- What am I *thinking*?
- What am I *feeling* emotionally?
- What *body sensations* am I experiencing?

1. ***Center Yourself and Tune in to Your Inner Process***

   Just as in a meditation practice, if you establish some sort of entrance routine, your psyche will recognize the cues, and you will find it easier to center and quiet yourself. So settle in and begin to observe your inner process, the thoughts crossing your mind, any emotions you may be feeling. Tune into any sensations going on in your body. Scan your entire body and see if you can experience really being in it. Breathe and release. See if you can just witness what is going on within you, without judging it in any way. This is how you move into your *Observing Self.*

2. ***Dialoguing with an Inner Character***

   Choose an *Inner Character* that you would like to dialogue with. I suggest that you pick an *Inner Character* tied to a situation in your life right now that stirs you up in some way. Allow yourself to experience what it is like to sit with this energy. It will have a very distinct feel and perspective. How does the world look from here? What are the thoughts, feelings and the body sensations you are experiencing in this particular place in your psyche? Sit for a few minutes and become familiar with the feel of this *Inner Character* so that you can recognize it in the future. If you haven't already *Named* this part of you, do it now.

   Now as You Sit in the Energy of this Inner Character, ask:

   – What am I *thinking?*
   – What am I *feeling* emotionally?
   – What *body sensations* am I experiencing?

3. ***Take what comes without judging or evaluating.***
Whenever you let an *Inner Character* respond, by writing or speaking, take whatever comes to you without judging it or drawing any conclusions about it. It doesn't have to make sense, or be consistent with your central values. What "he or she" says doesn't even need to be factually "true". The further away this material is from your established identity, the more important it is that you record it. In the chapter on *Shadow Work*, you will see how important it is to surface foreign or "unacceptable" thoughts, feelings, and sensations. Don't edit, just write down what comes to you.

4. ***Realizations and Discoveries***
After you have done a dialogue exploration, take time to read back over what you have written or listen to the recording that you made. Just the process of bringing this material to consciousness will shift your behavior, reactivity and choices. You will discover things you never realized before, and shed light on situations where you have been stuck before. Just giving your *Inner Characters* a voice and listening to them is healing and reduces internal pressure.

Gestalt "Two Chair" Technique

Another way of recording your dialogues is by using a recording device, answering the questions out loud, and listening back later. Here is how.

Sit two chairs across from each other and act as the interviewer from the first chair. Ask a question and then move to the second chair to answer as the *Inner Character* being interviewed. Go back to the first chair to ask the next question and then move again to answer. Alternating chairs helps you to shift your experience so that you can feel each *Inner Character* as a separate place within your *Inner Self System*.

If you record sessions and listen back to them, you will gain a lot of insight into how this aspect of you influences your perceptions, motivations, reactions and choices in life.

Patricia's Process

Let's see how Patricia used this exercise. So far we have three *Main Players* sitting at her *Inner Round Table*, each with a vested interest in her struggle. In *Step One*, she named them the *Dedicated Dieter, the Social Butterfly, and Coach Stern*. Here is an excerpt from Patricia's process journal as she let her *Inner Cast of Characters* express their thoughts and feelings about her health and weight loss goals. She also noted the sensations she was experiencing in her body while she was housing the energy of each character. The responses are written in the "first person," as if each *Inner Character* were speaking directly from the *Character's* perspective. This was what went on right after a friend called to ask her out to lunch.

The Social Butterfly
Thoughts: "Fantastic! Lunch with Marsha. I haven't seen her in ages. I can't wait to catch up on all her news!" I picture myself in a local restaurant talking and having a great time.
Feelings: Happiness, positive anticipation, excitement, security and well-being.
Sensations: When I am in my *Social Butterfly Self,* my body feels energized, lighter than usual, buoyant even. At the same time, there is a comforting warm feeling in the pit of my stomach.

The Dedicated Dieter
Thoughts: I can imagine this *Inner Character* sighing loudly now and speaking in a whiney tone. "Here you go again! You know you can't go out to lunch without breaking your diet and ordering something filled with calories! You never stick to the allowable

food list when you are out with friends, and you always order dessert! The only way you can control yourself is to decline these invitations, tie yourself to this miserable office chair and eat that boring bag lunch."

Feelings: A jumble of sadness, annoyance, anger, fear, hopelessness, loneliness, and self-loathing (wow!).

Sensations: Suddenly I feel tired and really heavy, like my body weighs about 500 pounds. It feels like someone pulled the plug and the energy just drained out of me. It's hard to move. I want to go to sleep. Suddenly I am aware that I have a strong craving for ice cream and cookies, my favorite comfort foods.

As Patricia's *Inner Dialogue* progresses, the argument heats up. The *Social Butterfly* tries to lift Patricia's spirits by taking on the *Dedicated Dieter* in the following interchange:

The Social Butterfly

Thoughts: (to the *Dedicated Dieter*) "Don't be a killjoy! Who wants to eat raw vegetables when you can be with friends eating garlic bread and cheese cake! Think about how much fun you will be having, the hustle and bustle of the restaurant and all those delicious tastes and smells. You don't want to stay here and be lonely! Come on!"

Feelings: When the *Social Butterfly* takes center stage, my mood brightens and I begin to feel relieved. The *Social Butterfly's* enthusiasm for life sweeps away the sad, lonely, deprived feelings I get when I stay inside alone, eating the boring food picked out by the *Dedicated Dieter.* I hate that food and I hate being alone!

Sensations: The heaviness lifts and I can feel an upsweep of physical energy.

When Patricia does not respond to the warnings of the *Dedicated Dieter, Coach Stern,* who has been listening in the background, steps forward with a much harsher, harassing approach. Patricia can picture this imposing *Inner Coach* standing, glowering with hands on her hips, as she begins to berate her.

Coach Stern
Thoughts: "Patricia, you disgust me! But I don't know why I'm surprised. This is precisely what you have been doing for years. You have no discipline or self-control. It's one excuse after another. You're hopeless!"
Feelings: I begin to feel a lot of fear, self-contempt and shame. Then I get a backlash of defensive anger from the *Social Butterfly*. She hates *Coach Stern*. She hates anything that brings me down or isolates me.
Sensations: My shoulders are tense and I have a knot in the pit of my stomach.

Patricia reported to me that after she wrote out this internal argument she felt very sad and defeated and almost cancelled lunch with Marsha. Then the *Social Butterfly* came flying forward once again.

Often in life, we ricochet from one extreme to another in the midst of an internal war. You can just picture Patricia's *Inner Characters* firing back and forth here, each trying to gain control.

Social Butterfly to Coach Stern
"Oh shut-up. You are such a kill-joy. Dieting is for bores and you are the biggest bore of all. Life is short; eat dessert first! Who cares about weight anyway? People love Patricia because she is so much fun. She celebrates life! She's not trying to look like some bone-thin model."

Dedicated Dieter
"This is not about looking like a model. You heard what the doctor said. The entire family is pre-disposed to diabetes and heart disease. This is life and death!"

Social Butterfly, rolling her eyes at Coach Stern and the Dedicated Dieter:

"You are both soooo melodramatic and up tight! If Patricia listened to you, she'd have no friends at all! I am sweeping her off to lunch and we are not listening to either one of you!"

The *Social Butterfly* won this argument. Patricia joined Marsha for lunch and forgot all about this little exercise. But when it came time for dessert, her *Observing Self* kicked into gear. She suddenly began to notice what was going on inside her. There was a tight feeling in her gut and she recognized that this came from the *Dedicated Dieter* and *Coach Stern*. She could picture them taunting her at that moment, "See, we told you that you couldn't go out to lunch without blowing your diet!"

At that moment, Patricia became aware that she felt a fullness that came from being with a dear friend. She separated the automatic linkage between lunch with friends and sweets and decided to pass on dessert. As she did this, she smiled to herself, the *Social Butterfly* making a smug little "so there" face at *the Dieter* and *the Coach*. Patricia returned to the office feeling a sense of self-mastery and hope. Perhaps getting healthy didn't have to mean being all alone, eating a bag lunch of yogurt and celery sticks.

Patricia's Realizations

Awareness is the first step to changing any automatic behavior. *Who* in you is acting and what is driving them? Patricia reported several realizations that came from her dialogue work:

1. She was beginning to un-link the automatic association between eating with friends and ordering dessert. By tuning in to the warmth of their presence, she found the feeling of fullness that she often associated with food.

2. It seemed that the *Coach* had the opposite effect of what was intended. When *Coach Stern* showed up, the berating undermined Patricia sense of confidence in herself and escalated her anxiety. This was a major trigger for cravings and subsequent comfort eating!

3. Patricia was also curious about the feelings of desolation that she felt when she ate alone at her desk. It seemed extreme for the situation, after all, what was the big deal if she ate lunch alone occasionally? This warranted further inquiry.

DEEPER DIALOGUES AND HIDDEN CHARACTERS

My all-time favorite inquiry of any *Inner Character* is *"Tell me about yourself."* Sometimes this opening will invite this part of your psyche to pour forth a river of information. You will discover things about yourself that you never knew before.

Patricia was puzzled by the deep desolation she felt when she ate alone. She wanted to explore it more deeply. Any time you have an emotional reaction in life that seems stronger than warranted, there is a history here. There are often hidden actors in the background that are weighing in on this situation, influencing you from the sidelines.

Patricia and I knew there was something important here. I asked her to sit with the desolation she felt when she was alone with her lunch in the office and just notice if any image or memory arose. Suddenly she looked up and told me about a scene from the third grade. She was sitting all by herself at a lunch table, watching everyone else laughing and running off to play. As she remembered this scene, she was overwhelmed with grief. She remembered that she had been unable to break into a tight knit group of girls and was always left on the outside. Eating lunch alone in the office felt just like that.

This was an important turning point in her work. We had just discovered a hidden *Inner Character*, a sad, lonely, vulnerable little girl behind the scenes. We named her the *Wallflower*. This is an example of a *Retired Self* from the past, left behind, but stirring up strong emotion in the present. We will talk about these *Kids Behind the Curtains* in chapters seven and eight. Patricia had all but forgotten the *Wallflower*, but the *Wallflower* had not forgotten her.

When we encounter *Inner Characters* that are troublesome, we often want to banish them, but it is really important that we seek to understand them instead. The information a troublesome *Inner Character* will reveal to you will give you keys to lifelong mysteries. With this understanding, you can address some of your deepest underlying needs to negotiate solutions and create strategies that will really hold up under stress. Our *Inner Characters* are trying to help us, but they sometimes go about it in a way that is not so helpful. Once you understand them, you will find you have more empathy for the ways in which they trouble you. Their energies just need to be re-directed.

Interview Questions — Seeking to Understand

Here is a list of interview questions that you can ask an *Inner Character* to gain more insight into how they operate. You can use your journal or a tape recorder. You can also dialogue with a trusted friend or therapist. Suggestions for being an effective dialogue partner are in the Appendix.

Begin with *"Tell me about yourself."* You may get an enormous amount of information with just this one inquiry. Write or speak as long as information flows. To delve deeper, you can continue on down the list of questions. Remember to hold the space of a neutral *Inner Moderator*. Take what comes without judging, editing or analyzing.

Interview Questions:

- *Tell me about yourself. What is your history? (How old was I when you came into being? What was going on at that time?)*
- *How were you a solution for me back then?*
- *How are you trying to help or protect me now?*
- *What are your fears or concerns?*
- *What do you want or need?*
- *Is there anything you would like to say to me?*

Additional questions you might ask them:

- *Who were your teachers and role models?*
- *What are the rules that you live by?*
- *What do you like to do?*
- *When and where are you active in my life?*

The Wallflower's Story

When I interviewed Patricia's *Wallflower,* she told us that she most wanted to feel loved and included and felt utterly desolate when Patricia turned down a lunch invitation, to eat that brown bag lunch, alone at her desk. It reminded her of grade school, when she sat and ate alone every day, excluded from the other girls. The *Wallflower* became very sad any time she had to eat alone. She pushed Patricia to accept lunch invitations to avoid these difficult feelings. She was afraid that if Patricia turned down lunch invitations, people would stop calling.

I asked Patricia how she had transformed from this shy *Wallflower* into the *Social Butterfly* she was today. Patricia smiled, "That would have been in the ninth grade, when we moved to a new town." She recalled how she was determined to re-invent herself in this new place and leave the shy *Wallflower* behind. The *Wallflower* had been sitting on the sidelines, studying the popular girls for years and she knew just what to do. Thus, the *Social Butterfly* was born.

The job of the *Social Butterfly* was to make sure that Patricia was never left out again. Once she became established as a *Main Player* in Patricia's *Inner Cast*, the *Wallflower* was not only retired, but banished to the shadow lands of Patricia's life, forgotten until now.

Patricia is not the first person I have met that recreated herself in a childhood move to a new town. A move is a chance to start over with a clean slate and establish a new reputation. At the new high school, Patricia birthed the *Social Butterfly* and learned how to make and keep friends.

The *Wallflower* is an example of a *Retired Self*. This one was hidden from her awareness until she began the dialogue process and rediscovered her. *Retired Selves* were *Main Players* on the stage of our lives at some previous time. We retire them when a chapter of life comes to an end. Sometimes we outgrow them, sometimes they represents a painful past that we would just as soon leave behind.

Moving the Process Forward

We will talk about the *Negotiation* and *Integration* steps of this process in more detail, but for now, here is a brief summary of how Patricia made peace with herself and got unstuck in her process.

She learned about the *Wallflower's* fears and concerns and knew she needed a lot of comfort, reassurance and connection. In her childhood, food and sugar had become the answer to feelings of sadness, anxiety or loneliness. When Patricia was sad and lonely, it was easy to finish off a pint of ice cream while mindlessly watching television, sabotaging days of progress. She learned to track her body for signs that the lonely *Wallflower* was getting stirred up. The *Wallflower* really liked ice cream, but in continuing to dialogue with her, Patricia discovered that there were non-caloric things she could do that soothed and pleased the *Wallflower* before she was overtaken by anxiety and cravings.

An important part of this process was the realization that Patricia lacked *Inner Comforters* and *Nurturers* who could help her calm and re-center herself when she felt anxious. She began to attend to examples of comforting, nurturing people in her life, in movies and television programs and eventually in her dreams. She selected an image that made her feel particularly safe and secure, and we conducted an inner visualization where Patricia placed the *Wallflower* into the care and keeping of this *Inner Comforter*. Patricia memorized what her body felt like when it was calm and peaceful and began a practice of becoming familiar with this inner state, so that she could travel there when she began to feel anxious. Whenever the *Wallflower* got triggered, she would imagine her being attended to by her *Inner Comforter*. She found a picture of a child sitting on the lap of a very warm, loving looking woman and posted this where she could see it regularly. It was a visual reminder that the *Wallflower* was loved, valued and included, always held in the arms of her *Inner Comforter*.

She retired *Coach Stern*, acknowledging her for her many years of service. She told the *Coach* that she could take a well-earned vacation, assured that someone quite alert and capable would monitor Patricia's health and weight.

As the *Wallflower* calmed down, so did Patricia. She began to be able to manage her emotional eating. At this point, the *Dedicated Dieter* could actually implement the success strategies she had known all along, but had been unable to put into action.

Within six months, Patricia lost twenty pounds. I spoke to her a year later and she reported that she had reached her target weight. Along the way she realized there were other things in her life she had kept herself from doing because of the fears and anxieties of the *Wallflower*. One of them was completing her education. She had not succeeded at college because she couldn't spend time alone with the books. Now that the *Wallflower* felt included, safe and comforted, Patricia found that she could be at peace while she was alone. She enrolled in school and was achieving another goal she had never considered possible.

Living from the Calm Core

Life changes significantly when you can observe your inner process rather than being swept away by it. The more you operate from the *Observing Self* and identify "who" is activated in you at any given moment, the more capacity you will have for directing your *Inner Cast of Characters*. Operating from your *Calm Core* makes it possible to negotiate between warring parts of self.

When you can stand in the midst of all the inner chatter and the impulses that are pushing you or shutting you down, you can begin to direct your life from a place of insight and power. Learning to observe your life from a centered, clear place is a true Spiritual Practice. The *felt sense* of this is important. Make it a practice to stop, tune in, and re-center yourself in your *Calm Core* throughout your day. The more you do it, the easier it becomes. Returning to this place of centered awareness throughout the day will reduce your anxious reactivity, improve your relationships, and empower your life.

Dialogue Retreat

When you have the time to do a deeper exploration, take this opportunity. Consider creating an evening or weekend retreat for yourself. If you are part of a group that does inner work, consider a group retreat, where you can share your process and discoveries with each other.

Caveats and Safety Precautions

Some people find the energy of certain *Inner Characters* a bit unsettling, particularly if other *Inner Characters* judge what they think and feel *as* "unacceptable" or bad". If you find that sitting in the energy of a particular *Inner Character* is too painful, disorienting or frightening, then don't do it. Try imagining that you are sitting *across* from this *Inner Character* and ask the interview questions, writing down what they say. This is still an effective way to work. Your psyche is indicating that you need this distance for now. If this still stirs up too much emotion for you, or you find that you can't get re-grounded or centered after this exercise, then you might need a companion on the journey. Find an experienced guide or therapist, who is trained in depth oriented work. Let them help you navigate the terrain.

CHAPTER 4

NEGOTIATING AT THE INNER ROUND TABLE

"Until you make peace with who you are,
you will never be content with what you have."
Doris Mortman

Have you ever made a decision that you later came to deeply regret? Do you wake up morning after morning hating your job and wondering how you ever got into this line of work? Are you disillusioned with your life partner, wondering what you ever saw in them? Perhaps your children are driving you crazy, and you can't figure out why you ever decided to have them! Women sometimes open a closet full of clothes, and finding that nothing suits their mood, declare, "I have nothing to wear." If you have ever found yourself despairing at the disappointing outcome of some important life decision, welcome to the human situation. This is what happens when one of your *Inner Characters* makes a decision and the rest of the *Inner Cast* has to live with it!

We Are Often at War With Ourselves

If you've ever had the experience of setting a goal, and then having one foot on the gas and the other on the brakes, you are experiencing the war between *Inner Selves*. We try to ignore these internal arguments or we attempt to resolve them by taking a firm position on one side or the other. Polarizing in this way may seem to work on the surface, but keep in mind that the *Inner Characters* who get ignored or rejected now feel hurt, sad, or angry. They wait in the background for another day in which they will assert themselves with renewed vigor.

Sometimes when we have opposing feelings about something, we swing back and forth between the two poles, confusing ourselves and others, full of frustration, despair and self-condemnation. Perhaps you want to be close to someone, but you also want your independence. Couples can vacillate between love and hate in one conversation. One part of you may want to achieve a certain goal, and another wants to lay around and do nothing. How do you reconcile being attentive and accommodating to the people you love, and being authentic and true to yourself?

We rarely make decisions in life that consider all aspects of who we are. Thus, we are destined to live with regret. We aren't taught to operate from a place of centered awareness, to develop an *Observing Self*. As kids, we learn to navigate life based on the rewards and punishments we receive. We reach a certain age and look back on roads not taken and the ways in which we sold ourselves short. Many people live with regret, convinced that they missed some golden opportunity or the relationship they always wanted, if they had only possessed the courage to go after it.

Any time you experience a general sense of anxiety, you will find two or more *Inner Characters* in conflict. Most decisions in life are made from the perspective of our *Main Players*, the *Inner Characters* we most identify with, who run our lives most of the time. Occasionally, we will have an outcropping of a less dominant *Inner Self*, who gets scared, frustrated, or needy enough to insist that we attend to them. Sometimes our *Shadow Selves* will do or say something completely "out of character".

Our psyches are systems of dynamic energy and the push and pull of all these inner agendas creates tension. The key to inner peace is learning to stand in our *Calm Core*, consciously directing the many possibilities of our lives. *Inner Characters* without a director leads to chaos. We often let one or two of our dominant *Inner Selves* silence the less assertive ones. Somewhere down the line, these quieter selves become very unhappy and there is upheaval and regret.

Remember that the entire *Inner Cast of Characters* has to live with the consequences of any important decision we make. A good *Inner Director* knows that everyone has a part to play. This *Director* makes sure that one actor does not step on the lines of another or hold forth too long on the stage.

STEP THREE
NEGOTIATING AT THE INNER ROUND TABLE

One of the major exercises of *Inner Peace Treaty* work is assembling and negotiating at an *Inner Round Table*. Your *Inner Round Table* is where you will gather all the *Inner Characters* that have a vested interest in a situation or goal at hand. Here is where you will seek to understand their differing perspectives and agendas. Here you will resolve inner conflicts and honor the gifts of these many aspects of self. You will *Negotiate an Inner Peace Treaty*.

In *Inner Peace Treaty* work, we don't banish our darkness; we call these troublesome parts of us to the table and harness their energies in constructive ways. Every destructive impulse you have ever had is part of that dynamic energy inside seeking expression in some way. It is an *Inner Character's* attempt to be a part of your life and to get his or her needs met. The *Inner Selves* that cause us so much pain and turbulence have valuable input, but the value is not always immediately evident while they are causing us internal stress.

Negotiations take time, but are worth the effort. When you can get an *Inner Committee of Selves* to agree on a plan of action, the synergy of this alignment creates tremendous momentum towards achieving a goal. That's what *Inner Round Table Work* is about.

Your Inner Round Table

From my first introduction to the realm of Camelot, I was enchanted by the stories of King Arthur and his Round Table. I loved the idea that Arthur would gather his best and brightest knights around that great table to discuss and debate ideas of the day and seek to create a more just and noble society. If Arthur had lived in this day, he would have included the wise women of the land as well. I am certain of it.

In my imagination, a large round table made from ancient oak sits in a great hall before a blazing fire. The scene is medieval; the room is lit by torchlight, with beautiful tapestries on the wall. Around the table sit chairs of different sizes and shapes, all hand carved. This is my vision of where I gather my *Inner Cast of Characters*. Here they will negotiate and mediate alliances, form committees that will solve conflicts, and build the goals and dreams of my life. I have found that the important thing is to take all aspects of my *Inner Self System* into account, not just the dominant voices of the day.

The Arthurian or medieval theme may not fit the experience of your inner world, so chose a scene that suits your personal style and *Inner Cast of Characters*. Perhaps you would be more at home sitting on a porch around a wicker coffee table in a cozy summer cottage, or at a round glass table, in a sundrenched modern structure, overlooking the Pacific Ocean. Perhaps what appeals to you is to be seated on the earth around a blazing fire in some sort of tribal counsel. Create a picture that works for you, but make sure that the gathering is circular, because the circle is the symbol for wholeness.

Charting and Grouping

Many of the people who do *Inner Peace Treaty* work chart their *Inner Self System* on paper, placing their *Inner Characters* around a central table so that they can see the full array of *who* lives in them. In weekend workshops, we often have a session for collage work, cutting pictures from magazines and pasting them on poster boards to represent our *Inner Cast*. This is a fun, easy way to explore your inner world.

We can resolve many of our inner conflicts by gathering the characters involved around an imaginary *Round Table* for interchange, understanding, and negotiation. An example of a simple chart is found in the Appendix, but you can easily create one by drawing a circle in the center that represents your *Inner Round Table* and surrounding it with any number of circles you need to represent *Inner Characters* seated around the table. Here are a number of creative things you can do with charting.

- *Draw different size circles to represent the weight and influence that each character carries in your life.*
- *You can show the faces that present themselves in public (your persona), and who is behind the scenes in private.*
- *You can show how your Inner Characters group together, according to alliances and oppositions or power and vulnerability.*
- *You might show their progression and development in a timeline.*
- *Pick different areas of your life and create specific character charts for each.*
- *You can create a pie chart that shows how much of your life each one takes up.*
- *You can add new characters as you discover them within you, or change the constellation at the table as your needs change.*

In every situation of your life, there will be a different set of *Inner Characters* who will have vested interests in certain positions.

You can conduct *Round Table Negotiations:*

- *Between two characters that have trouble with each other.*
- *According to a project, creating a subset of Selves as an Inner Committee.*
- *Looking at conflicted areas of your life: work vs. home, responsibilities to family vs. health or spiritual needs, etc.*
- *Exploring a decision you are trying to make, taking more aspects of self into account.*
- *To seek understanding about some area of hurt, confusion or reactivity.*
- *Changing the seating arrangement to create a new dynamic.*
- *Adding new characters from your dreams.*
- *Introducing new archetypal energies to the mix.*

You can explore:

- *Who is welcome? Who is not?*
- *Who gets along? Who doesn't?*
- *What are the natural groupings?*
- *Who are the Main Players? The Heavy Weights?*
- *Who plays the Supporting Cast?*
- *Who gets silenced by the stronger voices?*
- *Who holds the power?*
- *Who is happy? Who is not?*
- *What do they need?*
- *Are there Vulnerable Children, Shadow or Retired Selves in the background that are not welcome at the table?*
- *What happens if you rearrange the chairs?*
- *What happens if you rebalance the players to create space for other characters to express themselves?*
- *What or who is missing?*
- *What happens if you add some new energy to the mix?*

Recalibrating the Balance of our Lives

People often realize that a very important negotiation in their lives has to do with the amount of time and energy that certain *Inner Characters* are taking up. If you do a *Pie Chart Analysis* of your *Inner Characters*, you may see that there are crucial areas of your life that have become neglected because others are dominating the system. As the *Director* of your life, you need to evaluate if you are spending your time and life energy in the right proportions, in keeping with your deeper purposes. A major negotiation may need to take place to recalibrate the inner system and create space for neglected areas.

Missing Persons

Another way to look at the *Inner Round Table* is to see *who* is missing? Do you notice an imbalance of a particular type of *Inner Character*? For example, are there a plenty of *Power Characters* without any *Relationship Oriented Characters*? Are there mostly *Task Oriented Selves* without any *Creative Selves*? What might be needed in this group to balance it out or achieve a better result?

In the chapter on *Integration*, we will talk more about what people need to be whole and how we go about adding what is missing to our inner system. Who is missing in yours? Do you need more nurture, support, encouragement, toughness, courage, decisiveness, strength, tenderness, creativity, playfulness, sensuality, warmth, detachment, more flexible, flowing energy, or more dynamic "get it done" energy? If you are missing one of these energies, does it live in you anywhere? Is there *someone* in your *Inner Self System* that you can add to the *Negotiation* that would shift the dynamic towards a better solution or resolution?

Negotiating with Problematic Inner Characters

If you know that you have an *Inner Voice* or *Character* that causes a lot of trouble in a particular situation, you can imagine telling them that you are going to give them the afternoon off or leave them in a safe place, while other parts of you go and handle something.

Estelle

Estelle prided herself as being an assertive woman who didn't let anyone walk over her, especially men. She was aware of her rights and knew when a line had been crossed. She had a strong *Rebel Daughter* within her. The *Rebel* had no problem confronting people, but when she was front and center in Estelle's *Inner Cast*, the *Rebel* went in with both barrels blazing and blew up a lot of bridges that she might need to cross in the future.

When Estelle started doing her *Inner Round Table* work, she discovered that she had another *Inner Self* that did a much better job of establishing ground rules, setting limits, and taking care of things with strong, benevolent authority. It was the archetype of the *Wise Queen*. Estelle negotiated with her *Rebel Daughter* to let the *Queen* handle issues of transgression. The *Rebel* was willing to try it, provided there was a favorable outcome. Over time, the *Rebel* came to trust the *Queen*, because her wise, measured, strategic approach assured that Estelle maintained important alliances to build bridges to the future.

When Estelle lets the *Queen* handle things, she does not have to expend energy going back for damage control. The *Queen* thinks about the future of the whole kingdom, not just winning the immediate battle. The *Rebel* feels satisfied and safe (which was the issue all along), and everyone in Estelle's life is clear about expectations and boundaries.

YOUR TURN
CREATING AN INNER ROUND TABLE

Chose a situation in your life that you are currently unresolved about or a goal you would like to achieve.

The Inner Moderator

When you are *Negotiating* at the *Inner Round Table*, you will move into the role of the *Inner Moderator*. The *Inner Moderator* makes sure that all the *Inner Characters* who have a stake in the discussion will be heard and have their wants and needs addressed.

How do you activate this *Inner Moderator?* You do it with intention and imagination. We have talked about separating out the strands of inner conversation and not allowing one voice to interrupt another. As you begin the negotiation, you are entering into a place of observation, a quiet, aware, non-judgmental place, where you can look around and notice everything going on, without being caught up in it. From this place, you can moderate and facilitate the dialogue at the *Inner Round Table*, creating safety for all to speak, so they can get their point across and really be heard.

Stay aware of how other dominant *Inner Characters* will try to shove you out of this neutral space and pass judgment or silence what is being revealed. You will hear things like, "That doesn't make any sense. You can't do that. What will people think? That's stupid or immoral, etc." Hold the protective stance of the *Inner Moderator* and let each character speak their truth.

STEP ONE: NAMING

Trace your thought streams back to identify the *Inner Characters* at play in this situation. Name them and create an *Inner Round Table* chart. Explore the grouping. Play with the arrangement.

STEP TWO: KNOWING

If you haven't already gotten to know what drives these *Inner Characters*, do some exploration at this point. Understanding is the foundation for a successful negotiation. You have to understand where they are coming from and why they care about what they do. Refer back to Chapter Three for a list of exploratory questions. Here are some key questions relevant to the negotiation process:

- *How do you view this problem or situation?*
- *What are your fears or concerns in this situation?*
- *What do you want?*
- *What do you need?*
- *How do you view the others involved?*
- *What do you see as the solution?*

Review all of this. What did you learn that you didn't know before? How has this changed your view or experience of the situation?

STEP THREE: NEGOTIATING

When you understand what each party wants and needs and what their concerns are, you can look for the following:

- *Where is the common ground?*
- *What concerns can easily be addressed?*
- *Where can cooperation occur?*
- *Where can one yield, reassign jobs, or take turns?*
- *Where can compromises be made?*
- *What is missing in this situation?*

Solutions

Often times a solution will be clear at this point. One *Inner Self* needs a place to express themselves more. Another fears disapproval and needs reassurance that nothing bad will happen. One feels overlooked and needs attention. Another is tired of being in the spotlight. One *Inner Character* feels as if they are responsible for everything, another could care less about people or their needs.

Sometimes resolutions are easy. At other times it seems like the whole life needs a major restructuring. You have to identify the underlying needs of *all* the important characters, or the solution won't hold. Where is the system out of balance? Where can it be recalibrated? The more aspects of self you include in the collective bargaining process, the more successful the outcome.

Your Dream Life

We will talk more about the information and energies that your dreams bring you in Part Three. For now, pay attention to how your dreams are commenting on this process. As you learn about yourself and dialogue and get into relationship with that which was once under the surface of your awareness, your dream life will respond. You may also have a series of interesting coincidences in your life that seem related to a particular situation. In the Jungian world, we call these *Synchronicities*. They all serve to direct you to an increased alignment with your deepest potential, your *Soul Print*. This is an important part of the journey of *Individuation*.

CHAPTER 5

DOMINIC AND HIS DAD—
Characters We Left by the Side of the Road

*"You have to give up the life you planned
in order to have the life that's waiting for you."*
Joseph Campbell

Dominic worked for his father in a successful furniture manufacturing business that his dad built from the ground up. His father arrived in America as a penniless immigrant who worked day and night to build a successful company with a solid reputation for quality and service. It was always understood that Dominic would be his father's successor. His father was planning to retire, and Dominic would be at the helm by the end of the year.

Dominic came to see me after his second visit to the local emergency room. Over the past six months he had been experiencing escalating episodes of light headedness, chest pains and shortness of breath. He thought he was having a heart attack, but the medical evaluation showed that there was nothing wrong with his heart. His doctor had referred him to me to talk about his stress level and to discuss treatment for anxiety and panic attacks.

I took one look at Dominic's face and could see that he was indeed having heart trouble, but not of the physical kind. He carried the kind of resigned exhaustion I see in many men going through life, noses to the grindstone, trying to fulfill their many commitments to family, profession, and community. These are good men, but their faces and bodies are often braced under the weight of the responsibilities they are carrying. They soldier on until some illness, depression or crisis breaks them down.

The Good Son

As I listened to Dominic tell me about his life, he talked about how fortunate he was to have the opportunity to take over a thriving business. Many people would envy it, but I saw no "fire in the belly" when he spoke of it. As I got to know Dominic further, I took note that he rarely talked about work without mentioning his hard working father. Dominic loved and respected his father and wanted to be a *Good Son*. I introduced him to the idea that we are many faceted creatures and that anxiety is often created by two *Inner Characters* in conflict. We began to identify and explore his *Inner Cast of Characters*, beginning with the *Good Son*, whose duty was to please his father and to be what his father expected him to be. This had not been hard for him so far, but recently the *Good Son* had become concerned that he would not be able to live up to his father's expectation. He had a different personality from his father. What if he could not fill his father's shoes? At that point, I realized that there was another energy entering the picture that had a much heavier feel. We named him the *Heir Apparent.*

In a *Voice Dialogue* session, I interviewed Dominic's *Heir Apparent.* When he spoke from this archetypal energy, his face took on a gray cast. All warmth disappeared and his manner became serious and heavy. The *Heir* began to give me a list of things that Dominic would need to give up or change if he was ever to fill his father's shoes. He would need to work longer hours and miss more family dinners, he would need to be less friendly with his employees, he would need to give up coaching his son's little league and participating in community philanthropic activities. There was no time for such frivolities. He was also going to need to give up that vacation to Italy he was planning with his family next summer. You simply can't be away from a business for that long.

Dominic stopped and looked up at me after he had listed all these things. It ran completely contrary to the things he most valued as a *Family Man*. So we moved over and let the *Family Man* talk. He recalled, with sadness, that his father had rarely joined the family for summer vacations at the beach or thrown him a baseball or come to his games. Family and community involvement were high priorities for Dominic, the *Family Man*, who was frightened and outraged by the inevitable encroachment on family time that would occur once he became the *Heir* to his father's company. Dominic was stunned to hear that two such opposing energies existed inside him, and he began to understand why he was experiencing such anxiety.

Taking all Parts of Self into Account

The next week, Dominic came in for his session happier than usual. He reported that his old college friend Nick was in town, and talked with unbridled enthusiasm about the meal the two had prepared the night before. His eyes shone as he told me about Nick, who had trained at the Culinary Institute and was now head chef at an Italian restaurant in the wine country of California. "He works long hours, but he loves every minute of his life." Dominic sighed, "We had so much fun last night."

In that session, I saw the first flickers of a personal passion, a flame that might give him some life energy. I encouraged Dominic to keep talking and he reminisced about the Italian dinners he used to host in college. He would cook for friends with recipes he learned from his grandmother. He reminisced about how he grew his own herbs and gathered fresh ingredients at the local farmer's market. He would spend an entire Saturday chopping tomatoes, roasting peppers, making pastas and simmering sauces. Then, he would gather friends around a big old table and they would eat, drink, laugh and talk about their futures. "They called my apartment Dominic's Trattorio! La Dolce Vita! It was indeed a sweet life."

He spoke with sad nostalgia and yearning, for Dominic rarely cooked now. There was little time for friends, even less in the future, when he took over the business. "Nick did what he wanted with his life. He didn't have a family business to take over. I didn't have that choice." The energy drained out of him and he looked mournfully out the window.

We had just identified a long lost part of Dominic, a *Retired Self* that Dominic had left behind because of the growing pressures and responsibilities of his life. I knew he held an important key to Dominic's dilemma and we named him *Chef Dominic*. We spent more time dialoguing with him and experiencing his expansive, exuberant energy.

Retired Selves — Characters left by the Side of the Road

Dominic's story is an excellent example of what happens to so many people when an *Inner Character* gets left by the side of the road. Adult life is complicated, and we have very real responsibilities. We begin to prioritize in favor of the urgent and pressing tasks of the day. The guitar case sits unopened in the corner as we spend more time advancing a business career. We no longer sit on the back porch just listening to the crickets because there is laundry to do. Lazy Saturday mornings spent making love are now spent rushing kids to soccer games and music lessons. We haven't had coffee with a friend in months because we are caring for an aging parent.

It gets harder and harder to find time for things that were once important sources of replenishment and deeper fulfillment. Over time, we begin to feel sad and anxious for reasons we can't quite identify. The soul life is withering. We feel dull and deadened and wonder if we are depressed. If we ever tune in, we will hear what's wrong. It's the mourning of our long lost *Inner Selves* that brought us the zest of life.

Becoming Over-Identified with One or Two Main Players.

Dominic was naturally a very responsible person and he had become highly identified with the *Responsible Selves* in him. He took very seriously his role as *Good* and *Loyal Son* and *Responsible Provider.* He gained a great deal of satisfaction from being a *Family Man* and loved being involved in his community.

If Dominic's life became more focused on running the business, there would be less contact with his family, community and even the people at work. More and more time was spent with analysis, and budgets, and lots of problem solving. The *Good Son* was trying to be a fitting *Heir Apparent,* and these *Inner Characters* were pushing other important aspects of his life further into the background.

In the safe space of the counseling room, Dominic put his head in his hands and actually admitted that he really did not want to run his father's company. He was in a quandary because this had been understood as his "destiny" since he was a young boy. He loved his father and wanted to please him but he was overwhelmed by the burden of this future responsibility. He wanted to do what was expected of him, but his body was saying, "No!" He had no idea what to do.

CHARTING

Let's take a look at how we charted Dominic's *Inner Round Table.*

STEP ONE: NAMING

You can see we have *Named* the *Main Players* that are involved in this dilemma. There is the *Good Son* and the *Family Man*, who have negotiated a life balance thus far. We see the *Heir Apparent* on the opposite side of *Chef Dominic*. Both are smaller influences, pressing to become larger and creating tension in the system.

An Inner Round Table Chart for Dominic's Situation

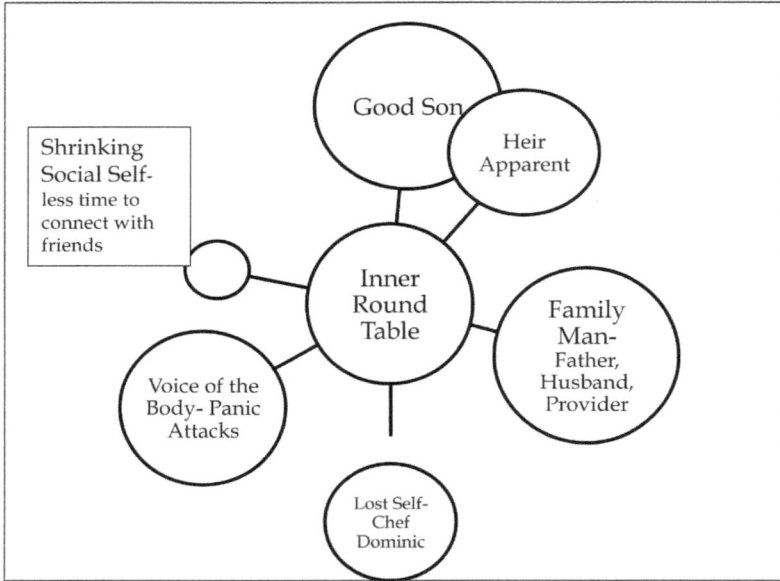

STEP 2: KNOWING

We spent time interviewing each of these *Inner Characters*, getting to know them and what made them tick. Dominic also began some journal work at home using the list of exploratory questions and generating some inquiries of his own. He began to tune in to the *felt sense* of each *Inner Character* in his body. Here is the list of questions he found most valuable when interviewing his *Inner Characters:*

- *What is your history?*
- *What are the rules that you live by?*
- *Who were your teachers and role models?*

- *What do you want and need?*
- *What are your fears or concerns now?*

He added the following questions:

- *What are the rewards of doing things your way?*
- *When are you happiest?*
- *If other people were not depending upon you, and you could wave a magic wand to make everything turn out, what would it look like?*
- *If you could do anything you wanted, without displeasing anyone, what would you do?*

His efforts to understand his *Inner Cast* and explore their differing needs, wants, values and concerns began to pay off as he separated the entanglement of the *Good Son* with the *Heir Apparent* and began to grasp that he was more than the roles he fulfilled, more than a player in his father's script. He had yet to write his own story, but now he had the realization that he could begin to write it. As the *Heir Apparent*, he felt only stress and a loss of enthusiasm for life. When he entered the realm of *La Dolce Vita*, he immediately began to feel inspired, released and relaxed. He began to explore how he could integrate more of the energy that *Chef Dominic* brought to him.

STEP 3: NEGOTIATING – *"Collective Bargaining"*

The goal of *Inner Round Table* work is to make a place for all aspects of self and to negotiate a way for their divergent energies to be expressed. Collective bargaining becomes possible when we stand in the center and take all parts of self into account. Dominic was standing amidst the tension of opposites and trusting that some new solution would emerge from the creativity that happens when we begin to tap into the wisdom of the deep collective unconscious. This way of approaching problems begins to seem almost mystical in its ability to bring about unexpected solutions. He was no longer afraid that he was going to polarize into any extreme, abandoning his family to work untold hours or dumping everything to run off to Culinary School.

Around this time, he decided to plant an herb garden and began cooking again for friends. He had dreams of his grandmother and little towns in Tuscany, and awoke from these dreams feeling inspired and refreshed. One Saturday, as he was standing at the stove stirring a sauce, he remembered a scene from his childhood. He and his sister Catherine were playing restaurant. He was cooking the food and waiting on the customers. His sister was counting the inventory and tallying up the money. He smiled at the thought that his sister had grown up to be a successful accountant. She would be coming into town for Thanksgiving.

When Catherine visited for Thanksgiving, they sat up late into the night and talked about their family. It was a very enlightening conversation. Dominic dared to voice his misgivings about taking over the helm of their father's business. He had never spoken these things to anyone in the family. Catherine shared with him the long term hurt and resentment she had felt that her father had never included her in the business plan. She waved it away, saying that she understood that dad was from the old country where the men ran things. She had established a successful career outside the family, but she only pretended that she had no interest in the family business. They both began to smile.

Over the next few weeks they began to explore the possibility of working together in the business in a way that suited both of their needs and talents. Catherine was gifted in administration and finances. Dominic preferred the creative end, marketing, and interacting with people. They both wanted flex time for family, with someone they trusted to cover for them. They hammered out a plan for partnering and prepared to propose it to their father.

Dominic's dad was upset and resistant at first. Dominic had to hold steady as the *Heir Apparent* lectured him on how he was not fulfilling his "destiny," and the *Good Son* in him nearly collapsed with anxiety. As he continued to re-anchor himself in his *Calm Core*, he was able to hold steady and sell the idea of collaborating with his sister. Based on a trial period, his dad conceded. He and his sister combined their talents and created a profitable and successful working relationship.

That summer Dominic and his children planted a chef's garden in their back yard. He began to gather friends in his home to share food and laughter and a celebration of the simple, good life. Life felt "right" when he acknowledged the intrinsic value that food, friendship and the simple things of life held for him. They fed his soul. He launched an annual charity food event called La Dolce Vita, where he could rub shoulders with local chefs and restaurant owners as they raised money for the community. Last year, he and his wife went to Tuscany for a romantic vacation, toasting to their good life and each other. Dominic's "heart trouble" has vanished.

Observing Self and the Calm Core

Inner Round Table work helps you to separate out from the dramas of living. Untangling the competing needs and agendas of your *Inner Characters* brings awareness and gives each one some breathing space. You will feel more confident and empowered as you learn to *Stop, Look and Listen* rather than reacting, pushed around by unconscious impulses and outdated scripts.

Listening to the messages sent by your body, the *felt sense* of each *Inner Character* helps you identify when they are activated in you. As you develop your *Observing Self* and have an increasing sense of operating from your *Calm Core*, you will find peace amidst the many demands of life. From your *Calm Core*, you can become the *Director* of your life's divergent energies, rather than be at their mercy.

Learning the *felt sense* of your *Calm Core*, this place of relaxed body and neutral observation, is a form of meditation. Seriously consider setting aside a few moments throughout the day to be still, breathe, and anchor yourself in this calm, centered place of awareness. Begin to observe how and when you get moved off your center and which *Inner Characters* are activated when you do. Learn to re-center in the flow of life. Develop this as a spiritual practice and notice how it changes your experience of living.

PART TWO

WHERE NEGOTIATIONS GET STUCK

CHAPTER 6

THE SCRIPTS THAT WE LIVE

*"We live immersed in narrative, recounting and
reassessing the meaning of our past actions, anticipating the
outcome of our future projects, situating ourselves at the
intersection of several stories not yet completed."*
Michael White

Human beings are story-making creatures and we love to tell the story of our lives. Every life has a script. It begins in our early years when we internalize "master stories" that help us interpret the things that happen and navigate life's challenges. Our *Inner Cast of Characters* develops to live out these guiding stories which answer questions like: What is my role and how do I play it? Who am I in the larger scheme of things? What is important? What can a person like me expect from life? Is my life a drama, mystery, comedy, tragedy or love story?

We draw our "master stories" from a variety of places, children's books, fairy tales, even cartoon characters add to the raw material of our master stories. In our make believe play, we try on costumes and explore how it feels to be a hero, princess, monster, witch, pirate, cowboy, nurse, teacher, etc.

Scripts get passed down from one generation to the next as kinfolk tell us stories of our family and cultural history. In our houses of worship, we hear stories of saints and sinners, loss and redemption. We go to school and hear examples of courageous, notorious, tragic, brilliant and talented people in history. We learn about the victors and the oppressed, and those who suffered and prevailed. We add more script material and possible characters from movies, television, and popular culture. As we listen to these stories, we identify with certain figures, vicariously experiencing their triumphs and tragedies. What we resonate with most gives us information about our own personal *Soul Print*, the archetypal patterns that are unique to us.

I know of few children who grew up in an environment where their parents encouraged an awareness of their individual *Soul Print*. Most of us had parents who told us who they wanted us to be. In our early years, our innate qualities were rewarded or punished and we adapted accordingly. Our conflicts, complexes and counterplots emerged as we complied or rebelled. This shaped our script and the development of our *Inner Cast of Characters* who have played out the unfolding drama of our lives. Our *Main Players* are not always representative of what is in our deepest and most authentic *Self.*

Script and Destiny

The scripts we develop as children can easily obscure our awareness of our deeper essence, and once in place, scripts are hard to change. They are woven into the fabric of our identity all along the way. A script becomes the lens through which we view the world and seems like the only possible reality. They direct and pull us to certain paths, relationships and careers. Until we surface and examine them, they operate automatically, outside of our awareness.

Winners

Some people's lives seem graced by a mysterious magic. The path opens before them. Everything they touch turns to gold. They are resilient and rebound from things that would destroy others. They develop *Inner Characters* named: *Gifted, Brilliant, Successful, Survivor, Visionary, Creator, Star, Leader, Hero, Saint, Empire Builder, Man or Woman of the Year.*

These are all "golden" labels. The problem comes if we become over-identified with them. They tend to be "power" characters. If these *Inner Characters* dominate the cast, it leaves no room for other aspects of the archetypal spectrum that move more slowly, may be softer, more relational, more sensual, more spiritual or intuitive. When you must always be *Special* or *Extraordinary*, when can you let down and just be *Ordinary*? If you are a *Brilliant Leader* or a *Creative Genius*, what do you do on the days when you feel *Lost or Dull*? Do you become *Nothing* on those days? If you are a *Saint*, what do you do on those days when you feel *Selfish, Hopeless, Angry* or just plain *Cranky*? Does the halo over your head become a noose around your neck?

Losers

Other people's lives seem to go from one failure and disaster to the next. No matter how hard they try, they can't win. The seeds of possibility and potential lay in the soil of their beings, unrecognized and uncultivated. When I interview them, I discover that they internalized limiting labels early on. I meet *Inner Characters* such as: *Damaged, Abused*, the *Disappointment, Problem Child, Black Sheep, Unwanted, Nuisance, Stupid, Lazy, No-good, Liar, Manipulator, Unstable, Delinquent, Defiant, Alcoholic, or Addict.*

The problem with these labels is that when people internalize them, they begin to believe that they define them in totality. When they become the dominant characters on the stage of a person's life, alternative story lines are not allowed to emerge. The seeds of winning, becoming "somebody," getting the love you want, or being recognized for special talents are trampled before they have the chance to grow. Bright possibilities get chased off the stage.

People have an uncanny ability to find situations that validate their scripts. Alternative plotlines end up like crumpled pages in a play-write's trashcan. I work with people all the time who limit themselves because their lives are dominated by *Main Players* who are *Victims* and *Losers*. The work with them is to get them to separate out from these identifications in order to allow their innate gifts and potentials to emerge, develop and to take their place on the stage of their lives.

EXPLORING YOUR SCRIPT FORMATION

List three of your favorite childhood stories from fairy tales, books, cartoons, movies, family, and religious stories. Were there historical figures or people in your family that you particularly admired? Make a list of these characters and individuals. Here is a list of exploratory questions. Take your time exploring these. You can ponder it a bit at a time, or you might want to schedule a dialogue retreat for yourself to delve more deeply into this material. It can be a rich focus for a group interested in inner work.

Stories You Loved as a Child

- *What were some of the stories you loved as a child?*
- *Who did you identify with in these stories and why?*
- *Who did you admire and why?*
- *What kind of challenges did these characters face?*
- *What resources (inner and outer) did they call upon to overcome their struggles?*
- *How did the story turn out?*
- *How are you like (or unlike) these characters in your life right now?*

In Your Childhood Play

- *What roles or characters did you usually play? (Main character, supporting cast, hero/heroine, villain, victim?)*
- *Did you choose these roles yourself or were they assigned by others? (Siblings or playmates?)*
- *What roles or characters would you have liked to play?*

- *How were the characters you played different from your actual childhood experience?*
- *In present time, how are you like, or unlike, the characters you played in childhood?*

Role Models

- *Who were the role models that influenced you?*
- *What did you learn from them?*
- *How did you seek to be like them?*
- *Have you succeeded?*

The Story of Your Life

- *If your life were a fairy tale, how would it be told?*
- *So far, is your life a drama, a comedy, a tragedy, or an ordinary story?*
- *What is the moral of your story?*

SCRIPTS WRITTEN BY OTHERS

The Script Monitor

Limiting scripts *can* be transcended if they are made conscious and rewritten, but this is no easy task. We all have an *Inner Character* that I call the *Script Monitor,* who watches and listens to us to make sure we are playing our parts as written. When we are "off script", the *Script Monitor* sets off alarms that create a great deal of anxiety.

Being "off script" feels wrong, but in some cases, wrong is right. Being "off script" may mean we are moving beyond previously constraining story lines. The tension of that wrong feeling needs to be tolerated while we are rewriting negative story lines. For a person who has always been a failure or an outcast, being "off-script" would mean experiencing success and belonging. We need lots of support when we are rewriting our script and inviting new players to our *Inner Round Table*.

Whose Life Are You Living?

In the previous chapter you met Dominic, who was living a script written by his father. This worked fine for him up until a certain point in his life, and then he could no longer deny his deeper yearnings.

Is it possible that you are living a script handed to you by others? A story which does not really suit your essential self? If you have come to the conclusion that you are living someone else's life, it can be extremely upsetting.

Many kids disconnect from their essential selves in order to gain their parent's love and approval. They pursue things that are important to their parents. To pursue what *they* really care about would betray their parent's expectations, and they fear the loss of their parent's support or attention.

Another version of this is parents that give their children an overwhelming avalanche of every experience they themselves couldn't afford, whether the child wants it or not: summer camps, designer clothes, sports, scouting, music, dance and tennis lessons. Unfortunately, many of these kids are burnt out by overscheduling. They never have a chance to feel their own inner rhythms or enjoy a quiet moment. Later in life, they may lack the capacity to tolerate frustration or delay gratification because everything was handed to them on a platter.

Transcending Your Parent's Expectations

If you are the child of a parent who worked two jobs to give you what he or she couldn't have, you know the pressure of living up to your parent's expectations. Your father may have told you not to work with your hands, to wear a white collar, not blue. I had a client whose mother refused to let her clean a bathroom because she was being groomed to marry a man rich enough to provide maid service.

Another version of a limiting script for the next generation is parents who don't want their child to reach too high, lest they be disappointed. Sometimes a parent sends the message not to achieve more than they did because they fear that the child may look down on them, as others have. They fear that this will somehow negate the value of their own lives. In my own life, I hit a ceiling for years that represented the limit of my father's career success. I finally realized that the *Good Daughter* in me believed that to surpass his success would be some kind of betrayal. I didn't want to show him up. Once I surfaced this internal "stop," I was able to move beyond it. He had moved beyond it as well and it turned out that my success made him proud.

Janice

Janice passed up a considerable family fortune because she decided not to follow her mother's controlling edicts about who she would marry, where and how she would live, and what she would do for a living. For years, she attempted to set respectful limits with her mother. Finally, they had a fierce confrontation about the constant undermining and criticism. After this conversation, Janice's mother broke off contact. Janice attempted to reconnect with her mother, but her mother would not respond.

She had feared this for years. It seemed that she had to choose between following her *Authentic Self* or being her *Mother's Daughter*. As she continued to do her *Inner Peace Treaty* negotiations she realized that she had been an orphan in her own home for years, never accepted for who she really was. She decided that living according to her own values was the most important thing in her life. She married a talented local carpenter, and now runs a coffee house, hosts local poetry readings, and teaches about organic gardening. Her kids attend public school, something her mother would consider an outrage. Her life is simple and rich in ways her mother could never support or understand.

Carl

Carl was a kid from "the projects." In middle school his science teacher recognized that he was a gifted student and began to open doors for him to attend the state's acclaimed High School of Math and Science. An IQ test confirmed significant gifts.

Carl's mother didn't want to hear anything about Carl's attending a fancy school. She distrusted educated white men and didn't want her son to be hurt or ridiculed by reaching for more than what she believed was possible. After many conversations with the teacher, who went to bat for him, she finally agreed to let her son leave home and enter this school for gifted young scientists. Four years later, Carl received a full ride scholarship to Princeton. Today Carl is a successful research scientist, exploring cures for cancer. He loves his work and earns enough money to live well and care for his aging mother.

The Script Payoff

When we live a script written by others, there is usually some promise of a pay off in the end. This makes us feel that it will be worth the sacrifice. We trade our hearts desire for what is acceptable or expected by others. Unfortunately, the promised script payoff does not always occur and when that happens, people find themselves in the midst of a serious crisis.

When the script we adopt does not match our innate *Soul Print*, the essence of who we are, we run into trouble. The greater the degree of difference, the more inner conflict we will have. We may get love and approval from the outside, but the flame of the soul life is extinguished. Some people resolve this by disconnecting completely from their inner experience. They decide to comply with the expectations of others, shutting off their inner guidance and doing as they are told.

Disconnecting from your essential *Self* can work for a while, but it often leads to a malaise that can't be named. This is what Thoreau was talking about when he said that "most people live lives of quiet desperation" and go to their graves never having sung the song that is in their hearts.

We don't purposefully undermine our happiness in this way. We do it because complying with the expectations of the people we depend on is both rewarding and adaptive. People who live lives defined by others often feel flat and depressed. They may go on anti-depressant medications, but it doesn't fix the real problem.

Sometimes when a person realizes how far they have drifted from what really matters to them, they have an overwhelming desire to escape their life and to free themselves. They may dismantle their entire life in an effort to "find themselves," quitting jobs, leaving marriages, or moving to a new place. While sometimes it is necessary to leave behind a life that no longer works, in many cases we can solve the problem by making a place for these disowned selves at the *Inner Round Table* of our life.

Judith, the Pleaser

Judith was a 50 year old, classy, attractive woman, with dazed eyes and a perpetual smile. She smiled all throughout our first session, even as the tears rolled down her cheeks. Her husband Don had just told Judith he was sick of their boring life and wanted a divorce.

Judith had lived the script of the *Good Wife* and *Devoted Mother* as closely as you could possibly live it. She had been smiling her entire adult life, being pleasing, following the rules, behaving properly, being supportive and accommodating to her husband. She kept an immaculate house, raised fine children, and maintained her figure. She had done all the right things. Now Don wanted a divorce. He had taken up with a thirty-two year old motorcycle riding waitress who had a tattoo on her ankle. Judith was bewildered. Her script was supposed to guarantee the happily ever after. What had gone wrong and what was she supposed to do now?

Many of you know this story. It may have happened to you, or a friend, or perhaps your own mother. An intelligent, college educated woman forfeits her own career and stays at home, devoting her life to family and husband. She does this sometimes because it is expected (the script), but often there is an *Inner Self* in her that believes in the calling of the *Good Wife* and *Devoted Mother.*

In the script there is an expectation of an exchange. She counts on a lifetime of security and love. When this script payoff evaporates, it is as if her whole life has gone down the drain. There is an upheaval of fear and suspicion as wives around her begin to wonder if their own well planned lives and successful marriages are as solid as they seem.

I know many a *Rebel Daughter* who became a successful *Career Woman* in reaction to watching their mother go through this kind of heartbreak and betrayal. "This will never happen to me," the *Rebel Daughter* says. This same woman can house a *Loving Wife* in the shadows who longs for love and intimacy, but is blocked from attaining them because relationships create too much vulnerability.

As Judith and I began to outline her *Inner Cast of Characters,* she saw how completely devoted she had been to the archetypes of the *Good Wife* and *the Devoted Mother.* Now she felt as frightened as an *Abandoned Child* and as hurt and angry as any *Betrayed Woman* has ever felt. In her marriage, Judith had never allowed herself to be angry. She had been taught that anger was not becoming in a woman. Now, a lifetime of hurt and anger began to come to the surface. She was no longer smiling.

I discovered that Judith had been an art major in college. Once a gifted painter, she had put her dreams of becoming a successful artist away after she got married. She had retired the *Gifted Artist* in exchange for the *Good Wife* and the promise of love, safety and security. In *Round Table Dialogues* including the *Betrayed Woman, Abandoned Child and Gifted Artist,* she began to reconnect threads of potential and possibility she had set aside in her earlier life to devote herself to others.

I encouraged Judith to channel her anger into some creative outlets and she decided to take up the ancient woman's art of weaving. She began to hand dye her wool, picking colors that expressed her emotions. She sent her anger into the pushing and pulling motions of the loom and through the shuttle, back and forth. She began to weave her rage, fear, betrayal and loss into the fabric of a new life. Her rage dissipated and she moved into a place of peace, joy and satisfaction. As the *Weaver* developed in her, she grew her hair long and allowed lovely streaks of gray to show. Judith has become quite a respected artist. She has retired her *Pleaser* and lives life on her own terms. Her work portrays the themes of women's lives and her journey of *Individuation.*

Living From Your Essential Soul Print Is Not Without Cost

Living from your essential *Self* is not easy or without cost. We face crucial decisions all along the road of life where we must balance what we love with practical considerations. How will we make a living? How will we honor the commitments we have made to people we care about as we seek to be true to ourselves? How will we deal with the disapproval or lack of support when others do not agree with our choices?

People often enter therapy at mid-life, when they begin to realize the cost of selling out what they really loved for the promise of acceptability and security. They can no longer ignore the gnawing emptiness of a life that has little meaning. When the promised script payoff does not arrive, they feel emotionally or spiritually bankrupt. A life lived without meaning can easily unravel when faced with illness, divorce, a mid-life layoff or the loss of your retirement nest-egg. At times like these we begin to ask "is that all there is?"

When Life Falls Apart: Crisis and Opportunity

Having a well scripted life fall apart is a major crisis. It is also a major opportunity to reconstruct your life on a more meaningful foundation. In order to do that, you have to do some real soul searching. You have to look beyond the script written by others.

DIALOGUE RETREAT
Scripts

Whose life are you living?

- *Do you have a sense that you are living a life defined by others?*
- *How did your parents and teachers encourage or discourage you in a particular direction?*
- *Did your parents ever discourage you from pursuing something you really wanted to do? What reasons did they give you?*
- *What outcomes or assurances do you expect for the life you are living?*
- *If they don't come about . . . . will it be worth the price you paid?*
- *In what ways are you living the unlived life of your parents?*

Uncovering Lost Story Lines

- *What did you want to do or be when you were little that you never had the chance to do or be?*

- *What reasons do you give yourself today for not pursuing things that you are drawn to, curious about, or strongly interested in?*
- *Make a list of people you admire or envy.*
- *What is it about their lives that appeals to you?*
- *How do you imagine you would feel if you were living that life?*
- *What are some possible ways in which you might have this experience?*

Dialoguing With the Script Monitor

Close your eyes and see if you can locate your *Inner Script Monitor*, that part of you that seeks to scare you half to death when you go "off script". Allow your *Script Monitor* to communicate to you. As the interviewer, you can ask:

- *How are you trying to help or protect me?*
- *When do you get upset with me?*
- *How do you signal me when I have gone "off-script"?*
- *What kind of warnings do you give me?*
- *What kinds of body sensations do you generate?*

Developing New Story Lines and Potentials

- *What callings and potentials have you been ignoring?*
- *What Possible Selves did you leave behind on your journey?*
- *What potentials might you develop in this time of flux and change?*
- *What new Characters might you add to the Inner Round Table of your life?*

CHAPTER 7

THE KIDS BEHIND THE CURTAIN:
The Innocent and the Orphan

"As soon as you trust yourself, you will know how to live."
Goethe

The two major archetypes of early life stay with us forever, the *Innocent* and the *Orphan*[1]. These *Inner Children* represent our vulnerable past, the children we once were. Every child is born innocent and all of us left parts of ourselves behind, like little orphans by the side of the road. Our *Inner Cast of Characters* developed to shield and protect these early selves from harm, fear, shame, hunger and rejection. We may have forgotten them in the process of developing our adult personas but they have not forgotten us. Like Russian nesting dolls, they are embedded deep in our psyches, hidden behind our *Main Players,* who take care of the business of life.

All of us have these archetypes within, but our lives will tend to be influenced more strongly by one or the other. They are behind the scenes, but we know they are there, because they generate such strong emotions. They can interfere significantly with the progress of *Inner Round Table* negotiations. If we are ever to make peace with ourselves, we must re-engage these *Inner Children*, value their input, and welcome them to the table of our lives.

---

[1]   Thanks to Carol Pearson, who introduced the idea of archetypes of early development in *"Awakening the Heroes Within: Twelve Archetypes to Help Us Find Ourselves and Transform Our World"*.

THE INNOCENT

All children are born innocent and we retain this important quality if we are:

- Welcomed into the world.
- Nurtured and protected as children.
- Celebrated and supported in exploring the world and developing our own unique qualities, gifts and interests.

None of us had perfect childhoods, but even the most traumatic childhoods had moments of innocence.

Exploration: Memory Lane—The Realm of Innocence

1. ***Close your eyes and think back to a time in your childhood when you remember experiencing pure delight.*** See if you can recall being quite young and discovering something amazing for the first time: a wild flower, a salamander, a butterfly. Do you remember the timeless feeling of summer, lying on the grass and watching clouds float by, or building sand castles on the beach? Did you ever create a magic world in a cardboard box? Do you remember a time that you felt totally safe and loved? Did someone read stories to you at bedtime? When you were little, did you ever get out of the tub and run naked through the house squealing and giggling as your mom chased you? This is the realm of innocence. Take a few moments to reconnect with the memory and feeling of this very young self inside, a self you may have lost touch with, your *Innocent*. What were the sights, colors, sounds, smells, temperature, textures and tastes? Stay there for a moment and really enter into the scene.

2. ***Tune into the energy of innocence.*** Most people describe it as light, free, expansive, joyful. What emotions are you feeling? Peacefulness, delight, wonder, curiosity, contentment? For some of you these feeling may seem very far away. Many people are often disconnected from this place of wonder and delight. Regardless of what has happened in years gone by, you can re-enter this wonderful realm and stay for a few moments.

3. ***While staying with the memories of innocence, let this feeling and energy permeate your entire body.*** This is a wonderful way of calming or inspiring yourself. Imagine breathing this feeling throughout every cell of your body. Notice how it makes you feel. Where do you feel it? Is it a sense of tingling, fullness, relaxation, floating?

4. ***Use this energy to heal.*** Scan your body and find any places that feel painful, heavy, sad or stuck. Imagine breathing innocence into these places and exhale the pain, tension, sadness, confusion, fear or anger that is stored there.

5. ***Notice if you have negative, more powerful Inner Characters that negate the value of these wonderful memories.*** They may try to muscle in and bring cynical thoughts or reminders of subsequent hurt and loss. Have your *Inner Director* instruct these negative *Inner Characters* to clear the stage for a few moments while we do some character exploration of the archetype and energy of innocence.

The Importance of Innocence

We never want to lose touch with our innocence, because some of our most precious potential is found there. This is where we access wonder and joy, spontaneous creativity, and the capacity to be open, uninhibited, and to delight in being sensually embodied.

We rely on our parents for protection when we are children. Tragically, not all of us find it there. If innocence is not protected, it can be violated and lost. A crucial task of growing into adulthood is to develop our own *Inner Protectors* and *Wise Ones,* who can discern the intentions of those around us, and determine where it is safe to place our faith and trust. When these protections are in place, we can continue to know the delight and wonder that the *Innocent* carries for us.

Innocents naturally gravitate to the spiritual path. The realm of spirit feels like home to the *Innocent.* This is what Jesus meant when he said that you must become like a little child to understand the kingdom of heaven. Mystical experiences and the sense of transcendence are born in this part of the psyche, but in order for the faith, hope and optimism of the *Innocent* to continue, it must be protected.

Innocents as Main Players in Adulthood

Sometimes a person will continue to carry this archetype into adulthood as a *Main Player* on the stage of their lives. Certain adults have a childlike quality to them. They tend to be very trusting and often depend on others to manage life for them. The traditional marriage is based on the idea that the woman would remain home in a place of protection, while the man went out and faced the hard, cruel world.

Those who maintain this archetype as a central character in adulthood will give their total, unquestioning devotion to people, organizations and religious institutions. This works well for some, provided the object of their devotion is responsible, ethical and benevolent, coming through with their part of the protective bargain. Unfortunately, this is not always the case, and the story doesn't always have a happy ending. Many great literary works are based on the drama of an innocent's betrayed trust.

The Wounded Innocent

We tend to think that people lose their innocence when they are young, but loss of innocence can occur at any age. People from protected childhoods are trusting and optimistic. They expect others to be honest and to have their best interests at heart. They can go through painful disillusionment when the world does not turn out to be as good and idyllic as they imagined. In my practice, I am constantly hearing stories of the devastating experiences that come when people assume without question that others will be there for them, and treat them with the same consideration that they themselves would. The wounding that comes from placing our trust and faith in people, organizations, and institutions happens to people of all ages, including a generation of employees who trusted that working for a lifetime would assure them security in their retirement.

Part of growing up involves relinquishing the childhood expectation of guaranteed protection, security, loyalty, honesty and fair treatment. When a person grows up with no reference point for dangerous situations, they wander more easily into the dark realm of the *Victim*. At this point their experience begins to shift to the *Orphan* archetype, which we will explore shortly.

If the wounding and loss of innocence is too traumatic or repeats too often, a person may banish this part of themselves permanently, and become cynical, bitter and controlling. Now the *Voices of Warning* police their inner world, preventing all forms of innocence, lest there be further wounding. There is something very tragic about people in whom all faith and idealism has been extinguished. We need *Street Wise Inner Selves* in our cast, who can help us be discerning about where to place our devotion, faith and trust.

Angela's Story

Angela was a classic *Innocent*. She was raised in a small town in the Midwest where everyone left their doors unlocked. Her hardworking dad and "stay at home" mom lived a simple life built around church and family. There was lots of love in her home, and Angela felt safe and happy as a child.

Angela went to college, where she met and fell in love with a handsome, intelligent young man named Andrew. They shared the same religious beliefs and seemed to want the same things in life. They married and Angela anticipated that they would live a life much like her parents. What she did not understand was how the wounding in Andrew's history would darken their future.

Andrew's father was a violent alcoholic, who left the family when Andrew was six and Andrew never saw him again. He grew up with a mother, who was exhausted and depressed much of the time as she struggled to make ends meet. Andrew had an *Inner Orphan* behind the curtain of his charming personality, and what he loved about Angela was her fresh innocence, her sunny disposition and how she showered him with love and attention. It never occurred to Angela that he would ever hurt her.

The problems began at the birth of their first child, when Angela's attention shifted to the needs of the baby. She was often exhausted. Andrew began to feel abandoned and resentful about the loss of attention. His *Inner Orphan* raged, and he began to leave the house and come home drunk. When he drank, he became violent, just like his father. Angela was scared and bewildered, but kept hoping that things would get better, if she could just be a better wife.

Six years later, Angela was referred to me by a women's shelter, where she was living with her two small children. She had big, childlike eyes and spoke very softly, apologizing for herself a lot. Frightened and confused, she wept in anguish over her broken dreams. She had done all the right things and did not understand how her life had gone so wrong. The script Angela had been following was the one in which the *Good Girl* marries the *Charming Young Man*, loves him and takes care of her family and lives happily ever after. In this case, the fairy tale had not come true.

Angela's Inner Round Table Work

Angela and I began to outline her story and identify who was sitting at her *Inner Round Table*. We talked about the archetype of the *Innocent* and the scripts they live. She described an image of herself, very young and curled up in a corner afraid to come out. She had been trying to be a *Good Wife* and had endured violence and verbal abuse for six years now.

Because the archetype of the *Innocent* was so central in Angela's psyche, her *Inner Round Table* was populated by several very young *Inner Selves*. Angela began to describe feeling so frozen with fear she couldn't figure out what to do. She couldn't think. She had always looked to others for the answers and doubted her ability to make decisions for herself. She had been brought up to believe that a man would supply her with an umbrella of protection, and she would rely on him. She wanted someone outside her, who was wiser and stronger, to direct her life. We named this aspect of her the *Dependent One*.

Another young self inside was an idealistic, forgiving, romantic *Inner Character* which she named *"Ever Hopeful."* This part of her refused to give up on the fairy tale ending, believing that love conquers all. *Ever Hopeful* trusted that Andrew would change every time he apologized for his violent behavior. He had an endless supply of chances.

Angela also had an *Inner Pleaser* who felt responsible for everyone's happiness. In interviewing her *Pleaser*, we learned that it was her job to know everyone's needs intuitively, respond thoroughly, and work out any conflicts in the mix.

As we continued to name her *Inner Characters*, we discovered a harsh, condemning *Inner Judge*, who had the face of a scary fire and brimstone minister from her youth. When we dialogued with him, he said things like, "Shame on you! A woman should obey her husband! When something goes wrong in a marriage, it's always the woman's fault. You are a failure as a woman. You need to go home to your husband and try harder."

When *Ever Hopeful*, her *Pleaser*, her *Dependent Self* and *The Judge* teamed up, Angela would collapse and become convinced that she *had* to return home and try to be a better wife. I asked her how many times she had been through this cycle of violence and apology with promises of "never again." She looked at the floor and solemnly told me she had lost count. She lived in a state of continual fear because Andrew drank constantly and she never knew what to expect from him.

Angela realized that she found her strength and courage from the powerful archetype of the *Protective Mother,* which came into being at the birth of her own children. The night Andrew had turned his violence towards the kids, the *Protective Mother* in Angela gathered her children up and walked out the door.

There are Two Round Tables in Every Relationship

We talked a little bit about how in any relationship, each person has an *Inner Round Table* to consider. When we meet people, we only see the *Main Players* that a person presents, while there are others offstage, behind the curtain and in the shadows. Andrew's shadow characters of the *Sad, Angry, Abandoned Boy* (*his Orphan*) and *The Drunk Abuser* (remnants of his father) had not come forward until after their children had been born and Angela was no longer showering him with her total attention.

Angela loved Andrew, his intelligence, his humor, his long lost tenderness, but she also became clear that he was a "package deal." Now she had met the darker and more disturbing *Inner Characters* that lived in him and came forward to ruin their happy life. She began to draw on the archetype of the *Protective Mother* to give her the strength to insist on safety for both her and her children. The *Protective Mother* set limits and refused to let her move back home until Andrew had done some healing work of his own.

Angela had always thought of Andrew as the intelligent one, but now she began to recognize her own innate intelligence. We began to cultivate a conversation with a clear, impersonal *Thinking Self* inside, inviting her to be a member of the *Inner Committee* that was determining her future. Angela began to claim her own capacity to solve problems, instead of looking to others. As she did this, her *Inner Children* calmed down and her two outer children began to relax as well.

Andrew was still refusing to consider that he had a problem. He told Angela that their Pastor had preached on forgiveness and she should forgive him and come home. This conversation threw her into a whole new bout of self-doubt as the *Judge*, the *Good Wife* and now the *Good Christian* went into a frenzy of anxiety. Her *Inner Pleaser* reminded her that she was responsible for everyone's happiness. *Ever Hopeful* reminded her of how wonderful things could be if she would just forget about the past. Angela's *Thinking Self* and the *Protective Mother* held firm.

As she began to think clearly, she realized the issue was not forgiveness or being a *Good Wife* or *Good Christian*. The issue was Andrew's need to look at the problems that came from his drinking and the unhealed wounds of his childhood. She was not going to raise her kids in a violent home. She began to consider the possibility that Andrew might not face his problems, and she might need to make it in the world without him.

Angela Grows Up

Angela was developing an *Observing Self*, that part of us that can stand back, with a neutral perspective and observe our inner process, the *Inner Characters* at play, what their needs and agendas are and what might be a wise way to proceed. While all her *Inner Characters* argued about what she should do, Angela held the tension of all this conflicting energy, remained anchored in her *Calm Core*, and no longer ricocheted from one extreme position to the other.

Angela faced the very adult realization that others do not always operate under the same values and standards as we do. We can't make other people do their inner work. So she got an apartment and enrolled in dental hygiene school. By now she had developed a quiet core of confidence and the *Voices of Judgment* and D*oubt* were getting softer and less convincing. *Ever Hopeful* turned her energy towards Angela's future rather than trying to resurrect a fairy tale dream. She accessed the energy of innocence in her play with her children and in the way she set people at ease in the dental chair.

Several months later, Andrew called to say he was attending Alcoholics Anonymous meetings, had a sponsor, and was working his program. Angela was happy for him, but explained that he would need a year of sobriety and some personal therapy before she would even consider putting their family back together.

Andrew and Angela are still in the middle of their story. At this point, Andrew will have to engage the confident, remarkable adult woman that Angela has become. She is engaging life and taking responsibility for herself. She is no pushover.

Innocents I Have Encountered

You may have several variations of this archetype in you. Over the years, in *Voice Dialogue* sessions, I have met many *Innocents* in both bright and dark variations. Here is a partial list:

The Idealist, Dreamer, Artist, Hopeful One, Visionary, Mystic, Sacred or Divine Child, Eternal Optimist, Pleaser, Polly Anna, Peter Pan, Authentic One, Gifted One, Special One, Naïve One, Dependent One, Good Girl, Boy Scout, Altar Boy, Adoring Daughter, Rule Follower, Favored Child, Teacher's Pet, Virgin, Persephone, (the young Greek Goddess). The *Puer (Eternal Boy) and Puella (Eternal Girl)* are archetypes well known in Jungian psychology that refer to this energy.

GETTING TO KNOW
THE INNOCENT WITHIN

Take some time and settle again into a childhood memory of wonder, safety, and delight. Remember that you may have several personifications of this archetype based on different times and memories in your life.

Dialoguing With Your Innocent

Center yourself by breathing quietly and deeply or by using some sort of entrance meditation. Enter into a wonderful childhood memory and immerse yourself in the sights, sounds, tastes, smells and sensations. Allow this experience to permeate your being. Imagine you are really there. Now imagine that you are having a dialogue with the little person. Take what comes.

   − *Tell me about yourself.*
   − *What shall I call you?*

- *What makes you happy?*
- *What do you like to do?*
- *Where do you feel most safe?*
- *Where do you show up in my life today?*
- *Is there anything I am doing right now that makes you upset or scared?*
- *What would you need to feel better?*
- *What gifts do you offer me in my life?*
- *Is there anything else you would like me to know about you?*
- *How might I protect you so that you can continue to bring me your gifts?*

After you have completed this dialogue process, take a moment to record anything that seems important to remember.

- *Did you have any new realizations about yourself or your life?*
- *What were the key images that came to you?*
- *What emotions did you feel?*
- *How and where did you feel them in your body?*
- *Are there any life changes you might want to make?*

Creating A Place in Your Heart

This is a really valuable part of this process. Imagine gathering this little person up in your hand and place your hand over your heart. Imagine saying to her or him, *"You are welcome here. I have a safe place for you in my heart."* This creates a touchstone of that memory. In the future, you can touch your heart and begin a conversation with them. They can awaken, open and engage with you.

Deepen the Relationship

You now have a relationship with your *Inner Innocent*. A way of deepening your relationship with this energy is to create some representation that you can see on a regular basis: a picture from a magazine, a figurine, something you draw or make in clay. Put it somewhere that you see often, on a shelf, the kitchen window ledge, your desk. You can also select music that evokes this hopeful energy in you, pick clothing that expresses it, or allow yourself to engage in activities where your *Innocent* can come out to play.

Remember to ask your *Innocent* to participate in some of your *Round Table Negotiations*. *Innocents* add fresh perspectives, creativity, hope and inspiration to our lives and *Inner Negotiations*. You can also make sure that they feel safe about the decisions you are making in your life.

Further Explorations for your Inner Innocent:

- *Where and with whom did you feel loved, nurtured, protected, guided, seen and validated, supported, even celebrated for your essential self?*
- *How well did you do when you first left home and encountered the "real" world? Did you feel prepared? If not, what new Inner Characters got constellated to help you survive?*
- *Have you ever had an experience where you were taken by surprise by someone's dark motives or dishonesty? Have you ever been used or betrayed by someone you trusted? What did you miss that might have warned you that you were in trouble? How were you wounded by this experience? How have you made sense of it?*
- *Has anyone ever told you that you were foolish, naïve, clueless, or overly optimistic? Do you have an Innocent as a major cast member?*

- *What aspects of being an Innocent have served you well in your life?*
- *How has an inner Innocent Idealist helped you to reach a dream?*
- *How has your idealism inspired others?*
- *Have you ever had a mystical or awe-inspiring experience? Revisit that experience and write about it now.*
- *Think of some characters or people in stories, movies and history that carry the energy of The Innocent. In what ways do you identify with them? What can you learn from their experiences?*

CHAPTER 8

THE KIDS BEHIND THE CURTAIN—
The Orphan

"You will love again the stranger who was your self. . . . .
Give back your heart to itself, to the stranger who has loved you all your life,
whom you ignored for another, who knows you by heart."
Derek Walcott

On the opposite side of the *Innocent* dwells the *Orphan,* the other main archetype of early life. Since none of us had perfect childhoods, and all of us have been hurt or rejected at some time, we all have experienced the sadness of being an *Orphan.* The following list of experiences creates an *Inner Orphan:*

- You were not wanted at your birth: you came at a bad time and there was not enough money, space, time or energy in your parent's lives. You were the wrong gender.
- You were neglected, abused, exploited, or abandoned in your childhood. You lost a parent to an illness or addiction.
- Someone in your family was disabled or seriously ill and their needs pulled all the family resources away from you.
- Your innate qualities, gifts and interests were overlooked, misunderstood, punished, or ridiculed.
- Something about you was different, and as you entered the world, you were treated as an outsider.

Orphans harbor no illusions about safety in this life. They have already experienced the dark side.

Exploration: Memory Lane — The Realm of the Orphan

Close your eyes and think back to a time in your childhood when you had an experience where you were not wanted. Were you ever abandoned, victimized, abused or betrayed? Did you ever feel misunderstood, left out, rejected, or picked on? Were you ever hurt by someone you trusted or loved? Did you lose someone that was particularly important to you? This is the realm of the *Orphan*. These memories may bring up strong feelings for you, including grief, anger and fear. See if you can just sit with these feeling for a few minutes.

This can be a very tender place in the psyche. Honor the sadness that it evokes in you. It is warranted. If opening this realm begins to overwhelm you with strong emotion, you can return to the exercises outlined in the *Innocent* and do some healing work; breathing the energy of Innocence into the places you have stored the pain of the *Orphan*. If you continue to feel overwhelmed by emotion, cease working by yourself, and find a therapist who can accompany you through this sad realm.

Orphans as Victims and Outsiders

While the *Innocent* is trusting and open, *Orphans* tend to be on guard for hurt and exploitation. They are slow to trust life or the people around them. At a young age, they learn that sometimes the wicked prosper. Sometimes cruel, incompetent or unethical people run things, and policies and trusted institutions are imperfect.

As outsiders, *Orphans* long for a sense of belonging, but they are so accustomed to rejection and abandonment they do not hope for much. They can become trapped in relationships, jobs and organizations that exploit them because they are afraid they can't do better. Their insatiable longing for love and nurture can't be filled by anyone and they tend to exhaust people with their need for constant affirmation and reassurance. They are seeking an experience that will make up for the vast deficits of their early years. While they are emotionally needy, they also tend to be suspicious, and are unable to recognize authentic love or meaningful involvement when they encounter it.

Because *Orphans* long to be connected and experience redemption, they are drawn to religious and spiritual organizations. While the *Innocent* comes to spiritual groups with idealism, an open heart and an easy faith, the *Orphan* comes seeking healing, belonging, and answers. They can be very loyal, but need a lot of reassurance that they are safe, appreciated and loved.

Sometimes *Orphans* compromise and adapt themselves to the values, beliefs and agendas of others in the hope that they will find love and be accepted. The dark side of this is the number of orphans who gravitate to groups with charismatic leaders that demand unquestioned loyalty and acceptance of their authority. This invites more exploitation and psychic harm. Gangs and cults are filled with orphans who have finally found a place to belong.

Image and Status

For some *Orphans*, image and status become very important to compensate for the deficits they feel inside. They can become high achievers and appear to be high functioning individuals. Underneath this carefully crafted exterior they may suffer from *Imposter Syndrome*. They hide a painful past or shameful secrets and don't really believe in their own worth or legitimacy. They fear being found out. I often hear them say, "If people knew me, they wouldn't like me."

Abandonment and Self-Alienation

Many orphans are out of touch with their essential selves. They suffer from a sense of self-alienation that comes from never having been seen or affirmed by those around them. When something

105

from their depths emerges, they tend to distrust it. They will often deny who they really are in exchange for fitting in and being admired. *Orphans* have a fundamental sense that something is wrong with them that can never be fixed and must be hidden.

Because they felt abandoned by others as children, *Orphans* tend to abandon themselves. They don't pursue their own dreams because they don't believe in themselves or believe that others will support them. They become agents of other people's dreams. They find it hard to claim an authentic, satisfying life that really fits them. Unsure of themselves, they make many false starts, constantly seeking reassurance that they are on the right track.

The Orphan and Depression

A growing number of people in our culture suffer from depression. In our media saturated world, there is little time to reflect on who we really are and what really brings us happiness. This leads to a disconnection from our essential *Self* and no matter how much we accomplish, how much stuff we get, it's never enough, because it's not what we truly need. The anti-depressants commonly prescribed today can be an important component of someone in a legitimate depression, but many people suffer from the malaise of self-alienation. Medication will not fix this. We need to be connected to our essential selves and connected to others in a meaningful way. This is a hard task for the *Orphan*.

Orphans in the Underworld

If the hurt and betrayal of an *Orphan* occur early enough and go deep enough, they may move into the criminal or antisocial realm, with no regard for others. Highly defended, they may believe that "the rules don't apply to me," and operate with a motto of "Look out for #1" or "Get them before they get you." They tend to divide the world into sheep and wolves, and the angry orphan is determined never to be a *Victim* again. Street kids, prostitutes and adult criminals are almost always orphans. Addiction programs are filled with *Orphans*. They use drugs, alcohol and sex to numb the pain inside.

Soul Orphans

There is a particular kind of "hidden" *Orphan*. On the surface they were given everything a child could want or need, but their *Soul Print* was never acknowledged or nurtured. They were treated like pawns on the stage of the parent's lives rather than unique individuals. When a child's essential self is never seen, embraced or reflected, it withers through soul neglect.

Since the attention they get is based on performance, they never feel truly secure. They fear that if they fail to fulfill their parents' expectations, they may lose their parents' love. When kids can't quite make the grade, or figure out how to be what their parent's want them to be, they are in big trouble. They know they are disappointments and they are hurt and angry, and often move into self destructive behaviors, constellating the archetype of the *Misunderstood Rebel*.

In my practice as a therapist, adult *Orphans* talk about feeling that they never belonged in their family of origin. Artistic children are born into athletic families, football players are born to intellectuals, and scientists to artists. Their parents never understood them and constantly attempted to reshape their natural inclinations. Some of my clients wonder if they were secretly adopted.

Healed Orphans and their Great Potential

Most people who house *Inner Orphans* don't like them. Our *Inner Orphans* stir up difficult emotions and distressing body sensations. We wish these troublesome *Inner Selves* would just go away and we often try to banish them. This only makes the

Orphan feel worse. Once again they are unwanted. The *Orphan's* greatest need is to belong and find a place in someone's heart. Here is the key; as much as the *Orphan* seeks to be valued and included in the outside world, the healing of an *Orphan* will only take place when the person in which they reside recognizes and embraces them. Each of us has to welcome our *Inner Orphans* to the *Round Table* of our lives. Only then will they feel safe, secure and loved.

Healed Orphans are really valuable. They are very observant, street smart, discerning, intuitive and bring a lot of energy to our lives. Yes, they can kick up suspicions, anger, insecurity and emotional turmoil in times of stress. Yes, they are prone to over-reaction and regretful outbursts. But has ignoring their inner presence really made things better for you? Orphans settle down when we acknowledge them and get into relationship with them.

When a person with a strong *Inner Orphan* gets healed, they have the potential to become powerful leaders and healers. The archetype of the *Wounded Healer* is a powerful archetype of a healed and transformed *Orphan*. You will find restored, healed *Orphans* working as social workers, therapists, clergy, health care providers, coaches, teachers, lawyers, and volunteers, and service-oriented workers in all possible fields. They invent products that improve people's lives. They work quietly in private practices, healing people one at a time. They are at the forefront of social change movements, visionary and courageous. They found organizations that advocate for those who are weak, forgotten, exploited and marginalized. They find answers to problems that no one else can find and implement changes that are long overdue.

Maureen — The Story of a Soul Orphan

Maureen was born into an intellectual, achievement oriented family. Her father was a doctor and her mother was an attorney. They were thinking people, certainly beyond any kind of irrational faith. Maureen was a deep feeling, introverted child, prone to mystical experiences. She remembers coming to her mother at young age reporting that she had just seen an angel. Her mother scolded her for making up stories and explained that no such thing was possible. As a teenager, Maureen's father once found her reading a book on world religions and threw it in the trash.

Although her parents strongly discouraged any expression of her mystical leanings, the archetype of the *Mystic* and *Spiritual Seeker* were strong in Maureen's innate *Soul Print*. She kept her books on the spiritual path in her locker at school and quietly began to practice meditation. She did not discuss spirituality with her parents.

Maureen was an excellent student and her parents were pleased when she was accepted to a prestigious university. Away from home, she began to attend a church with a strong emphasis on social justice and a ministry to the inner city poor. In this place, Maureen felt like she was with her people and had found her home. She began to feel a call to become an ordained minister. When she spoke to her parents about this, they were appalled. They refused to pay for seminary, but encouraged her to pursue her interests academically through a Ph.D. in philosophy or religion. A professor in the family would be quite acceptable to them.

Maureen's Inner Cast of Characters

Maureen came to see me in her second year of a Ph.D. program in philosophy. Her parents were pleased with her path. She was depressed and felt trapped and panicky. As we began to untangle the threads of her life, we began to identify the underlying scripts and *Inner Characters* that were at war within her.

We began our sessions by talking to her *Philosopher,* an *Inner Self* that had been center stage in her life for the past two years. Maureen's *Philosopher* was confident and powerfully articulate, intrigued by discussions of ethics, social theory and historical movements. It was all quite lofty and interesting, and you could feel the brilliance of Maureen's good mind as the *Philosopher's* energy filled the room. When I asked her where she felt the *Philosopher* in her body, she replied that "he" did not want, need or have a body, only a brain.

I asked her how her interest in poverty began and suddenly she became sad. We began to engage the *Soul Orphan* within her. I asked the *Orphan* to tell me about herself and her history. Maureen's *Soul Orphan* began to recount stories of growing up in a home full of intellectual conversations and political debates. Such conversations felt like a chilly maze to Maureen's *Soul Orphan*. Any time Maureen's *Soul Orphan* attempted to talk about her spiritual wonderings, or mystical stirrings, her mother would change the subject and her father would look at her disapprovingly, warning her not to become one of those "pathetic navel-gazing people." She was painfully aware that she was not welcomed in that home and retreated into the background.

Maureen's *Soul Orphan* was tender, sweet and shy. She was so delighted to find someone who was interested in her and honored the beauty of her mystical insights. One of the most beautiful things about the *Soul Orphan* was her capacity to see value in all people regardless of their race, status, education or background. Her energy was warm and soft, so opposite the hard, bright energy of the *Philosopher.* It was difficult to imagine that they existed in the same *Inner Self System.* The pull between these two *Inner Characters* clearly created tremendous internal tension.

Sitting beside her *Soulful Orphan* was an interesting *Inner Character* that we named *Mother Theresa—Servant of the Poor. Mother Theresa* believed in selfless devotion. She did not like privilege and informed me that Maureen's parents should sell all their earthly belongings and give their money to the poor. She was deeply distressed by Maureen's current path. "Throw out the books. Roll up your sleeves," she declared, "hands on service, that's what counts."

In overhearing all these idealistic declarations, Maureen's *Good Daughter* got stirred up. We engaged her and discovered how much she longed for her parents love and approval. She wanted to make her parents proud, and they were so happy with her current path. They had been so concerned when they found out that she had actually worked in dangerous, inner-city neighborhoods. The *Good Daughter* had a heavy, sad, resigned feel to her. She explained how it was worth exchanging what was truly inspiring to Maureen, so that she would not concern or disappoint her parents. She explained how a lot of important work could be done in academia, a much safer environment. Maureen could lecture and publish brilliant works on important social issues. She might influence whole groups of people rather than just helping the small number she would touch by doing hands on helping. It was very convincing.

One night, Maureen came into my office excited and disturbed. The previous night, she had a powerful dream, in which she was working side by side with *Jane Adams*, the famous social worker. This was Maureen's dream:

I am with Jane Adams. Her eyes are deep and warm and have a wonderful sparkle of life to them. She looks deeply into my eyes as she tells me about my destiny. I am to follow in her footsteps, to live and work humbly, side by side with the poor, just as she did. I will receive help and protection from the other side. I am suddenly filled with a deep sense of peace, and I know my life has meaning.

During this session, we decided it was time to begin an *Inner Round Table Negotiation* involving her *Soul Orphan, Mother Theresa*, the *Philosopher*, and the *Good Daughter*. We added this recent dream figure of *Jane Adams* whose message was still resonating so strongly. I gave Maureen suggestions for a *Dialogue Retreat* and she went to the beach for a weekend. We had been naming and getting to know her *Inner Cast of Characters*. Now she was to call an *Inner Round Table* meeting and see what could be *Negotiated*. At the beach, she asked each *Inner Character* the following questions:

Inner Round Table—Information Gathering:

- *How do you view this problem or situation?*
- *What are your concerns?*
- *What are your needs?*
- *How do you view the others involved?*
- *What do you see as the solution?*

After these questions were answered, she was to look to see:

Negotiating:

- *Where is the common ground?*
- *What concerns can easily be addressed?*
- *Where can cooperation occur?*
- *Where can compromises be made?*
- *What are the real needs? How can they be addressed?*
- *What is missing in this situation that might be solved by the introduction of a new Inner Character? Who might that be?*
- *Does this character exist in the Inner Self System, or does he/she/it need to be developed?*

Resolutions

When Maureen returned, I could tell she was in a whole new place. She had decided to leave school. The dream experience with *Jane Adams* had given her a new resilience and had spoken deeply to her, healing a sad emptiness inside. The dream took place in a settlement house, and she had the realization that a "settlement house" was a place where the soul was doing what it most longed to do. Wherever that was, when you were doing it, you were settled, at home.

Maureen had loved her experience of being part of a church outreach team in the inner city. She knew that while her parents were appalled at the idea of her becoming a minister, they could deal with her being a Social Worker. In surfing the internet one night, she had "happened" onto a program that combined a Masters in Divinity with a Masters in Social Work. She decided that she was going to pursue this path, even if she had to pay for her own education. This made *Mother Theresa,* her *Soul Orphan* and *Jane Adams* happy. She made peace with her *Philosopher* by promising him that he could use his talent for ideas and language by expounding brilliantly from the pulpit. She positioned her *Good Daughter* with the *Soul Orphan* for comfort. The *Orphan* knew a great deal about the grief of being on the outside and had learned ways of staying connected to people without having to be understood.

Maureen is now a minister in a large church staff, with an outreach program to the homeless and the inner-city poor. She is a happy, confident woman, living from her heart, in alignment with her *Soul Print.* Her *Orphan* loves to go and sit in the quiet of the hundred-year old church in the late afternoon and watch the colored light filter through the stained glass windows. She feels a sense of awe and wonder and gratitude in those moments.

Maureen's parents still do not entirely understand her, but they appreciate her passion and her dedication. She loves them and has let go of the need to be fully understood. When she visits home, her *Philosopher* engages with them in lively debates about politics and religion. They both enjoy this. Her parents see how happy she is and how much good she is doing in the world. They have decided she is a pretty *Good Daughter* after all.

Orphans I Have Known and Loved

Orphans come in many forms. Under the umbrella of this archetype you will find:

Victim, Cast Aside, Exile, Disowned, Sad, Angry, Bitter, Invisible Child, Overlooked, Refugee, Misunderstood, Abandoned, Nihilist, Cynic, Rebel Son and Rebel Daughter, Hothead, Loner, Mercenary, Manipulator, Criminal, Walking Wounded, Renegade, Cowboy, Reformer, Advocate, Martyr, Movement Leader, Wounded Healer, Rugged Individualist and Social Justice Crusader.

People give all sorts of names to their *Inner Orphans* that originate in books, movies, and fairy tales.

WELCOMING THE ORPHAN TO THE TABLE OF YOUR LIFE

Exploration

Take some time to look behind the curtain of your early life and get to know the *Orphan* within you. For some of you this realm will be quite familiar. Others of you have distanced yourself from these kinds of painful memories.

If you have a history of trauma or abuse, or if you find that these kinds of explorations cause you to become overwhelmed by emotion, then you should probably enter into this work with the support of a therapist. Even people without a history of trauma will do well to have a friend to call, just in case you happen into a painful, unexpected place.

Most people find that they can do this work if they proceed gently and allow themselves adequate time to process the emotions that may arise. Set aside some uninterrupted time in a quiet place so that you can delve into this tender place in your psyche. Using an entrance meditation will deepen this exploration and signal the psyche that you are undertaking something important.

You can use the same methods of exploration that you used for the *Innocent:* writing in a journal, using the two-chair technique, or working with a therapist or trusted friend who will ask the questions and just receive what you have to say. Remember that if you are the "asker," you should refrain from adding anything or trying to fix your partner. Just hold the neutral, non-judgmental space of the *Moderator.* After you do this exercise, it is especially important that you reground in the body, in present time. Do something that involves movement to process the emotions that may kick up. Stretch, take a walk, dance, do some yoga, take a shower. Drink water and perhaps eat something to get grounded.

Meeting your Inner Orphan

Close your eyes and allow yourself to enter into a memory of a time when you experienced being an *Orphan.* Re-enter that memory as much as you feel able. If the emotions you feel are too much, back out and imagine you are viewing the experience as if it were an event on a television screen in front of you.

If you have done this kind of deep inner work before and feel able to enter in more deeply, allow yourself to remember the details of the sights, sounds, tastes, smells and sensations of that time. When you have pulled in the energy of your little *Orphan,* you can begin the dialogue process. Remember that you do not have to ask every question listed here. Pick the ones that feel most resonant to you.

History:

- *Tell me about yourself.*
- *What were the circumstances that caused you to come into being?*

- *How old were you?*
- *How did you survive?*
- *How did you make sense of what happened to you?*
- *Did you make any decisions about life based on what happened?*
- *What would you like to be called?*

Questions for the Present Time:

- *Where do you show up in my life today?*
- *Where do you feel safe?*
- *Where do you not feel safe?*
- *Where do you feel loved?*
- *Where do you not feel loved?*
- *What makes you scared, sad or angry?*
- *How can I help you feel safe, loved, and included?*
- *How are you trying to help me?*
- *What gifts do you bring me?*
- *Is there anything else you would like me to know about you?*

Creating a Place in your Heart

You have now established a relationship with your *Orphan*. Now imagine gathering this little person up in your hand and place your hand over your heart. Imagine saying to them, *"You are welcome here. I have a safe place for you in my heart."* You have now created a touchstone, hand over heart. At any time, you can touch your heart, remember your vulnerable *Orphan* and have compassion for them. They can feel safe and engage with you.

Deeping the Relationship

Welcoming our *Inner Orphans* to the *Round Table* of our lives is probably one of the most important things we can do to heal the deep wounds of the past. A way of honoring and deepening your relationship with your *Orphan* is to create some representation that you can see on a regular basis. Clip a picture from a magazine, purchase a figurine, draw or make something in clay to represent this important *Inner Character.* Put it somewhere that you see often, on a shelf, the kitchen window ledge, or near your desk.

Remember to ask your *Inner Orphan* to participate in your *Round Table Negotiations.* They have great intuition and are keen watchdogs for potential problems. They tend to view things negatively, with suspicion, and often over-react, but they also pick up warning signs for things that are not quite right. Their warnings are to be held in perspective with their vulnerability and balanced with the input of older, more secure *Inner Figures* who can protect and discern well. If you disregard the input of the *Orphan,* you will find yourself trying to move forward with one foot on the gas and one foot on the brakes. The more included and loved *Orphans* feel, the more they begin to look like redeemed *Innocents,* bearing gifts instead of anxiety.

Further Explorations of the Inner Orphan:

- *In what ways have you experienced being abandoned or Orphaned in your life?*
- *How did you make sense of what happened to you? What conclusions did you reach about yourself, others, and life?*
- *Have those conclusions served you or limited you?*
- *What people and institutions have you trusted that turned out not to be trustworthy?*
- *What gifts, interests or personality qualities did you banish in childhood because they were not welcomed?*
- *What kinds of compromises have you made in your life in order to belong or to find love?*
- *How have you settled for less than your dreams because a Voice of Cynicism told you that what you wanted was not possible?*

- *Think of some characters or people in stories, movies and history that carry the energy of The Orphan. In what ways do you identify with them? What can you learn from them?*

CONCLUSIONS

People are often surprised by what they learn when they spend time, get quiet and go deep with these exploratory questions. The face we show the world is in front of the curtain, each of our *Main Players* holds a solution and a protection for the needs of the vulnerable selves we once were. They are in the past, behind the scenes, but they still influence us today, more than we realize. If you look at the early experiences of the *Innocent* and the *Orphan,* you will have a deeper understanding of why you have developed your particular *Inner Cast of Characters.* Many of the mysteries of your life will be solved as a result of this work, and you will begin to experience a significant increase in self-compassion.

- *What is the relationship between the Main Players in your Cast and your early experiences of hurt or vulnerability?*
- *How have the Main Players in your cast protected you? Helped you survive? Succeed?*

"Who's Upset?" versus "What's Wrong?"

Any time you are upset in life and can't quite figure out why, remember to ask the question "Who's upset?" rather than "What's wrong?" What's wrong is not immediately evident. Often there are vulnerable children in the background who are kicking up anxiety.

Sometimes you will find that the braking mechanism of your vulnerable *Inner Children* actually holds great wisdom. Perhaps only one set of *Inner Characters* is making this decision while ignoring important aspects of self in disregarded parts of the psyche. Perhaps the intuition of an *Orphan* has kicked in signaling that you are missing some hidden factor that would change your mind if you knew it.

We have all experienced wanting to move forward in some goal or endeavor and feeling somehow paralyzed to do so. When we surface the fear or the hurt of our *Inner Children,* and address their needs, often times the resistance evaporates and we are able to move forward.

For When You Feel Stuck:

- *Name the Inner Characters in the forefront.*
- *Look behind them to see who might be hiding in the background. Are there vulnerable children with unaddressed needs and concerns?*
- *Pull them up to the table and get to know them. What are their wants, needs and concerns?*
- *Begin to address these using the Negotiation Steps outlined in Chapter Four.*
- *If differences are extreme and seem unresolvable, practice the wisdom of waiting. Learn to stand in the midst of what is unresolved and wait for creative solutions not yet conceived of.*

CHAPTER 9

THE NOT SO SUPPORTING CAST—
The Inner Voices That Undermine Us

*"People lead lives of quiet desperation
and go to the grave with their song still in them."*
Thoreau

Myths throughout time have told us stories of *Guardians at the Gate*, monsters, dragons and other scary things that must be overcome before the hero or heroine can complete their quest. This mythological theme echoes the process of change in the psyche. Whenever we stand at the threshold of change, we face our own version of the *Guardians at the Gate*.

As you become increasingly aware of your *Inner Self System*, you gain the power to direct your life in a more conscious way. As you gain a sense of your essential *Self, you* are less likely to follow other people's scripts. Once you experience living a life that really suits you, it's hard to go back to the small box that once contained you.

In spite of the promise of living a richer, more meaningful life, it is difficult to deal with the anxiety of moving into unknown territory. You are making choices that others may not understand, fighting the dragons of fear and self-doubt that stand at the threshold of change. You feel "not quite yourself," and unsure of who you are becoming. Many people have dreams of being lost or wandering in a wilderness. Robert Frost reminds us that when we are deciding between two paths, taking one means we will not take the other. Will you take the familiar path of safety and approval, or the road less traveled, in search of a more authentic life? At the threshold of change, our *Inner Script Monitor* calls up the *Guardians at the Gate.* We have talked about the *Script Monitor.* Let's look at some other members of our *Inner Cast* that limit, discourage and harass us. To continue with our theater metaphors, we will call them the *Not So Supporting Cast:*

- **The Rule Keeper** (Deeply embedded Do's and Don'ts, Controller)
- **The Voices of Warning** (What will happen if you disobey the script or break the rules?)
- **The Inner Critic** (Judge, Evaluator, Comparer, Challenger, Doubter)

If you are stuck in your negotiations, look to this group. Their job is to enforce the status quo. They want to keep you in line and out of trouble, to see to it that you follow the rules, stick to your script, fulfill given roles, and play them in a particular way. Any time you are in a growth process, they will get very stirred up. If you don't stay in line, they warn you about the terrible things that will happen to you. Where are *you* in this mix? Where is your *Soul Print?* They are not interested in that.

They Masquerade as Helpers

They operate under the guise of advisors and protectors. They would be so wounded if you suggested that they have evil intentions. "We only have your best interests at heart!" And this is true, they are not intentionally treacherous. They are simply unaware of how much havoc they cause. They act as guard rails on the road of our lives. Never mind that they drain our enthusiasm, douse our courage, and do not allow us to savor the sweetness of success.

Whenever I am working with creative people who are blocked, I look to this set of *Inner Characters.* Their influence can grind creative people to a complete halt, second guessing, doubting their abilities, hesitating to put themselves out into the world. When I am working with people who are underpaid, I look to these *Inner Characters*. They prevent the hardworking secretary from asking her demanding boss for a raise. When I encounter people who don't have the relationships they want, I look here. They undermine successful relationships in all sorts of ways.

Anytime you are stuck in your *Negotiation Process*, or unable to resolve something, look for the influence of these *Inner Voices*. Personify them as *Inner Characters* and get them out so that you can openly negotiate with them. The *Not So Supporting Cast* can convince us that what we want isn't possible. "Who do you think you are?" they taunt, "to think you can do that?!" Whether they are whispering in the background or berating you mercilessly, they will not leave you in peace. In the process of pleasing all of them, you may become quite disconnected from your essential *Self.*

As you wade through the material in this chapter, do not despair. This is a tough chapter and some people find the content depressing. The reason I go into this material is because I firmly believe that you can surmount any of the challenges presented here. You can deal with the underlying anxiety that the *Not So Supporting Cast* generates when you want to make life changes. You *can* negotiate with them, addressing their needs and concerns. You can integrate new material and write new rules and scripts. You do not need to slay these dragons; you can redirect their energies in constructive ways. You can also appreciate their "counsel" while balancing their energies with *Inner Characters* who protect, discern, support and encourage. So let's take a look at the *Not So Supporting Cast.*

You will find your own unique names for this set of inner energies. Each can be fleshed out in the same way you have done other *Inner Characters*. They can look like *Inner Demons, Dragons, Ghosts of the Past, Dark Inquisitors, Bullies, Hijackers, Judges and Controllers, The Inquisition, Drill Sergeants, Slave*

Drivers, Policemen, Jailors, Tyrants, Wicked Witches, Dark Queens, etc.

THE RULE KEEPER-
The Do's and Don'ts of Life

From the time you were a child and became aware that there were consequences for your actions, you began to develop an inner *Rule Keeper.* The job of the *Rule Keeper* is to memorize all the do's and don'ts thrown at you as you were growing up. "Be Good. Be Pleasing. Be Strong. Be Nice. Don't hit your brother. Don't question authority. Don't whine. Be thankful for what you've got. Don't tell Aunt Madge she is fat. Be honest. Don't talk about dad's drinking outside the house. Make your parents proud . . . . but don't make a big deal of yourself. Sex is dirty, save it for holy matrimony."

Many of the things we learned in childhood were very confusing and contradictory. If you never examine or reconsider the rules you learned as a child, they can seriously undermine your happiness and success in life. We got these rules from all sorts of authorities: parents, grandparents, teachers, coaches, books, clergy, religious institutions, and the culture we live in.

If you have an inner *Good Girl* or *Good Boy* or a *Rule Follower,* you will have difficulty breaking any given rules and can become fairly outraged when others do. Think about how you felt the last time you watched someone run a red light or cut into a line! If you are a *Rebel* (especially without a cause), then you may have trouble following rules even when it is in your best interest to do so!

Take a moment and list some of the rules you internalized as you were growing up. The longer you interview your *Inner Characters,* the more you will encounter this list. They are embedded in your script, like the air we breathe, outside of our awareness. Everyone has their unique list. The *Do's* compel us with "shoulds and musts," the *Don'ts* constrain us. Both cause tremendous havoc for us when we are unconscious of them. As adults, we need to surface and examine them. And if they no longer serve our greatest good, we need to neutralize them and move beyond them.

THE VOICES OF WARNING

Warnings come when we break the rules. They can come from any of our *Inner Cast of Characters*, and can be contradictory, because each of our *Inner Characters* has a differing set of rules! There are many competing agendas. Is it any wonder that we find ourselves in internal conflict? During times of stress or change, when we are anxious anyway, the warning bells in us can get quite loud.

Here are some of the things I have heard the *Voices of Warning* say. You can see how they team up with your *Inner Critic* to stop you in your tracks. See if any of them sound familiar to you.

Who do you think you are?
What makes you think you can do that?
What will people think?
You don't have the proper credentials!
You've never done anything like that before.
Don't embarrass yourself.
Don't make too much of yourself. Be humble.
Don't be selfish. You need to think of others.
Your husband will leave you if you do.
Your mother and father will be devastated.
People will talk about you behind your back.
You will burn in hell if you do that.
You don't want to offend people, do you?
If you do that, you may ruin your professional reputation.
What if you fail or make a fool of yourself?
What you are considering is downright reckless!

That sort of thing is just not done by people like us.
You're not good enough, intelligent enough, appealing enough,
talented enough, capable enough, sexy enough . . . etc.

What Triggers Them

All forms of inner work trigger the *Voices of Warning*. Change costs something. It always requires that we let go of the old and embrace the new. Living a life in alignment with your *Soul Print* has a reward and a price. We have settled into certain dance steps with people in our lives, and they don't like it when we change the steps. Sometimes the changes we make lead to recasting our *Inner Characters,* with a different set of players on the stage. Sometimes we recast the outer players as well. When someone in your outer life is about to be "fired or retired," they may not like it much. This creates tremendous anxiety in us. This is when we need to step up on *Round Table Work*, develop our *Observing Self,* learn to center and soothe ourselves and anchor ourselves in our *Calm Core.*

The Voice of God

The most imperious *Voice of Warning* you will hear masquerades as the *Voice of God*. Over the years, I have conducted many interviews with the *Voice of God* and heard the litany of commandments, demands, rules and requirements. The threat of divine punishment is always hovering over such a person's life, should they violate or fall short of these edicts. As we delve a little deeper into the origin of this voice, we find that it begins to sound more like *Reverend Fire and Brimstone*, the scary preacher from a person's childhood, or perhaps *Sister Cruella* from Catholic School.

The Twelve Dangerous Don'ts

Bob and Mary Goulding[2] identified twelve *Don'ts* that show up in the scripts of people who have difficulty in life. They are: Don't be close, Don't be a child, Don't be important, Don't make it, Don't grow up, Don't be you, Don't be well, Don't belong, Don't think, Don't feel, Don't exist, and just Don't (try, risk, hope, dream, etc.).

BREAKING FREE

Do's and Don'ts:

- *List some of the Do's and Don'ts that operate in your life.*
- *How old were you when you learned them and who taught you?*
- *What will happen if you don't comply?*
- *Whose love or approval will you lose?*
- *Who will be threatened (inside and out)?*
- *Who will get mad (inside and out)? What might they do?*

Developing New Potentials and Possibilities:

- *What do the Voices of Warning tell you that you aren't capable of doing in your life? Who said? Why?*
- *Look around your Inner Round Table. Is there anyone who believes differently? Let them speak.*
- *What kind of reassurance or support would you need to move forward?*
- *Who in your Inner Cast would be able to supply this support?*
- *Who on the outside world would support you?*

---

[2]   See bibliography for Goulding, M & Goulding, R., *Changing Lives Through Redecision Therapy*; and Joines,V. and Stewart, I., *TA Today: A New Introduction to Transactional Analysis.*

Negotiating with the Voices of Warning

We are largely unaware of the amount of energy and inspiration that we lose by complying with the *Voices of Warning*. Look around and see where they are coming from. *Who* in you is generating them? Is this *Inner Character* dominating your inner stage? Are they stopping you from doing something important in your life? Are they keeping you from living into your true purpose and potential? Once we address needs and concerns, we can garner inner and outer support and cross the threshold into new territory.

THE INNER CRITIC

The *Script Monitor* and *Voices of Warning* may interfere with us when we break "given rules," but the *Inner Critic* gets after us when we are following them! If you tune in, you will notice that your *Critic's* voice has a familiar ring. You will hear echoes of the words and the tones of the early authorities in your life, particularly when you were in trouble. *Critics* say things like, *"What's wrong with you? Are you an idiot? Can't you do anything right? God is going to punish you. What will people think? You're hopeless. Will you ever think of anyone but yourself? No one wants to hear what you have to say. Surely you can do better than that!"*

Once again, the *Critic* does not see his or her efforts as antagonistic or mean. The *Critic* wants to protect you. The *Critic* wants you to survive! The problem is that nothing is *ever* good enough. Every time you leave work, a meeting, a date, a party, this insidious voice will start up. "Why did you say such and such? You sounded like an idiot! Why didn't you do such and such? What's wrong with you?" You have your own version of this litany.

Banishing the Critic?

I have heard some people talking about banishing their *Inner Critics*. Good luck! You may think you have gotten rid of them, but they are very clever. Often they just go offstage and return in a different costume.

The Inner Peace Treaty Solution

Get to *Know* your *Inner Critic* in all its many guises. You may have several, each operating in a different situation! *Critics* love attention and they love to talk. After all, they believe they are experts on your life. So, begin a dialogue with them. Observe yourself and identify how this aspect of your psyche works. You can utilize any of the interview inquiries, such as:

Getting to Know Your Inner Critic:

- *Tell me about yourself. What is your history?*
- *What are your fears and concerns?*
- *How are you trying to help or protect me?*
- *What assurances do you need to feel safe or satisfied? (Keep in mind that your Critic may be one who is perpetually dissatisfied.)*

Negotiating with your *Inner Critic* means valuing their input, but considering it in light of more positive, supportive *Inner Round Table* members. This voice always needs to be balanced with *Inner Supporters, Encouragers* and *Wise Ones*. Where we get into trouble is when we let the *Critic* be an authority over our lives.

Sometimes, I tell my *Critic* to take the day off. I have negotiated with them to let someone else attend to the important stuff. I have found that comforting and reassuring them works really well. I always thank them for their input. With deft directing skills and compassionate understanding, you may actually come to appreciate the value that this difficult character brings.

So give your *Critic* some direction! Put them to work on projects and tasks that require evaluating, checking for details, or looking for pitfalls in your plans. A well-directed *Critic* can be beneficial in times when a little extra push could take you to the next level of excellence.

Inner Critics as Dark Queens

Before I could move forward as a writer, I had to face a formidable *Inner Critic*. She surfaced and appeared in a series of dreams right around the time that I began to seriously consider that I might have something to say. This *Inner Character* appeared to me as a tall, stern, aging *Russian Ballerina*. Her energy was that of the *Evil Witches and Dark Queens* who appear in so many famous fairy tales.

Fairy tales tell us stories of imperious *Dark Queens*. Mine had constellated at the thought of making my writing public. As she appeared in my dreams, she stood with her arms folded, gazing down her nose, cold and compassionless. Her hair was pulled up into a tight, black bun, which made her look even more severe. She disdained amateurs and beginners and had determined that I was one. In her presence I withered. I felt that my new attempts at writing were foolish and stupid. I felt ashamed for thinking that anything I could produce would be worth showing to the world.

As I traced back the history of this suppressive energy, I discovered that I had been under her evil thrall for most of my life. Fear of negative evaluation had kept me from pursuing paths that would have been immensely rewarding for me. I continued to trace the strands of this dark complex and remembered an early experience playing the piano for a panel of judges. Until that point, music had been a source of incredible, expansive joy. That day, I was told that while I played with great feeling, my technical proficiency was lacking. I was handed a report card with various categories that needed improvement.

This experience shattered the idyllic relationship I had with my music and with my creativity. It taught me that when you expose the work of your heart to the harsh scrutiny of the world, others will judge it, and will not value it in the same way that you do. This hurts. The *Russian Ballerina* knew this. She was trying to protect me!

As I interviewed the *Russian Ballerina*, I learned that she was aware of the inevitable critique and judgment that comes from others when you put your ideas out there. She knew I was writing about things that mattered deeply to me. She did not want me to be hurt. As I dialogued with her, I realized that her intent was not malicious after all. She was being protective, in the only way she knew how.

So often, we are unconscious of that which binds us and keeps us from reaching our full potential. Shedding light on this once hidden constraint had the same effect as throwing water on the *Wicked Witch of the West*. It broke the spell and the fear began to melt away. At that point, I was able to garner the support of *Inner* (and outer) *Encouragers* and move forward.

The Inner Patriarch[3]

Sidra Stone, PhD has outlined a particular version of the *Inner Critic* found in women. Because we have grown up in a culture defined by masculine rules and values, the rules of men pervade our unconscious and manifest in an *Inner Self* she calls the *Inner Patriarch*. We have internalized cultural norms and this voice will constantly remind us of the acceptable range of behaviors for women, warning us of the consequences of stepping outside of "our place." Even women who are "liberated" or surrounded by

---

[3]   See bibliography for Sidra Stone's work-*The Shadow King*.

loving, supportive, enlightened men will feel this dark internal presence. It sets limits on our achievement, creative expression and certainly on our sexuality.

During my *Luminous Woman Weekends*, we name the *Do's and Don'ts* generated by the *Inner Patriarch*. We realize that we were often coached in these constraints by our mothers. As we create this long list, we begin to recognize how ridiculous and contradictory they are. Together we see how we were silenced and immobilized. As the list gets longer and the edicts get more and more outrageous and absurd, years of pain disappear inside gales of laughter.

CHAPTER 10

THE NOT SO SUPPORTING CAST—
The Voices of Pressure

"One does not become enlightened by imagining figures of light but by making the darkness conscious."
C.G. Jung

The last category in the *Not So Supporting Cast* is the *Voice of Pressure*. In this category, I include:

- The Pusher/Producer
- The Pleaser
- The Perfectionist
- Super Human Strong One

These characters can insert themselves into every transaction of our lives, driving us relentlessly, worrying us constantly, and undermining our health and joy.

The Pusher/Producer

Hal and Sidra Stone call this intense *Inner Self* the *Pusher*. Other names for this archetypal energy are the *Producer, Performer, Over Achiever, Competitor, Slave Driver, Explorer, Dare Devil, Empire Builder, Hero, Saint, Savior, Corporate Climber, Social Climber* and sometimes *Super Mom* or *Super Dad*. It doesn't matter how much money you make, how high you climb in your profession, how powerful, beautiful or saintly you are, the *Voices of Pressure* will want you to do more. There is no end point at which you can rest, or consider yourself "arrived." If you do enough today, tomorrow is another day with new requirements.

It is constantly reminding us how much is at stake should we let up or slow down. Push, produce, the clock is ticking, others are getting ahead of you! You are running out of time! Linked up with the *Critic,* you will constantly compare yourself to others and come up short.

If you let this ever expansive, ever demanding part of the psyche take center stage, you will run yourself into the ground. The *Pusher/Producer* has no limits, no awareness that you live in a human body, no awareness of feelings, or soul, or that there are only 24 hours in a day.

Exploration — Your Inner Pusher/Producer

- *Do you find it difficult to relax or enjoy your achievements?*
- *Are you allowed to have fun or take a day off?*
- *Do you feel guilty enjoying the simple pleasures of life?*
- *Are you allowed to do the things you really enjoy, even if others don't value them?*
- *Is everything you do related to building your career or making money?*
- *How often do you find yourself asking, "Where will this get me?"*
- *Is it difficult for you to take time out for quiet reflection or a spiritual retreat? What does the Voice of Pressure say to you during times like this? What kinds of sensations get stirred up in your body?*
- *Can you take a morning or an evening off to enjoy pure pleasure?*
- *Do you ever just sit and "do nothing?"*
- *Where do you feel most pressured to achieve in your life?*

- *What does the Voice of Pressure say about why it is important to push, perform, achieve and do more? What will happen if you don't?*
- *What kinds of things might you do if there was no pressure to earn, achieve or accomplish anything at all?*

This *Pusher/Voice of Pressure* can be as tricky as the *Critic* in terms of changing costumes. If you are not after worldly power and glory, it can easily move into the realm of your artistic or spiritual life. Give these internal pressures *Names* and look for how they are creating problems for you. Any time you are feeling anxiety, discontent, conflict or unhappiness they are probably lurking somewhere in the background. Invite them to the table and *Negotiate* openly with them so that you can get on with your life or relax into enjoyment!

The Saint, the Spiritual Achiever, and the Cosmic Pusher

People who shift their values away from power, career achievement and material acquisition are susceptible to an insidious kind of inner pressure that comes from the desire to "achieve" (notice the telltale word) spiritual transcendence, sanctification, or enlightenment. This usually requires some form of practice or discipline.

Spiritual practices are wonderful, but when the *Spiritual Achiever* gets into the act, it moves the sincere *Seeker* into the same dangerous energy as those who are in the material realm. When this energy takes over, your life will adopt a lot of rules, "should's and must's." You must follow a particular diet, you must meditate a certain number of hours on a strict schedule, you should tithe, or give money to spiritual causes, you must be sexually chaste or celibate.

If you are in the Christian realm, the archetypes that you might inhabit are that of the *Saint*, the *Renunciate*, the *Social Justice*

Crusader, or the *Monastic Contemplative*. I have my own particular version of this energy, which I have named *Poor Clair* after the Medieval Franciscan nun who renounced her family's wealth to become a servant of the poor. *Poor Clair* believes that I should give everything I have to the poor and devote my life entirely to sacrificial service. Whenever I am around any Catholic religious order devoted to working with the poor, she forgets that I am married and wants to join them!

When the *Saint* teams up with the *Inner Critic*, he or she will begin to review and grade a person's spiritual growth with scrupulous rigor. The *Spiritual Pusher* keeps a report card on our spiritual depth, practices, integrity, prayer life, etc. reminding us that if we were more devoted, more sincere, more disciplined or self-denying, we would be progressing faster. This is the same over-achieving, joy-erasing, wolf-like energy dressed up in spiritual clothing. It will still eat you alive.

The *Spiritual Pusher* can become very self-righteous and judgmental of others. The *Spiritual Pusher* can escalate into omnipotent dimensions. Now we have a *Savior Complex,* with the cataclysmic sense that it is up to us to solve the world's problems. We begin to feel like there are not enough hours in the day to do the work that needs to be done. We begin to take on the role of God. Hal Stone likes to call this energy the *Cosmic Pusher.* According to the *Cosmic Pusher,* you should sacrifice everything you have to the cause, because the cause is more important than your insignificant little life. You should pray without ceasing and work without stopping.

Another related *Inner Character* in this group might be named the *Self Improvement Junkie* or the *Consciousness Achiever.* When people realize the benefits of personal growth work, they can get carried away with learning everything they can, getting better and better, and more and more conscious. Suddenly the *Inner Growth Pusher* will get into the act and say things like, "surely this next book, workshop, or spiritual teaching will hold the ultimate answer for me."

When you become aware that you are being carried away by any of these "well meaning," achievement-oriented selves, you can get your *Inner Director* back in charge. You might want to repeat this mantra: "One task at a time, one experience at a time, one day at a time."

THREE PRESSING THEMES

One or more of the following themes play out in most people's scripts[4]. Take a moment to consider how they play out in your world.

- *You must please others*
- *You must be perfect (or quite excellent)*
- *You must be strong (superhuman, beyond personal needs)*

You Must Please Others

This theme is especially common for women, but you find it in men as well. *Pleasers* put the happiness and approval of other people first in their lives. They do for others constantly and often do not know what they want for themselves. *Pleasers* feel safe only when the people around them are happy. They have a difficult time saying no or setting limits. Many are seething with suppressed hurt, anger and resentment, but they don't show it directly. That would be displeasing. The *Pleaser* must be nice and accommodate

---

[4]   I consider these three to be the most crucial. The foundation of this thinking is drawn from the work of Taibi Kahler. He has a larger list, as outlined in Stewart and Joines *TA Today: A New Introduction to Transactional Analysis*—see bibliography.

others. They are the ones who must be flexible. Sitting behind a person's *Pleaser* might be a *Martyr, a Sad, Needy or Angry Child, a Jealous Woman, an Angry Man*, a *Hidden Manipulator, or a Time Bomb*. *Pleasers* are often secretly critical (or envious) of those who are "selfish" and do exactly what they want, without caring what anyone thinks!

You Must Be Perfect (or at least really excellent)

The *Inner Perfectionist* will put constant pressure on you, and create a lot of suffering. Perfectionists team up with the *Inner Critic*, who grades every move you make in life. You are always falling short. When the *Perfectionist* dominates your *Inner Cast*, your life will be filled with overwork, over-responsibility, anxiety, depression, and guilt. You may often feel angry because no-one else cares as much as you do, or works as hard. Relaxing, pleasure, and socializing may be considered a "waste of time." Change is scary. Forget spontaneity! You might be able to go on vacation, but you won't enjoy it unless it is perfectly planned and executed. Accessing the realm of the *Inner Child* is almost impossible, because of the pressure to control outcomes. Too risky, and there is just no time for such "frivolity."

The *Perfectionist* will keep you up late into the night working and reworking some project. Your *Perfectionist* will also try to prevent you from doing new things that you may not be very good at because you are not allowed to be mediocre at anything. That would be shameful. You must be an instant expert at everything.

You Must Be Strong—Don't have needs

This is a very subtle but important script theme in people's lives. People with a "Be Strong" script are often admired by others. This is very rewarding for them and keeps them going. They tend to be responsible, reliable, and even *Saintly*. They *Soldier* on regardless of the troubles that beset them. The "Be Strong" theme can go hand in hand with other script themes because you can push yourself mercilessly to be even more pleasing or perfect. When you don't attend or acknowledge needs of your own, you can devote all your energy to the needs of others. Strong people can hold entire families together, possibly even save the world, if they don't get bogged down in their own needs. They are great in emergencies.

People who operate with this script theme seem almost superhuman, until they push themselves past the point of endurance and fall apart, emotionally or physically. In order to be this strong, you have to disconnect from your own needs and discomforts. They are prone to illnesses that come from constant stress and overwork. Mundane things like adequate sleep, healthy food, regular exercise, and "down time" are low priorities. People with a "Be Strong" theme can also experience profound despair if they encounter something beyond their capacity to fix. We don't usually see these *Saints* and *Heroes* in their moments of desolation and despair. They suffer quietly and in private. After "pouring themselves out" as *Suffering Servants* they can become *Martyrs*.

Many people who have a "Be Strong" driver started taking care of other people at some incredibly young age, like five. They often took care of the parents who were supposed to be taking care of them. Going numb helps negate underlying emotions like anxiety, loneliness and the longing to be loved and cared for themselves. They bear unspeakable burdens for long periods of time with the deep hope that eventually, someone will notice that they have needs too. They long to be cared for without having to ask. Asking for help or support induces shame in *The Strong*.

Sometimes, when they have been stretched beyond the limit of endurance, they may become angry that no one cares for or helps them. People around them are often surprised by their angry, hurt declarations and respond by saying, "I had no idea you needed anything. You are always so self-sufficient."

EXPLORING SCRIPT THEMES

Look inside and see where these themes play out in your life. See if you can find your *Inner Perfectionist, Pleaser,* or *Strong One.* Dialogue with them to get to know them better.

- *Tell me about yourself. What is your history?*
- *When did you come into being?*
- *What rules do you live by?*
- *Who were your teachers and role models?*
- *What kinds of things do you push me to do?*
- *How are you trying to help or protect me?*
- *What do you want?*
- *What do you need?*
- *Where and how are you activated in my life?*

Pleaser

- *Who is it important to please and why?*
- *What might happen if you don't?*

Perfectionist

- *How do you know when something is good enough?*
- *What might happen if it isn't?*

Strong One

- *Who depends on you?*
- *What might happen if you show that you have needs or weakness?*

If these script themes are strong in you, it is important to include these *Inner Characters* in your *Round Table Negotiations.*

They will influence you more than you know and their needs and concerns must be addressed by other *Inner Characters* who can calm their fears and make them feel safe. Follow the *Negotiation* model outlined in Chapter Four and mediate between these warring parts of self.

True Inner Helpers

Remember that our sense of vulnerability in life is tied to our *Inner Children*. Their needs and concerns must always be considered in any negotiation. They hold the key to a vast store of information about why we do the things we do. They may be stuck in a time warp, frozen with fear, unable to grow up and handle the realities of adult living. The *Not So Supporting Cast* developed out of an attempt to protect them. You have to address the needs of the children before you can cross the threshold into the person you were born to be. *Negotiating* with *Inner Children* involves bringing in *Positive, Nurturing, Protecting Inner Parental* figures who can comfort in times of fear and distress, problem solve, structure time and resources, and provide encouragement to risk and grow.

Sometimes we have not yet developed these positive *Inner Characters* that can counter balance the *Not So Supporting Cast*. Remember that all these potentials exist in the archetypal seedbed of the psyche. The more you listen and align your life with your *Soul Print*, the more resources you have available to you and the more you can identify and transcend all of the unconscious programming that limits you and drains your life energy.

CHAPTER 11

RELATING FROM THE CALM CORE—
Scripts, Secrets, Shame and Sexuality

"Fool said I, you do not know. Silence like a cancer grows."
Simon and Garfunkle

Insecurity in Relationships

Our *Scripts* and the *Not So Supporting Cast* can undermine us as we seek love and connection in personal relationships. They overwhelm us with rules, warnings and self-criticism, driving us into a childlike ego state where we need constant reassurance and validation. The *Critic* tells us we are too fat, ugly, boring or bothersome to deserve someone's love or fidelity. If things are going well, the *Voices of Warning* whisper, "Don't trust this. It's too good to be true. Nothing ever works out this well for you. He or she is probably comparing you to his last lover, who was far more attractive and sexier."

Our *Script* dictates that we must *Be Pleasing*, or *Perfect* or *Beyond Needs*, so we never acknowledge our needs or ask for what we really want. Over time, our *Inner Children* get increasingly sad or angry as we long for someone to see that we have needs too.

Many mid-life divorces stem from living for years in a "scripted" relationship that is flat and lifeless, doesn't feed our souls or fulfill the longings of our heart. We think the problem is with the other person, but more often the problem is with ourselves. How can we connect with another person when we are disconnected from ourselves? We are acting out a part in a script rather than relating authentically.

As young people, we often enter relationships with idealized hopes and unrealistic expectations. We hope that our partners will always be kind, attentive, giving, loyal, faithful, romantic, responsible and employed. Very few people know how to navigate the realities of a real relationship.

Single people in mid-life, re-entering the dating scene, bring baggage from the past. They often place heavy burdens on new partners, hoping that they will be different from previous lovers. When our unconscious scripts are unexamined, we tend to repeatedly pick the same actors and play out certain story lines, again and again.

There are two *Inner Round Tables* in every relationship. Relationships become more successful, fulfilling and pleasurable when we are aware of who sits at each partner's *Inner Round Table*. Then, we can negotiate what kind of relationship we want to create! What is needed and wanted? What is possible? How can we be responsible for ourselves and still address our mutual needs and vulnerabilities? How can we make it safe for our *Inner Children* to come out and play?

Sylvia

My client Sylvia was a confident *Career Woman,* re-entering the dating scene after a difficult divorce from an unfaithful husband. With each new man she met, the first few dates went fine, but then the *Scorned Woman* and her *Hurt Inner Child* would kick in and sabotage her. She would begin to feel scared, insecure, needy and then angry. This energy would cause her to act in ways that drove potential partners away. Sylvia found her *Scared, Insecure Inner Child* asking questions like, "Do you like me as much as your last girlfriend? Do you really find me attractive? Do you really want me around?"

Even when things were going well, the *Voices of Warning* would get going in her head and say things like, "Men can't be trusted.

He doesn't really care for you. He's only out for sex." She would start to wonder if she was being played for a fool *again* and then get angry and accusatory. The *Vulnerable Child* in Sylvia wanted each of these men to take on the role of *Reassuring, Protective Father*, making her feel safe, so that she could overcome the fear that all men were like her ex-husband. What she feared most would happen; the man would be overwhelmed by her insecurity and neediness and withdraw. This confirmed to Sylvia that no one would ever love her and that men could not be trusted.

Relating from the Calm Core

Cultivating our *Calm Core* is essential for good relationships. It is the only antidote for fear and insecurity. Relationships produce vulnerability! When you are caught in the hold of a *Fearful, Frantic, Needy Inner Child,* the first thing to do is to reclaim your center and re-establish your *Inner Director.* Then, you can navigate the challenges of a relationship. When you find that someone is not on the same page as you, you have to hold steady and begin to seek understanding. You have to know who you are and what you want to be able to negotiate with another person. Our *Inner Children* start to quake and we tend to get thrown off balance into fear and anger and unmet needs. This is a crucial time to do some *Inner Round Table* work.

Relationship Explorations

- *When I am upset, are my intuitions and reactions warranted, or am I responding to past hurts and old script material?*
- *Do I know my own needs and vulnerabilities?*
- *"Who" in me is upset? Do I have an Idealistic, Indulged or Frightened Child inside, who has been hurt, angry or frightened?*
- *If so, how can I comfort, reassure and calm them?*

- *Do I have an Inner Adult on board who can see things clearly and problem solve?*
- *Do I expect the other person to see things like me?*
- *Where is the misunderstanding in this relationship? What needs to be negotiated, or sorted out? Who at their Inner Round Table is reacting to me?*
- *What do I actually want here? "Who" in me wants it?*
- *What is actually possible rather than just wished for?*
- *Am I anchored enough in my Calm Core to know that I can be OK regardless of the outcome?*

When you are in your *Calm Core*, distortions drop away. You can look, see and sense what is actually going on around you. You will be able to figure out who is worthy of your love and trust, and who is not. You will be able to figure out who shares your values and wants what you want. When you have your entire *Inner Cast* at your disposal, they can look around and discern things really well! When you are anchored in your depths and know your value, you can feel confident about yourself and handle life as it comes. People who no longer fit in your world may leave. Let them. As your *Inner Resonance* becomes clearer and more harmonious, you will begin to attract the people you really want in your world.

The Imposter Syndrome

Many people express the fear that they are inadequate or unqualified to be in the positions they occupy. They express fears of being found out, exposed and humiliated. Their *Voices of Warning* are in high gear, reminding them that eventually they will be shown to be nothing but a fraud or a pretender.

- *Do you ever feel like an imposter? Do you ever feel that you are not qualified for the work you do?*

- *What do your Voices of Warning say about why you are not qualified to be, do or have something?*
- *Have you ever stopped yourself from doing something because you feel that you don't have the "proper" credentials?*
- *Who in you says this? Is this really valid or is it old script material?*
- *Is there another Inner Character who has a different opinion?*
- *If you legitimately need more credentials, how might you achieve this?*
- *Do you have Inner Supporters and Encouragers?*
- *Who in your outside world believes in you and supports you?*

SECRETS, SHAME AND SEXUALITY

Almost everyone has things in their past that they would just as soon keep hidden. If the *Main Players* in your current cast hold a very different set of values from the person you once were, alarms may go off when someone gets a little too curious about your past.

What do your *Voices of Warning* say about some of your *Retired Selves* and how your current spouse, friends, co-workers, boss, church, country club, or children would view them today? This is a very important negotiation, because the fear of being "found out" can create a tremendous amount of inner stress in people. It is one of the primary reasons that people keep their distance and never really feel close to others.

Go through your history and *Name* the *Inner Selves* you have banished in order to fit in and be acceptable. Ask them to tell their stories and give them some time. Remember that every *Banished or Shameful Self* was trying to get some need met. Sometimes they were expressing a beautiful aspect of your *Soul Print* and were humiliated, exploited or punished for doing so. They went into hiding to survive. Find out why. Validate that and thank them for how they were trying to help. Ask them about the gifts they might bring you today if they were allowed to be a part of your *Inner Round Table*. When we close the door on certain *Inner Selves*, we may eliminate the pain and trouble they caused us, but we also lose their energy and their gifts.

- *What Inner Characters from your past did you retire or banish when you "grew up?"*
- *What Inner Characters do you hide or negate to be acceptable in your current career, social group or relationship?*
- *Do you come from "the wrong side of the tracks," have a criminal record, or a past "rebel" that you hide?*
- *What do the Voices of Warning say would happen if your secrets were found out?*
- *Take a moment and ask "who" in you is concerned about all of this? Is this a valid concern or is it old script material? Dialogue with them.*
- *What gifts or energy might these Banished Selves bring to your life if they were welcome at your Inner Round Table?*

Sandra and Jamie

Sandra and Jamie came to see me. Jamie was threatening to leave because Sandra had become distant and sexually avoidant. When they did have sex, Sandra was unresponsive. What Jamie did not understand was that Sandra was hiding a traumatic secret.

In a private session with Sandra, she revealed to me that she had been repeatedly sexually abused by her stepfather during her teenage years, and when Jamie touched her in certain ways, she began to feel horrible feelings inside. Her solution was to avoid being touched or go numb and dissociate, just like she had during the original terrifying experiences. Sandra had never spoken about her past to anyone. This information was locked behind a steely wall. She believed that if anyone knew about this, they would view her as irretrievably damaged. She believed that somehow she was to blame for what happened to her. She was fundamentally "bad" and this disqualified her from ever being loved.

As we began to work together, we named this terrified *Inner Character "Damaged Goods."* Before *Damaged Goods* would even speak to me, I had several negotiations with the fierce *Voices of Warning* that had been silencing Sandra for her whole life. They had many good reasons for not speaking of such things, including the fact that when Sandra had tried to tell her mother about this, her mother became furious and told her to stop making up lies.

Then there was the church, with its strong emphasis on the importance of purity and virginity. Since her virginity was gone, Sandra decided she wasn't of much value, but if she never spoke of it, only she would know. This secret led her to silence herself in other areas as well.

Over the years she had many unwanted sexual experiences, because she didn't feel able to speak up or set limits. She was grateful for anyone's attention. She felt lucky that anyone wanted her at all. She always numbed out during sexual encounters. This relationship was different. Jamie was the first person who was really good to her, and she didn't want to lose this one chance for love.

Sandra and I spent many sessions dialoguing with her *Inner Self System,* surfacing the distortions she had come to believe about her value and what was possible for someone like her. As she began to understand her history and the role that numbing out had played in her life, she became increasingly able to inhabit her body and mediate the torrents of fear, anger and grief that coursed through her in intimate situations. Her heart was very guarded because she had been so devalued and hurt, but she found that when she entered the realm of her soul, there was a place in her that had never been damaged or hurt.

In a guided visualization, she engaged her *Keeper of the Flame*[5], a protective, wise woman who could support and protect her. She began to realize that her flame was not extinguished. She began to reclaim the inner light she had lost.

In working with the couple, each partner had an *Inner Cast of Characters* who were interacting very negatively when things went wrong in bed. Both of them had frightened, hurt, angry *Inner Children* that got triggered when things were not going well. In beginning to cultivate a *Calm Core*, Jamie was able to find a patient, compassionate *Inner Self* who did not take Sandra's distancing so personally. This gave Sandra the time and safety she needed to work through the traumatic dissociation that had always accompanied their sexual interactions. As we explored the many archetypes from which we can express ourselves sexually, and the many differing meanings that we bring to sex, Jamie and Sandra discovered ways of connecting that felt safe and pleased them both. As they continued to explore new ways of interacting and new potentials in their *Inner Cast of Characters*, they healed the wounds of the past.

Over time, Sandra began to integrate a new *Soulfully Embodied Self* that experienced touch and connection in a wonderful new way. As she began to trust Jamie's love and compassion for her, she was able to open her heart and her body. She discovered that she had a deep capacity to be responsive when she felt safe and honored. In this way, she was able to reclaim the birthright of her innate, joyful sexuality.

Making Peace with Your Sexual Selves

- *Have you made peace with your sexual history?*
- *Who in you carries your sensuality? Who carries your sexuality? Do you have Sexual Selves? How well do they get along with*

---

5   See bibliography and resource list for the work of Gina Ogden, PhD. This is drawn from her book *The Heart and Soul of Sex*.

the rest of your Inner Cast? Who in you is comfortable or uncomfortable with your sexuality?

— *Dialogue with your various Inner Characters and uncover their thoughts, feelings and beliefs about sex. What are the rules around sex? What is your sexual script? Who, What, When, Where, and How Sex is OK? Where do these beliefs come from? What do the Voices of Warning in you say about your sexuality? If you are a woman, what does the Inner Patriarch say? If you are a man, what does the Inner Matriarch say?*

— *Do you have unlived longings that you are afraid to reveal to yourself or anyone else? What does the Not So Supporting Cast say about these longings? Have you made peace with your sexual orientation?*

— *How do you view, experience and express your sexuality from the differing realms of heart, mind, body and soul? Are these realms integrated or compartmentalized? In harmony or in conflict?*

— *How would you experience your sexuality if it was aligned and sourced from your Soul Print?*

Transforming Your Relationship with Shame

Shame is a huge issue in people's lives. John Bradshaw's transformative work on shame teaches us that healing the shame that binds us is probably one of the most important pieces of work you will ever do. Shame has to do with exposure and being "found out." Shame separates us from others. Because you are developing an *Observing Self,* you will notice times in your life that you experience rushes of shame. We usually push these rushes of emotion down fairly quickly, because they are so painful. When you feel that flush of shame, look around for "who" is so frightened and why they are in hiding.

If you have not made peace with your past (or your present) and want to do some work in this area, use the Inner Peace Treaty Process to begin dialoguing with the *Inner Characters* that carry shame. See if you can reach some new insights and self-compassion as you bring them out of the shadow realm. Sometimes you will need the help and support of a therapist, particularly if it involves childhood abuse or trauma. Most of you can begin this work on your own if you are gentle with yourself, hold off the *Not So Supporting Cast,* and keep *Inner Comforters, Protectors, Nurturing Parents, Wise Persons and Encouragers* involved in the *Negotiation* process.

PART THREE

INTEGRATION—
SHADOW WORK
DREAM WORK

WHAT PEOPLE NEED TO BE WHOLE

CHAPTER 12

THE SHADOW REALM

"Do not neglect to show hospitality to strangers,
for by so doing some have entertained angels
without knowing it."
Hebrews 13:2

The Shadow realm is a place of quagmires, the source of many dark and difficult situations in our lives. It is also a place of buried treasure, but the stuff of this realm does not look like treasure to begin with. Initially, it looks and feels like stuff to be avoided or gotten rid of. In its worst form, it seems more akin to radioactive toxic waste, with a dangerous half-life, difficult to manage or contain.

The term *Shadow* originated with Jung. He used the term to refer to material in the unconscious that has been rejected as unacceptable, dangerous, uncivilized, or immoral. We splinter off these parts of ourselves early in life, in order to be safe, loved and accepted. They get relegated to a *Shadow* pile. Over time this pile is swept away and forgotten, dumped into the basement of our unconscious.

We don't remember these early decisions to rid ourselves of our shadow qualities, longings, or tendencies, but they still affect us. We avoid situations that evoke disowned qualities and judge others who exhibit them. In distancing ourselves, we feel safer. We like to think that we are above those things.

In his book, *Owning Your Shadow*, Jungian analyst Robert Johnson describes how our *Shadow Characters* develop. Johnson says that sorting out what is acceptable to a society is necessary, and "there would be no civilized behavior without this sorting out of good and evil. But the refused and unacceptable characteristics do not go away; they only collect in the dark corners of our personality. When they have been hidden long enough, they take on a life of their own, the shadow life."

Dark Shadows

The nightly news is filled with examples of men and women who are not able to control their dark impulses. We are horrified, but also fascinated by the mild mannered person who suddenly goes insane and guns down innocent co-workers. We are curiously amazed by the quiet book keeper who has been discovered embezzling a million dollars over the course of twenty years. We are sickened by stories of the mother who drowns her own children, outraged by trusted financial institutions who gamble with our financial security, appalled by moral crusaders caught consorting with prostitutes. Most disturbing are the inconceivable stories of priests who molest innocent children. All of this comes from the shadow realm.

We condemn these actions vehemently, proclaiming our moral superiority. Most people would assert that they would never be tempted to exploit the innocence of a child, and yet most of us would have to admit to occasional brief moments of murderous rage, sexual fantasies about someone other than our spouse, or the temptation to compromise some important value in the face of financial need.

We know from prisoners of war that we do not know for certain what we would do in situations of extreme pressure, punishment and deprivation. If we are truly honest, we are frightened by our own dark, primordial impulses. We learned as children to be civilized, not to hit, bite, scream, steal or destroy things. That doesn't mean we don't want to.

Bright Shadows—Abandoned Gifts and Underdeveloped Potentials

It is important to note that we don't just disown the negative or uncivilized parts of ourselves. Over the years, I have met people who also disown their most positive qualities. Sometimes the people around us can't handle too much brilliance, beauty or creativity, and so we dull ourselves down. We disown intelligence, artistic talents, intuition, emotional sensitivity, spiritual gifts, even our deep capacity to love if they are too threatening for the people around us.

People who disown their gifts suffer greatly because these energies then go underground and have no healthy path of expression. The result can be a low-grade depression, a chronic sense of restless anxiety, or addictive and compulsive behaviors. When someone comes into therapy with one of these problems, I always look to see if they have not disowned some *Bright Shadow Gift*. An important part of making peace with yourself is to reclaim gifts once abandoned, and develop the potentials you disowned.

One way of identifying *Bright Shadow* material is to notice the people you admire or idealize, even envy. What is it that attracts you? What qualities does this person carry that you value so highly? What opportunities or experiences have they had that you long for? Look around to see who makes you angry or resentful. What seems unfair? What is someone getting away with? If you were just a bit more like them, how might your life be better?

A very quiet client of mine expressed the exasperation she feels when she works so hard on a company project and a self-promoting co-worker walks off with the credit. She so dislikes people who are self-promoting that she won't take credit where credit is due. She is angry at her co-worker but she needs a bit of the shadow entitlement he carries.

Sometimes we find ourselves envious or resentful of those who have had the chance to develop certain gifts. I know actors and musicians with tremendous talents who have worked for years and are still unable to sustain themselves with their art. When they talk about certain commercially successful artists, they are critical, commenting on performances they perceive as "mediocre, shallow, pandering to the unsophisticated masses." Behind this is the shadow of envy, a longing for their own commercial recognition, which has yet to arrive.

Whether our shadow material is dark or bright, these disowned constellations of energy have an impact on us. They shape our personalities, perspectives, moods, career, recreation and relationship choices. The shadow realm can determine the entire direction of a life for good or ill.

How We Judge What We Disown

We all want to think well of ourselves and to be thought of as acceptable. We shape ourselves according to the values of the groups we belong to, trimming off our rough edges, learning *who* in us is welcome and *who* is not. After we reject certain qualities in ourselves, we judge, criticize, and sometimes envy them in others.

For example, it is not uncommon for those devoted to human service to have limited finances. Occasionally they will exhibit some shadow self-righteousness in questioning the ethics and values of those who have money and power.

Every society or community has basic agreements about what is good and bad. We judge the actions of those who do not match our values and standards as unenlightened, dangerous, immoral or even insane. If these "others" are too frightening, we mobilize to subdue or destroy them.

History is filled with examples of one group determining that they were superior to another. We killed the infidels during the Crusades. Christianity has clothed the "savages" in any number of resource rich places. In our current political rhetoric we hear the arguments over who is *good and righteous* and who is *destructive and evil*. This is how every holy war and genocide gets started. Our very righteousness often becomes the launching missile of our shadow projections as we do evil in the name of God.

Sexuality and Aggression

We are particularly afraid of the two most primordial energies in life, creation and destruction, which manifest as sexuality and aggression. Most of us are taught to suppress these instincts as a way of managing them, and so they are particularly subject to shadow activity.

We are not taught how to work with these energies creatively, with responsibility and consciousness, and so we disown them, suppressing, controlling, and punishing their expression. "Good girls are not sexual." "Nice people don't get angry."

Split off, these energies go into the unconscious and become dark and destructive. Our current struggle with pornography and sexual addiction are examples of what happens to the natural instinct of our sexuality when it gets split off and relegated to the *Shadow* realm. The violence in the streets and in our very homes and the devastation of war throughout the world shows our inability to consciously direct the primal instincts of aggression.

How to be Non-Judgmental

Many spiritual people today are trying to live from a place of compassion. They do not want to be angry or resentful or judgmental. Our attempts to disown judgment only drives it into the shadow realm. There is a better way. The secret to being less judgmental is tied to the capacity to stand with awareness between opposing energies and experience both sides of the spectrum.

You cannot disown your *Inner Judge* or *Critic*. This discriminating part of the psyche is present in all of us. It helps us survive, but we need to be conscious of who wrote the script and what the agenda is. Everything in the psyche is energy in motion. How we direct that energy is our choice. For example, if we judge all aggression as dangerous and wrong, there will be times when it is appropriate to be in *Warrior* mode, to set a strong boundary, or put an end to something, and we won't be able to do it. Conscious awareness and responsibility are the only ways we can begin to direct our instincts for good or for ill.

Any time we become over-identified with a role, value or way of being, we will judge what is on the opposite side. Being over-identified with something is different from consciously choosing a well-considered way of being. Being over-identified means that we believe this defines who we are. It is an unconscious stance and pulls us into a state of imbalance. We become reactive to that which we have disowned. Reactivity reduces our capacity for wisdom and conscious choice.

Part of being a responsible person is owning and creatively directing our own shadow energies and our capacity to do harm. As we realize that all possibilities dwell within us, we learn to stand between many opposing energies. When we can stand between opposites and see both sides, judgment falls away.

The bottom line is that people who hurt others are operating out of a state of unconsciousness. They don't know or can't grasp any other way to be. The more personal work you do, the more you realize how unconscious you were, just yesterday. One day, it occurs to you that, if this is the case, then there is something you are unconscious of today. Even those of us with the best intentions unintentionally hurt others and create chaos. This awareness brings humility and a new commitment to do our inner work.

We Are Unconscious of Our Shadow Characters

We can see the shadow characteristics of others, but we are utterly blind to them in ourselves. As Jung wryly stated, "the unconscious is unconscious." Each of us is unconscious in a different way and when we realize that this is an inescapable part of life, we experience an increase of compassion for ourselves and for others. Conscious awareness means that we know we have an *Inner Cast of Characters*, but we are more than our *Inner Cast* or the drama of our lives. We are the theater in which they play.

The unconscious makes no delineation between good and bad, bright and dark. It is all just energy. It is our *Inner Cast of Characters* that decides what is good and bad. We are looking through their eyes when we evaluate things. We are not necessarily noticing that the color of the lens is shading the view. We are not considering what shadow needs might be influencing our choices.

Any time we are being dominated by one *Inner Character,* we are subject to shadow influences. Because they are disowned, our *Shadow Characters* wander in our psyches like orphans and refugees. If they get hungry, scared or angry enough, they rise up and take over. They are experts at masquerades, sometimes presenting themselves as the *Voice of God* or a *Demonic Force.* We feel helpless to resist such omnipotent influences.

Sometimes we make simple or careless mistakes that affect the direction of our lives. Sometimes we act in ways that are so completely "out of character" that it turns our world upside down. Once the *Observing Self* comes online and begins to look at what is driving our actions we are doing *Shadow Work.* We are bringing what is hidden into the light where we can understand it and transform it for our creative good.

Unfortunately, we are a culture that worships the bright side of existence. We tend to avoid the dark. We want to achieve, not reflect. We want to learn how to win friends and influence people, not how to swim in a dark abyss. We want a quick medication fix rather than to look at the cry of the soul beneath our distress.

The Inner Police

If we choose not to face our fears and shadow tendencies, we develop *Inner Police* that avoid the people and situations that stir them up. Life becomes increasingly constricted. We take fewer risks. Sometimes we stand at the gate of the Garden of Eden and refuse to enter because we are afraid of one tree that carries some forbidden fruit. We fear the *Shadow Serpent*, who might tempt us to partake.

For each person the forbidden realm is different. The *Voices of Warning* caution us like dragons at the gate of that garden. If we cross the threshold, we will enter the realm of fearful emotion, which must be faced before we can harvest the good fruit.

The Observing Self

As we begin to experience the presence of an *Observing Self*, which witnesses life, and the dynamics that play out within us, we realize that we are not merely our *Inner Cast of Characters*. We begin to experience ourselves as the theater in which all of this plays out. From this observing stance, we sit in the director's chair of our lives.

We cannot control others, but we can make choices about how we will live. We can hold certain values, and live by certain standards, but as we become more conscious, our values and standards begin to emanate from a deeper place of conviction, our *Soul Print*.

We know that in the primordial realm of the psyche, we house all possible life energies, which could manifest as a wide variety of *Inner Characters*. Some are more fitting than others to play out the life which is most in tune with our *Soul Print*.

That which truly belongs to us does not need to be so rigorously defended. We become less judgmental. We begin to relax. Life unfolds more easily as we trust the process. Each of us must discover the path we were born to walk, make our own choices, and ultimately be responsible for our lives.

Why Would You Want To Do Shadow Work?

You will never make peace with yourself until you own all of who you are. You must learn how to direct the many energies that live in you as *Inner Characters*. If you have spent most of your life disowning your *Shadow Characters*, the idea of seeking them out may seem absurd, reckless and dangerous. You may have early religious training that taught you to "flee evil and hold to the good." This childhood edict may create a *Gatekeeper* who warns you against doing shadow work.

Many people try to repress and deny their shadow material, but the *Shadow Characters* that carry these submerged energies inevitably show up. Denied on the inside, we end up marrying people who carry these disowned qualities, or we end up working with them as a co-worker, or worse yet, a boss. Some people have children who live out the unresolved and dark contents of their parent's *Shadow Characters*.

Perhaps you remember the mafia wisdom in the movie *The Godfather,* to keep your friends close, but your enemies closer. That's the thinking here. Not being aware of our darker capacities sets us up for some disturbing surprises. That which we run from follows us. Our suppressed shadow material has the potential of derailing the most carefully crafted life.

Michelle's Story

Michelle is on a spiritual quest to simplify her life. Last year, she left a prestigious marketing job in New York and moved to the mountains. She wanted to leave behind her elite upbringing, become less attached to material things, and spend more time pursuing a contemplative life.

The reason she was in my office was to figure out what happens to her when she visits her mother. Her mother lives in an opulent house filled with her father's wonderful art collection. On this last trip home, she had tried to explain to her mother about her new direction in life. Her mother frowned and with a long suffering look said, "I have no idea why we spent all that money on an Ivy League college education." Then her mother laughed and suggested they go shopping. Michelle didn't want to go shopping, but she saw how happy it would make her mother, and off they went.

In the dressing room of her mother's favorite boutique, Michelle recalled how her mother cooed over her as she brought in elegant outfits that suited the professional *Retired Self* Michelle had just left behind in New York. In that moment a shadow *Runaway Shopper* spent $500 on two outfits she would never wear in the mountains.

As Michelle and I explored *who* triggered the *Runaway Shopper* to purchase these clothes, we uncovered an *Orphan*, hiding in the shadows. As we began to dialogue with the *Orphan,* she told us that she would do anything to win her mother's love and attention including buying clothes that pleased her mother, but Michele would never wear. Michelle wanted to retire her *Pleaser* and her need to impress others.

As Michelle became more conscious of the shadow forces that were driving her, she called an *Inner Round Table* meeting. She began to provide support for her *Lost Orphan* who always felt unseen and unheard by her mother. She spent more time hiking in the mountains, and began to discover a strong, independent aspect of herself who needed no one's approval. She named her *Mountain Woman*. On a subsequent visit, she entered her mother's house strongly grounded in the energy of *Mountain Woman*. She had her *Orphan* safely tucked behind this confident, independent *Inner Character.*

This time, when her mother wanted to go shopping, Michelle suggested they take a walk instead. On the walk, she spoke from her *Calm Core* about her new direction in life. Michelle had reached a place where she was OK about herself regardless of whether her mother understood her or not. She realized that the insecurity and defensiveness she had been emanating in past visits evoked anxiety in her mother. Now she was speaking from a place of strength and confidence, and her mother relaxed. She realized that with her *Orphan* feeling safe, the shadow *Runaway Shopper* ceased to be an issue.

Devin's Story

Devin sat in my office with his head in his hands. He was depressed about his life. We had outlined some of his *Inner Cast of Characters,* the *Faithful Husband* and *Responsible Father* and *Provider.* He described his wife Beth as a *Good Woman* and *Devoted Mother* who was deeply committed to church work and the children. Beth was not that interested in him, personally or sexually, and she was unaware that behind his office door, he was spending an increasing amount of time viewing internet pornography. He was deeply conflicted about this, and as we talked, I could see the guilt and confusion in his eyes. I could also see the sadness he felt in his lonely marriage.

Devin sat in church on Sundays listening to the preacher talk about the evils of carnal lust and feeling increasingly sad and guilty about his "shadow life." The sermons told him that he was "sinful and bad," but offered him no helpful suggestions on how to deal with his deep loneliness or his sexual longings.

In our sessions, he talked about growing up in an emotionally detached home where no one shared their feelings. His eyes lit up when we talked about his early relationship with Beth and how connected they seemed to be, sharing deep thoughts and feelings. Somewhere in the midst of raising children and making a living, they had lost that connection.

I invited Devin to stop condemning himself with a broad brush and to explore his *Inner Cast of Characters* to discover *who* it was in him that was watching the pornography. We interviewed the *Inner Judge* who had determined that everything in his instinctual realm was to be condemned. He talked about being bored with his life and resentful about being ignored in favor of the children. The *Responsible Father* in him felt very guilty and selfish about this resentment. Devin decided to name the shadowy *Inner Character* that carried his pornography involvement the *Sex Junkie*. As we began to dialogue with this *Inner Character*, Devin realized that this unwanted behavior was driven by deep hungers. He recognized that there was a parallel between eating junk food and having what he called "junk sex." It relieved stress and got his mind off his problems for the moment, but didn't really nourish him. His real hunger was for a meaningful connection with the woman he married.

I asked him if he had talked to Beth about this and he said no. He was living out of a childhood script that told him that men should be strong and stoic. They should not have needs. This *Strong, Stoic Man* was convinced that if he expressed his longings to Beth that she would lose respect for him or tell him he was being selfish.

One night Devin had a dream about the early days of his marriage. He remembered being an impetuous, open hearted *Young Lover*. When he woke up, he was filled with a longing for that time. He began to talk to Beth about his sadness and how much he missed the romantic connection they once shared. As he opened his heart and reached out to her, she was moved by his tenderness and they began to re-engage sexually. As Devin's need for a deeper connection was met, the hungers that were driving his shadow sexual life diminished. He found he was able to free himself from the compulsive grip of the *Sex Junkie* that had once held him captive.

Making Peace with Your Shadow

If you are ever going to really make peace with yourself you will need to go into shadowy corners and clean out the basement of your life. This includes integrating your primal instincts and reclaiming the *Lost Children* that roam uncomforted in the dark corners of your psyche. We spend an enormous amount of life energy monitoring and controlling our shadow aspects. In spite of all of our efforts, these creatures of the deep claim us in our moments of weakness and hunger, when we are too tired or pre-occupied to police them. They all want a place at the *Inner Round Table* of your life.

When we bring this energy to consciousness and learn to work with it, we can harness its power for good. Some of our greatest gifts are tied up in shadow material and the only way to access them is to face the dragon at the gate that guards the treasure.

SHADOW WORK
TO DO OR NOT TO DO

Three Reasons People Don't Do Shadow Work

1. We don't know that we have *Shadow Characters* or how much they impact us.
2. We are taught to "flee evil" and avoid our dark impulses. In this teaching we learn to fear our shadow and not to face it. We don't know where to start or how to proceed. How do we identify our shadow energies? What do we do with them once we discover them?
3. We fear that if we own and take responsibility for our darkness, we will be required to make difficult changes. We decide that it is better to remain unconscious.

Three Reasons To Do Shadow Work

1. To stop creating chaos in our lives and in the lives of others. To solve the mystery of why we undermine our true happiness and fulfillment.
2. To free up the large amounts of energy currently being spent policing, avoiding, denying, and repressing. To redirect these energies to creative endeavors.
3. To tap into the "gold" of our shadow, accessing the hidden gifts and treasures that reside there.

CHAPTER 13

INNER PEACE TREATY
SHADOW WORK—
Naming, Knowing, Negotiating, and Integrating

"The Shadow is the door to our individuality.
Insofar as the Shadow is our first view of the
unconscious part of our personality,
it represents the first state toward meeting the Self."
Edward Whitmont

We often avoid doing shadow work because we are afraid of what we may find. We might have to face some dark aspects of ourselves or discover a terrible secret. We fear the swirling mystery of the unconscious.

Entering this realm is not without risk. The power of our *Shadow* is great and demands respect. We are taking a look behind the familiar image of ourselves. When doing this work, it is advisable to have someone with whom you share your inner journey, a soul friend or therapist. That way, if you become overwhelmed, you will have someone to stabilize you.

In addition to the safety that a co-traveler provides, it is immensely satisfying to share your journey with someone who will honor the hard work you are doing and hold your treasured discoveries as sacred.

If you have a history of trauma or abuse, it is crucial that you enter this terrain with the support of a therapist who can help you process the emotions that will inevitably surface.

That being said, the psyche seems to know how much new material we can integrate at one time. It brings us small doses of shadow material each night in our dreams as characters and themes that invite us into unfamiliar territory. We will talk more about dream work in the next chapter. There is plenty of shadow material in waking life.

SIX WAYS OF KNOWING YOU ARE IN THE SHADOW REALM

1. *You are mysteriously and strongly attracted to someone or something.*
2. *You have a strong negative reaction to someone or something.*
3. *You keep experiencing mysterious obstacles to happiness or success over and over again.*
4. *You feel compelled to do something that is very unlike you.*
5. *People keep giving you the same feedback about problems you create, but you feel misunderstood or wrongly judged.*
6. *You are over-identified with some wounding experience and you cannot move beyond it.*

1. *You are mysteriously and strongly attracted to someone or something*.

It might be a cause, job, teacher, lover, even a place. There is nothing more compelling than the experience of finding a "perfect fit," something that feels destined to be. You may feel like you found your true home, or that something in you has awakened for the first time. Something *has* awakened. Something that was once unconscious is moving into consciousness. You are experiencing yourself and life in a new and wonderful way. Naturally, you think it is the person, place or thing that is creating this wondrous feeling. However, in actuality, you are experiencing the awakening of something that has been sleeping in your archetypal depths. Once awakened, this experience is yours forever.

People get very stuck here. They get attached to the stimulating cause of this awakening, particularly with people and work. Now certain experiences and people are truly wonderful, but I am talking about over-valuing here. I am talking about *Bright Shadow* projection. When we begin to idealize people and situations, thinking they are "perfect," we are not seeing the whole picture and setting ourselves up for a painful disillusionment. The enchantment becomes a bitter dis-enchantment. It is the children in us who do this. They long for perfect love, protection and provision. Every person, cause, career, organization and place has a shadow side. This is part of the human condition. Inevitably we meet the shadow and if we have been living in a state of innocence, this can be devastating.

When we fall in love we are in the *Bright Shadow* realm. We feel as if lightening has struck, like we are star crossed. When we are swept away like this, we are unable to see the whole person, in their humanity, as they really are. All we can see for a while is the *Bright Shadow* projection and how wonderful we feel when we are in love with our projections!

When our rose colored lenses finally fall from our eyes, it is shattering and frightening. We want perfect love and mountain-top experiences. We hate the valleys or the ordinariness of life. Some people become addicted to this rush of excitement and continue to search for the dream ideal, moving from one job or relationship to the next, trying to re-recapture that first blush of love. As we grow up, we realize that life contains the full spectrum of experiences, bright and dark, joyful and painful. Not every day is a transcendent day and that's as it should be.

So yes, we are awakened by experiences and teachers and love and life. But ultimately they are awakening something that was already in us, in our own archetypal seedbed. What was once unknown has become known, what was submerged has now become conscious. Once awakened, we own it. It does not belong to something or someone outside of us.

Exploration—Strong Attractions

The following inquiries are for an attraction to a person. The same questions would apply if it were an attraction to a situation, place or cause.

- ***Who in you is so attracted to this person or situation?***
  Name this Inner Character now.
- ***What about them is so attractive?***
  What qualities does this person have that are similar or different from you? How do you experience yourself in response to this person? Imagine that you are involved with them. How does it feel? How does this fulfill you? What need does it meet? How would your life be different?
- ***What is awakening in you?***
  Often people or causes we are attracted to represent an Emergent Self, something undeveloped, but coming into being. Over-idealizing another negates our own capacity to develop what they carry and can cause us to become dependent on them. Developing these longed for qualities in ourselves reduces that dependency.
- ***How might you make space for this emergent energy?***
  Is there anyone at your Inner Round Table who would object to you integrating the qualities, talents or energies you have been idealizing? Dialogue with these Inner Characters and find out what their concerns are. What assurances do they need to make space for these new potentials to your Inner Round Table?

2. *You have a strong negative reaction to something or someone.*

When you find yourself judging, hating, envying, resenting, ranting or raving, you know you have hit pay dirt for shadow work. This form of shadow can also cause you to avoid things. Notice if you stay away from certain people or situations, because you get too stirred up and can't manage your emotions. It is a tremendous opportunity for shadow work.

Exploration

- *What are you judging in another and why?*
- *What are the feelings they evoke?*
- *How are the qualities you are reacting to different or opposite from you?*
- *Is there anything about this person or situation that you secretly long for, but believe that you cannot have?*
- *Which of your Inner Characters are involved in this negative reaction? What is the threat? Are any of your Inner Characters attracted rather than repelled?*
- *Explore the history of your reaction with your Inner Characters. How did they come to feel this way?*
- *How would it change your life if you integrated some of this rejected quality?*

3. *You keep experiencing mysterious obstacles to happiness and success over and over again.*

It may be that every job you get, you end up with the same abusive boss. You may have a pattern of dating people who are emotionally unavailable. If either one of these is true, try working the questions outlined in #1 and #2.

You may constantly undermine your health goals. You may be on the verge of success repeatedly and then things mysteriously fall apart. The names and faces change, but the dynamics keep repeating.

Other examples of self-defeating patterns are saying stupid things in front of people you want to impress or getting sick right after you make an empowering life decision. Perhaps people tell you about certain gifts and talents that you have, but you refuse to claim them. This indicates that some sort of unconscious activity is playing out. These are all indications of shadow activity in your relationship with power and success.

It looks like it is happening on the outside, but it is really generated from inside, where *Inner Characters* are playing out self-defeating scripts. Everyone gets taken advantage of occasionally in life and people do encounter legitimate challenges, but when bad things happen to good people, over and over, shadow activity is at play. *Who* in you is picking untrustworthy or abusive people? *Who* in you is setting events in motion that undermine your success? *Who* is not seeing warning signs?

The way to put an end to these frightening and heartbreaking situations is to surface the unconscious material that is operating. It is time to look more carefully at your *Inner Players* who are setting these events in motion.

Exploring your script material around success:

- *What would it mean to be successful?*
- *What do you like or dislike about successful people?*
- *Do you have an Inner Character who is concerned with how you might change were you to succeed?*
- *What do the Voices of Warning tell you about success?*
- *What assurances would these Inner Characters need to allow you to move forward?*
- *Might your success upset or threaten someone in your outer life?*

- *Whom do you respect and admire in the outside world that you could use as a role model for success? Consider adding an imagined version of this person to your Inner Round Table. What kind of input would they have for your life?*

Committee Work for Success

It often helps to form an *Inner Committee* to explore a mystery in your life. Determine which of your *Inner Characters* have a vested interest in this situation. Gather them at your *Inner Round Table* for the purpose of solving a problem or working towards a goal. Maintain the position of neutral *Moderator*, insuring that everyone has a chance to speak. Begin the dialogue by asking each one:

- *Which of your Inner Characters picks your jobs, friends, lovers, cars, clothes, etc.?*
- *Look to see where your Inner Children might be influencing you. What are their needs?*
- *Do you have Thinking, Problem Solving Inner Characters on this committee?*
- *If you are having trouble with money, which of your Inner Characters is managing your money? If they are spending to meet emotional needs, how might you negotiate with them to get their needs met in a better way?*
- *Do you have good Inner Protectors, who warn you when they sense problems ahead? If so, do you listen? If not, why?*
- *Go around your Inner Round Table and ask each Inner Character how they view the situation and what they think should be done.*
- *If you are missing Inner Nurturers, Supporters, Protectors, or Strategizers in your Inner System, who is someone you can use as a role model? Have you had any dream characters that have brought this energy to you? Imagine inviting them to join you as a member of your Inner Round Table Committee.*

4. *You feel compelled to do something that is totally unlike you.*

It's hard to know sometimes whether these compelling urges are "good" or "bad." If your life has been unhappy and failure ridden, doing something completely "out of character" may be a good thing! It may indicate that you are outgrowing a self-defeating script. Some people really do need to leave a marriage or career. Sometimes an urge to change your life indicates the emergence of a true calling, so an *Inner Round Table* meeting is important, to take a deeper look.

People also derail their lives by following compelling urges without examining their origins. Sometimes people tell me that they are following their hearts, but when we look a little deeper, we see that they are really seeking to meet some deep need that has gone unaddressed for a long time. One of their *Inner Characters* has been ignored, become very unhappy and has stormed the stage of their lives, insisting on being heard. Long term unaddressed needs are open doors for the entrance of *Shadow Selves*.

A great example of this is the stereotypical mid-life crisis. People leave long-term marriages, quit established careers and go in search of "who they really are." Discovering who you really are is one of the most important things you will ever do, but this can be navigated in a dedicated process of conscious change.

One of the most disruptive things people do in mid-life is fall in love with someone other than their spouse. Romantic attractions indicate that a person's life has gotten too small for the size of their soul. We need to keep growing across our lifespan, and years spent in an unfulfilling marriage or career become intolerable at midlife.

Midlife is when a lot of people come into therapy. They are in crisis and they don't know what to do. Midlife is a time of integrating the disowned or uncultivated parts of ourselves. Powerful new archetypal energies are at work. So in response to irresistible urges to change your life, ask yourself:

Exploration

- *Is my Observing Self involved in this process? Can I just sit, with awareness, in the midst of competing agendas without polarizing to one side or the other? Can I stand in the tension of two opposing energies, exploring what is going on?*
- *Regarding the course of action I am considering, what tension will it relieve? What need will it meet? What problem will it solve?*
- *Do I feel compulsive or overwhelmed? Can I wait until I feel I could move freely to either side of the argument?*

Inner Round Table Meetings

- *As I survey my Inner Cast of Characters, can I gather an Inner Committee to explore this? Who should be here?*
- *Do I have my Inner Moderator operating so that all parties can be heard and negotiations can take place?*
- *Survey each member of the committee and ask them how they view this course of action. Who is for or against it and why?*
- *If I believe I am being called to do this, how will it help me to live more deeply or purposefully?*
- *What will it cost me and who in my Inner Cast of Characters will pay that price? Have I negotiated with them so that they are in agreement?*
- *Have I looked around to see what deep needs might be driving this?*
- *How are my Inner Children involved?*
- *Does this have anything to do with needing to feel safe, loved, comforted, included, nurtured, powerful, desirable, resolved or vindicated.*
- *Are you trying to undo a former hurt?*

- *Is this a repeat of an old pattern? Who in me plays this pattern out?*
- *If you determine that this is a crucial action to take in service of your growth and greatest good, then how will you need to rearrange your life to make the space for this change? Who in your Inner Cast of Characters will support you in this process?*
- *Who in the outer world will support you?*

5. People keep giving you the same feedback about problems you create, but you feel misunderstood or wrongly judged.

If people keep giving you the same negative feedback and you keep insisting that *you* are the *Victim*, you might want to do some *Shadow Work*. Somewhere within, unconscious dynamics are going on that are creating problems for you. We don't like to admit our faults, failings, and dysfunctions, but we all have them. Becoming conscious of them and claiming them does not reduce you to a terrible person. It empowers you to have more of what you deeply want in your life. If you want to stop the madness, take a closer look at yourself.

Feedback is important in life. It is important to differentiate between the two kinds of feedback we get from people. The first comes from those who are upset because we are not living according to what suits *them*. They want us to play a part in *their* life script. The second kind of feedback comes from those who care enough to tell us where we are messing our lives up. They are giving us clues about our shadow aspects.

People Who Can't Take Feedback
Many people who appear arrogant or entitled are actually quite insecure. That's why they can't take any negative feedback whatsoever. They are continually looking for reassurance that they are OK. Some people are so tormented by an *Inner Critic*

that they can't tolerate any criticism without falling into shame and self-loathing. We all need *Inner Supporters, Comforters and Encouragers* that will uphold us when life tears us down. We also need them to support us when we are hearing difficult truths about our lives. Every distorted perception, dysfunctional life strategy or defensive personality adaptation is driven by an unmet need. Behind these problematic defenses sits our vulnerable children, trying to protect themselves, or seeking love and support. We need a lot of self-compassion to face the errors of our ways.

Exploration

- *What is your preferred image of yourself?*
- *How would you like others to think of you?*
- *Consider some feedback that you have received from more than one person. If it were true, what conclusions would you draw about yourself?*
- *What does your Inner Critic/Judge tell you about this?*
- *What might be the needs that are driving these behaviors? Who in you carries these needs?*
- *Are the strategies you employ to meet your needs working out well? Who in you came up with those ideas? Who in you might take a different approach?*

6. You are over-identified with some wounding experience and you cannot move beyond your history.

People survive some horrific life experiences. When you have survived something very difficult, it is important to tell your story to someone who can honor the struggle and the hurt these experiences caused you. There is also a time for transcending a story that has limited and defined you, to move into a larger story. When we can't get over something that has happened to us, we are attached to the wound in some way. There is shadow activity at work.

Sometimes we don't know who we would be without this wound. The wound is the defining identity of an *Inner Character*. For example, if you were abused as a child, is the *Main Character* on the stage of your life still the *Abused Child*. If your husband left you for another woman, are you still the *Betrayed Woman* or the *Victim?* How does having this story, this wound, help you to be cared for, protected, or special? Does it excuse you from doing the hard work of re-defining yourself, or taking full responsibility for your life? Would moving past an old wound feel like you were letting the person who hurt you "off Scott free"? Do you have *Inner Characters* who need justice, vindication, an apology or restitution before they can let go?

Exploration

- *Has a particular Wounded Self or Victim become a primary part of your identity?*
- *Who would you be without this identity?*
- *If an apology or restitution is not forthcoming from someone who hurt you, what can you do to experience closure from your end? What would your Inner Children need to cut the chords that tie you to a painful past?*
- *Whom can you imagine adding to your Inner Round Table that would provide you with a sense of being Protected, Validated, Understood and Loved?*
- *How might they help you write the next chapter of your life?*

INTEGRATING OPPOSITES

Hal Stone's Homeopathic Shadow Tincture

Over the years, I have listened to Hal Stone explain his famous remedy for integrating shadow material and reducing reactive judgments. A workshop attendee will begin to describe some awful person who really disturbs them. Hal will ask about specific qualities that this appalling person carries. We hear things like, "He is so self-centered." or "She is so weak and dependent." or "He is always so negative about everything." or "She is so brazenly seductive!" Hal then asks the workshop attendee about how they see themselves. What are their qualities? Invariably, the person who hates selfishness is usually very kind and giving. The self-sufficient person hates weakness and dependency. The proper woman can't stand seductive, openly sensual women. Notice that we are dealing with opposites here. Whenever we move too far to one end of an archetypal continuum, we will either be attracted or repelled by its opposite. Our reactivity is signaling us that this is the very medicine we need to move to a more integrated center.

Hal's solution for this reactivity is to imagine boiling the offending person down into a homeopathic tincture. He then prescribes a certain number of drops of this remedy every day. The purpose of this is to integrate just a little bit of the rejected quality and to watch what happens. It doesn't mean that we are going to become that which offends us: selfish, uncaring, dependent, negative, or slutty. It means that we are going to move out of our position at the extreme end of the archetypal spectrum and integrate some of the opposite. It allows us to see the unique way in which this energy lives in us. This reduces our judgment and reactivity and gives us the capacity to be in the presence of this energy with equanimity.

How would you be different if you became just a bit more like the person that you find so disdainful? One man said that if he were more like his selfish stepmother, he would set better boundaries with people's requests and do more of what *he* wanted to do with his life. He smiled and realized that this would make him less resentful of others. The woman who hated weak, dependent people commented that her last boyfriend left her saying, "I feel useless in your life because you don't need me for anything." The woman who criticized the seductively dressed woman at the center of attention at the cocktail party said, "Last week I saw a red dress I really liked, but I did not allow myself to buy it, because I was afraid I might draw too much attention to myself."

All of these people realized their lives would be better off if they integrated just a bit of the qualities that they found so negative in others. That which we judge and disown is often just the medicine we need to move ourselves to a place of higher potential and greater wholeness.

Embracing Light and Dark

I have a picture of a woman with an angel on one shoulder and a devil on the other. She looks stressed out. The message is about the age old struggle between the good and evil, black and white, clearly split into two obvious categories. The picture poses the question, "which one will she listen to?"

This is how we typically view our shadow material. We see what is in the light as good, and what is hidden in the shadows as bad. The older we get, the more we realize that some events that seemed like the worst possible tragedy at the time brought about change and growth that would not have occurred otherwise.

Likewise, we sometimes make decisions with the best of intentions and the results are very negative. It's hard to tell whether an event is good or bad until much time has passed and all the consequences have played out. That is the nature of shadow material. All shadow contains gold if we will only mine it. The work is hard and takes time, patience, and self-compassion. The rewards are great.

CHAPTER 14

DREAM WORK

"A dream is a theatre in which the dreamer is himself the scene, the player, the prompter, the producer, the author, the public, and the critic."

CG Jung

When I began to study Jungian psychology, I discovered that the process of dialoguing with sub-personalities was something that Jung himself practiced. In fact, he had great reverence for it. Jung's *Red Book* is an account of his journey through the archetypal realm as he encounters the surprising *Cast of Characters* in the depths of his psyche. In the Jungian world, engaging in an experiential dialogue process with dream characters is called *Active Imagination*.

I was so pleased by the discovery of *Active Imagination* that I entered Jungian analysis and began a lengthy study of Jung's work. Jungian theory gave *Inner Peace Treaty* work its theoretical foundation. Adding dream characters to my *Inner Peace Treaty* process deepened my self-understanding and accelerated my personal growth in a way I could never have foreseen.

Jungian analysis introduced me to *Shadow Work*, which I consider a major spiritual practice. Doing our personal *Shadow Work* is one of the most significant contributions we can each make towards healing a broken world. We begin by working on ourselves, making peace with our own warring *Inner Characters*. Then, we can make peace with others.

Dream work dovetails with *Inner Peace Treaty* work. I have taught *Inner Peace Treaty Dream Work* for years at the Haden

Institute and in other workshop settings. Many dream workers have told me how much they enjoy adding this method to their existing practices. It gives them a simple way to unlock the wisdom of a dream and to access the archetypal energies held there. Each night the psyche presents us with a different *Cast of Characters* as the soul unfolds the deeper story of our lives.

The nightly stage of my dreams shows me what kinds of archetypal energies are stirring in my psyche. I am noting the symbols and what they might represent, but most importantly, I am noting the energies. *Who* is showing up and how are they commenting on the unfolding of my life? What are the feelings, the story lines and themes? How does the action progress and resolve? What is moving through my psyche in response to my attitudes, and life direction?

Over the years, I have included characters from my dreams as *Inner Round Table* participants. When I first started dialoguing with my *Inner Characters*, I interacted with them as if they were seated outside of me. Eventually, I began to experiment with entering into my dream figures, inhabiting them and experiencing things from inside their world. In this process, I would be looking at me through their eyes! This provided an amazing set of insights.

Hal and Sidra Stone taught me how to separate out and distinguish the energy and perspective of each *Inner Character.* As we become more aware that we are the theatre in which our *Inner Characters* are acting out the scenes of our lives, that awareness helps us separate out from the drama. We can rest in the quiet soul space of our *Calm Core* and direct our lives with more clarity. We still get triggered, captured by domineering complexes, swept sideways by new archetypal currents, but we navigate with greater skill and regain our center more quickly.

Archetypal Fluency

Learning the skill of how to move in and out of a range of archetypal energies is what I call *Archetypal Fluency.* When you are fluent in a foreign language, you can speak it with ease and also understand the nuances of the culture. When you are fluent in archetypes, you can recognize and inhabit a wide spectrum of energies.

Most of us become identified with a narrow range of archetypal expressions that match our roles and the cast of *Inner Characters* we have adopted, but the possibilities of what our *Inner Theatre* can house is endless. Each of us has the capacity to expand our archetypal range of being and to explore new territories in the psyche. This is one way to transcend the limiting definitions we have of ourselves.

Dream work is a profound way of developing *Archetypal Fluency*, integrating new material from the realm of the personal unconscious and beyond. As we open ourselves to this vast realm, we discover resources we never knew we had.

When you expand the range of archetypal energies you can inhabit, you begin to understand others better. You become a wiser and more compassionate person. People who can be with a wide variety of energies are less judgmental or reactive. Things bother them less and their fears and anxieties dissipate.

Every dream character that comes to you carries a different archetypal energy. If you begin to explore your dream characters from the inside out, you will continually expand the range of archetypal energies you can inhabit.

Conducting the Inner Orchestra

I once had a dream in which a master engineer adjusted the levels of a multi-channeled mixing board, to produce the perfect final mix. It reminded me of how we can direct our *Inner Self*

System, adjusting the volume of certain *Inner Characters* up or down depending on the situation. I like the way Hal and Sidra Stone liken it to being the conductor of a large orchestra. We are in control of who is playing and how loudly. A skillful conductor decides if there needs to be a bit more from the percussion section or if the violins need to quiet down.

WHAT ARE DREAMS AND WHY DO THEY MATTER?

Dreams have been important to all cultures throughout time. They have generally been interpreted by designated members of a tribe or group who were considered intuitively gifted to know their meaning. Dreams can be considered postcards from the soul. They send us pictures of where we are on our journey. They constantly invite us to grow into something more.

Jungian Dream Work

Jungian psychology teaches us that we are far more than our roles, our history, or the *Persona* we present to the world. In Jungian analysis, dreams are used as inroads to deeper processes. They transcend the narrow confines of our ego identity, bypassing our defenses, programming and scripts. They show us the path to undiscovered inner resources, soul material that lies hidden under the surface of our awareness. As this material emerges, it can be explored and integrated into our waking life. Dreams move us beyond our need to conform or rebel. They show us where our thought distortions lie and how we might be fooling or limiting ourselves.

Dreams lift us into a larger frame of reference. They help us to reconcile conflicting parts of our personalities. In life, we sometimes get stuck in a corner, unable to see another point of view. The dream world introduces creative alternatives, experiences that break us out of our fixed ways of being. These dream experiences can be disturbing. They create a kind of heat that melts our frozen perspectives and helps us to view situations with a new attitude.

Dreams point the spotlight on our shadow material, those parts of our personalities which we have split off and rejected. Our disowned shadow material is not just dark, it also contains the most beautiful aspects of our being. Dreams bring us back into contact with these lost parts of ourselves. In the midst of the rubble, we discover hidden potential, waiting to be awakened.

In Jungian theory, every person and every symbol in the dream is a part of the dreamer's psyche. So when we dream of others, it is important to consider how we characterize them. What are their qualities and where do we find these in us? How do these qualities relate to our current life situations?

Dreams also give us information about our reactions to our outer life. They show us how we are projecting our own unconscious material onto others, often amplifying the content, to get our attention. Every aspect of the dream is chosen by the unconscious to shed light on something in our lives.

What Purpose Do Dreams Serve?

There are many methods of working dreams. All of them have value. Many people wonder what purposes dreams serve. Here is a list of possibilities:

1. *Dreams help us process the events of the day.*
2. *Dreams offer us creative solutions for living.*
3. *Dreams alert us to the unconscious forces that are driving us.*
4. *Dreams show us where we are out of balance.*
5. *Dreams provide compensation, wish fulfillment and pressure release.*
6. *Dreams give us Yes and No guidance.*

7. **Dreams bring us what we need for our healing and wholeness.**

8. **Dreams inform our lives. They tell us who we are today and invite us to become something more.**

1. *Dreams Help Us Process The Events Of The Day.*

It is helpful to view dreams in the context of our waking lives as they frequently contain "day residue," fragments of our daily lives that get mixed into our dreams. Life comes at us fast, and we do not have time to process everything that happens to us. When we sleep, we sort through the day, locating things that were emotionally charged. To use a computer metaphor, our psyche goes through an interior system check, filing things into categories and defragging our lives. Experiences that had an emotional charge get revisited and reworked.

Some dreams help us to achieve a sense of closure where none was possible in waking life. An example of this might be a conflict in a relationship that you cannot seem to resolve. Your psyche may return to that unresolved situation and rework the events that took place with a different outcome. You may feel differently about the situation when you awake. This internal shift may or may not change the situation on the outside, but as you change your approach, people and situations have been known to change as well.

2. *Dreams Offer Us Creative Solutions For Living.*

Dreams offer us creative solutions we wouldn't consider with our waking mind. Many inventions have been sourced from dreams. Artists create from their dream life on a regular basis. Our waking mind tends to solve problems according to its most familiar values and strategies. This causes us to filter out approaches that don't fit our current frameworks. The dreaming mind is creative and unrestrained. During the night, we wander into new internal territory, and view problems and situations from a new perspective. We come up with "out of the box" solutions not previously considered. That's why we say that a person should "sleep on it" before making a final decision.

Jim's Story

Jim was experiencing a lot of frustration at his job. His boss was placing impossible demands on him without the resources to accomplish them. Jim felt anxious, trapped and angry, but afraid to protest, lest he be fired. The archetype of the *Victim* was highly constellated in him, and he had a long history of being taken advantage of. The *Voices of Warning* were loud in his head, "Don't complain. Try harder to make things work." He was exhausted.

One night, he had a dream in which he played the part of the *Brave Hero.* In the dream he discovered a dangerous factory condition that would kill hundreds of workers. He approached the industrial tyrant who owned the plant in a way that appealed to his profit motive. Repairs were made and he saved hundreds of lives.

When Jim woke up from this dream, he felt a shift in himself. He had moved out of the energy of his *Victim complex.* Infused by the archetypal energy of the *Hero,* he could see a solution to his problem that hadn't been evident when he looked at it through *Victim's* eyes. He was able to go into work and communicate with his boss from a place of confidence and clarity rather than anger and fear. What he had to say made business sense to his boss, but more importantly, the energy from which Jim communicated evoked a cooperative response and led to positive change.

3. Dreams Alert Us To The Unconscious Forces That Are Driving Us.

Each of us has our own set of wounds, longings and unmet needs. We are often unaware of how these things drive us. We get overtaken by *Inner Characters* with powerful hidden agendas. In Jungian psychology this is referred to as a *complex*. A *complex* is a long-standing tangle of unconscious reactivity that distorts our perceptions and drives our behavior.

To be stuck in a complex is to be hijacked by one or more *Inner Characters*. This creates distorted perceptions of life. When we have been captured by a complex, we believe that we are "right." We feel clear about how things should be and what to do. Later, we see the folly of our ways, but this is long after the scene has played itself out and the curtain has come down.

Everyone has complexes. They are part of the human condition and your particular set of complexes will follow you throughout your life, activating from time to time. One of the goals of a good psychological analysis is to become more aware of what your complexes are and which *Inner Characters* play them out. That way, you can catch yourself more quickly when you are under their spell.

Dreams create amplified illustrations of our complexes to get our attention. The more highly charged the drama in our dreams, the stronger the message that we are not dealing with something important. Recurrent dreams indicate that there is something deep within us that has yet to be addressed. If we do not attend to the message the dream brings, the drama may escalate into disturbing dimensions.

4. Dreams Show Us Where We Are Out of Balance.

Complexes create imbalances in our *Inner Self System*. Each *Inner Character* has a different history, agenda and way of working. Some are quite young, quite needy or angry and have very distorted ideas about life. They can be highly reactive and create a lot of drama.

Some of our *Inner Characters* get very upset when they are neglected. Just like people in life, who become hurt and resentful when their needs are ignored, our neglected *Inner Characters* will soon generate dreams that illustrate their displeasure. This is how they show us where we are out of balance.

Case History — Lorraine

Lorraine described herself as "the only one around who takes responsibility for anything!" She was angry and exhausted and complained that no one else carried their weight. One night her psyche generated the following dream scene:

> *I am the commander of a military regime, enforcing a cruel occupation in a village of frightened, vulnerable peasants. The peasants have been turned into slaves and all celebration is forbidden, punishable by death. I look into their sad, pleading eyes, and feel no compassion.*

Lorraine awoke from the dream disturbed by how cold she could feel towards the poor peasants. She identified strongly with them in her waking life. They worked so hard and had no joy. In working the dream from the perspective that all dream characters represent a part of us, it suddenly dawned on her that she was also a cruel tyrant who drove herself mercilessly!

We began to explore her need for perfection and control, and she talked about her early life, recounting memories of growing up in an alcoholic home, where she dared not relax. She was ever vigilant in her early years, in an attempt to keep everything under control. There was no time for play or simple pleasures. Lorraine touched into the grief she felt over her lost childhood and realized that she needed to put an end to the reign of her cruel *Inner Tyrant*.

She began to cultivate a relationship with her *Inner Peasants* who loved simple pleasures. She began to allow herself to participate in activities that brought her true enjoyment rather than doing everyone else's work. As she did this, the *Frightened Child* in her began to relax. As she became less angry and judgmental, people became more willing to engage with her and support her. Her improved relationships and a growing connection with her *Inner Peasants* brought a whole new sense of pleasure and meaning to her life.

5. *Dreams Provide Compensation and Safety Valves for Pressure Release.*

When we move too far into one attitude of life, our dreams may play out a scenario where we embody the opposite orientation. We do things in our dreams that we would never do in waking life. Someone who is usually very contained and reserved may dream about being wild and free. A free-spirited artistic type might dream of wearing a suit and running a large corporation. Dreams act like the roll stabilizers on a big ship. When we begin to tilt too far in one direction, they seek to pull us back to the center.

Dreams also provide a safety valve for the pressure that builds up from suppressing our impulses. We inhibit these impulses because we are attempting to live according to certain rules of society. Dreams operate in a part of the psyche that is not governed by rules, morals or religious constraints. One example of this is celibate individuals, who are known to be plagued by sexual dreams. In medieval times, it was thought that the monks were being visited by evil spirits when these dreams occurred. Viewed as compensatory material, these dreams are a healthy way that the psyche is mediating the instinct to procreate and releasing the pressure of inner sexual tension. Sexual union in a dream can also be the psyche's way of taking in some energetic quality that the sexual partner carries.

People who strongly identify with loving kindness can be very disturbed by dreams of committing murder or other cruel acts. Again, the psyche is compensating for repressed aggressive instincts and inviting us to look at how we may have moved too far into being passive to the detriment of our purpose and wellbeing.

6. *Dreams Provide Yes And No Guidance For Our Lives.*

When making an important decision in life, it pays to attend to your dreams. Dreams do not always give an obvious "Yes or No" in response to "what should I do?" but they often inform us about important factors and deeper motivations that we may be overlooking. "Yes and No" dreams express the needs of *Inner Cast* members who were not consulted. Other disturbing dreams are warnings that we are in danger. If you believe a dream is warning you about something, check it out. Change your direction, and see how your dreams respond afterward.

I can think of several warning dreams that I did not heed and lived to regret later. Here is a personal example of a No dream where I listened and followed the guidance.

I was offered a job in community mental health where it sounded like I could make a big difference in the lives of people in need. It appealed strongly to the heart oriented *Inner Characters* in me that carry my *Rescuer* and *Savior* energies. I went home that night and had the following dream:

I am at the bottom of the ocean trapped underneath a huge, gray military tanker. I am pinned under the weight and realize there is no way to get out from under this ship. I am going to die here. Suddenly I realize that this ship is not a multi ton tanker. It is just a large inflatable raft. I push it off of me and begin to swim to the surface. I can see the sunlight filtering down through the water and know I am going to make it.

You don't have to be a master dream worker to get the message of this dream, a warning that this job would bury me. Dreams sometimes speak in puns. The next day, as I was telling this dream

193

to a friend, I caught the dream pun of the inflatable raft as it highlighted the inflation of my *Savior Complex*. The military tanker represented the impersonal, immovable governmental system that my *Savior Self* thought it could redeem.

When we "helper types" go into these inflated states, we forget that we are mere humans, having only 24 hours a day and actually living in a body that needs food and rest. This *Savior/Rescuer* complex has cost many devoted human service people their health and relationships and ultimately undermined their capacity to do good work in the world. I declined that particular job offer and joined a counseling agency where I was able to work directly with disadvantaged kids and families in a way that was meaningful, but did not bury me.

7. *Dreams bring us what we need for our healing and wholeness.*

If you care about anything in life, you are going to experience loss. Loss brings grief and pain and some losses can be very difficult to recover from. The dream world is a place where such healing can occur.

You may have lost a treasured relationship through death or disagreement, or a coveted position through a job layoff. You may revisit these losses in your dreams, sorting through them over and over. If you watch the progression of these dreams, you will see that the psyche is working through different aspects of the situation, helping us resolve pain and move forward. Many bereaved people are visited in dreams by a deceased loved one who comes with words of comfort and reassurance.

Dreams help us to heal the wounds of childhood. Even people with a childhood they remember as "happy" have some repair work to do. Because no parent is perfect, we all have things to heal. Some of my clients have had a childhood so horrific that I cannot imagine how they got as far as they did in life. I am continually amazed at the history that people transcend.

People can get healed through restorative life experiences, but the healing power of dreams can be so fast and so deep as to be considered miraculous. Healing dreams are like spiritual balm on our deep wounds, providing the transformative energies we need to move forward.

As I work with people on their dreams, certain dream images are so profound we can only sit in awe and reverence of them. Sometimes I am so moved by the magnitude of the healing power they carry that tears come to my eyes. The healing happens in the dream world, but people awaken changed. The change resonates in the body and remains. One dream can infuse a person with enough energy to move them into an entirely new sense of what is possible in life.

Case History–Carla

I worked with a client who suffered from repetitive dreams of trauma from early abuse by her mother. Her mother had refused to let my client be baptized. As we worked together, it became evident that the completion of the ritual of baptism was still important for Carla. She was not a traditional Christian, but we worked together to construct a deeply meaningful baptismal service, with poetry and sacred writings and a ritual that resonated with her spirituality at that point. With a small circle of her friends, Carla was baptized. The experience had a profound impact on her psyche, and she began to believe that she could transcend the limits her mother had placed on her. It was as if she had broken an evil spell that had kept her captive all her life. Several weeks later she had the following dream:

I am in the midst of the same repetitive dream with my mother. She has me backed into a corner when suddenly smoke begins to form between us. The smoke becomes a huge man with a great beard. He stands between me and my mother and gathers me in his arms.

Then the house begins to rumble and split open. He carries me out of the house into the sky, up and up, until we can see the earth below. I see the scene of my baptism. He continues to carry me out into the universe, holding me close, shielding me from the heat of the sun. I feel utterly safe and loved, and I realize that I am in the arms of God.

This dream repeated itself over a period of months in which she is held by a loving and protective God figure. In each dream she got progressively younger. At one point she jokingly said that if the trend continued, she would be an embryo. It was as if she were being healed at all ages and stages of her early life. God had inserted himself between her and her abusive mother and provided the protection and love she had missed as a child. Carla began to feel a greater sense of safety in her life and to experience herself held in God's hands, having a place in the universe.

8. *Dreams Inform Our Lives and Tell Us Who We Are Becoming.*

Dreams tell us about who we are becoming. They invite us further into our *Individuation* process where we integrate opposites and open more possibilities. They expand our *Archetypal Fluency.*

I have kept a journal from the time I was a pre-teen. Even before I began to "work" my dreams, I recorded dreams that made a big impression on me, dreams where I awoke feeling changed, healed or guided in some mysterious way. They often occurred at pivotal points in my life. In retrospect, I see how they were revealing the paths I was to take, the struggles I would experience, and how I would overcome them.

The Jungians call these *Big Dreams*. *Big Dreams* tell you about your destiny. They involve a change in your *Inner Cast of Characters* and invite you into a bigger story. Here is one example:

> *I am a gazelle, running in a large herd of gazelles, across an open landscape. As I run, I lift off the ground and become an eagle. I soar high above the earth where I can look down on the running herd and watch the beauty of their shifting, synchronous movements. I am aware of the expansive silence of the skies and my lofty perspective. I am also aware that I am alone and want to rejoin the group. I descend and become a gazelle again, happy to be running amidst the collective herd, but aware that I can ascend as an eagle at any time, and return to the skies.*

Here is a beautiful portrayal of opposites, the contrast of the lofty sky and the grounded earth. In the sky, I feel space and inspiration, a sense of perspective as I look down onto the earth. On earth, I feel embodied, with a sense of belonging to a collective group. This dream outlines a theme that has woven throughout my whole life. It continues to inform me about how to move between the energies of the lone eagle and the herd gazelle. Both realms are important, becoming over-identified with either creates an imbalance. The lesson is about how and when to move from one to the other.

I can use the wisdom in these dream images in *Inner Round Table* explorations. The experience of being the eagle or gazelle can inform me about what will help me resume my sense of wholeness. The *Eagle* often tells me that I am stuck in an old framework and need to enlarge my perspective. She may tell me that I can pick a goal or target in the distance and with singular focus, I can swoop in and claim it. The *Gazelle* may tell me that it is ok to be grounded and ordinary, a non-descript member of a collective or that there is protection in numbers. When I remember this dream, I can still feel the movement of the running gazelle, pounding the earth. She reminds me that being embodied on the earth is an amazing thing and I need to remember to take care of my body.

Growing and Becoming Pot-bound

Sometimes our lives and the stories we tell about ourselves become too small to contain the beauty of our souls. The people around us are often unsettled when we begin to change. The system tries to push us back into our previous state of being. "You are not being yourself," the system says. These definitions can hold us in place, constrained in ways that can become painful. We can drift along for years following the script of others, out of alignment with our *Soulprint*. Dreams invite us to re-imagine who we are.

Sidra Stone uses a wonderful metaphor that there are times in our growth when we become "pot bound," where our life container becomes too small for who we are becoming. We need to be repotted into a larger container, for just like a plant, our roots become tangled and tough.

Sometimes, the *Self* cracks the old pot open, in an effort to free us from its constraints. In these cases, the *Divine Director* begins to arrange experiences and situations that move us out of our comfort zone into a more profound and purposeful path. An unexpected illness strikes us, a failed relationship, or a lost job. Disorientation and depression can occur as the internal system shifts and our life takes on a new direction.

There is often suffering in letting go. At times like these dreams can comfort us and direct us, bringing in the energies we need to move forward. Dreams can lead us through the wilderness into the next stage of our becoming.

A few years ago I had a series of dreams that indicated that I was to teach in the larger culture. As I began to move out into a larger arena, I had dreams of commissioning and instruction about where to go next and with whom to align myself. I held these dreams close, and they provided me with tremendous energy in their affirmation of my current direction.

Out of this process I created the *Luminous Woman Weekend,* a workshop in which women can explore their unfolding story in relationship to archetypes of the feminine. I had to choose to invest more time in this pursuit and let go of other opportunities that had been meaningful up to that point. During my decision making process, I had the following YES dream. Two of the women whose books and teachings have been formative in my journey came to me and said, *"You are standing on the shoulders of the work we have done. We are commissioning you to carry our work forward."* They instructed me to walk into unknown territory and let the path unfold. The dream conveyed an amazing infusion of affirmation, support and confidence. It continues to uphold me as I live into this calling.

Precognitive Dreams

People have pre-cognitive dreams. There were people who received dream images about the events on September 11th. They dreamt of the date, twin towers, planes crashing, terrorists, firestorms, but they did not know the meaning of those dreams until the inconceivable event had actually occurred.

If you work your dreams over time, you will see in retrospect, that certain dreams precede significant events in your life, as if they were preparing you to face that event. These dreams are alerting us that changes are coming, helping us to make the interior shifts required to face them.

Jeremy Taylor

Jeremy Taylor has been teaching dream work for over thirty years. I often recommend his books, *Dream Work* and *Where People Fly and Water Runs Uphill.* They are excellent resources for new and veteran dream workers alike. Jeremy's passion is the use of dreams in community building. Here is a summary of ideas I have learned from Jeremy's teaching that apply to individual dream work:

- All dreams come in the service of healing and wholeness. Even our most terrifying nightmares carry important clues to our healing.
- Dreams have intelligible meaning, conveyed in the language of symbol and metaphor. The images, people, creatures, settings and story lines selected by an individual's psyche are purposeful. It is useful to view all aspects of the dream as if they were an aspect of the dreamer.
- There is no such thing as one ultimate interpretation, as each dream has many levels of meaning: personal, collective, archetypal, physical, emotional, spiritual, etc.
- Only the dreamer can say what the meaning of a dream is. A meaningful interpretation is usually accompanied by a "tingle-pop" sensation in the body, accompanied by something that might be called an "aha."
- Dreams come to expand our understanding. They are not telling us things we already know. Even if the content seems familiar, we should be careful about jumping to the smug conclusion that "I know what this dream means."
- Even in nightmares, dreams do not present "unsolvable" problems or inescapable situations. Answers and solutions are embedded somewhere in the dream material.
- Dreams indicate the cutting-edge growth of the personality. They give us pictures of things we do not yet understand and open us to experiences that are not yet "speech-ripe."
- Like a holograph, even a small fragment of a barely remembered dream can unfold into significant guidance.

- If you miss the message of a dream, the psyche will bring it back again (and again) in subsequent dreams until you finally get it.
- Symbol and dream dictionaries can add additional associations for dream material, but it is best to begin your dream work with your own personal associations.

In the next chapter we will explore how to work your dreams using the *Inner Round Table* approach in the *Inner Peace Treaty* model.

CHAPTER 15

INNER PEACE TREATY
DREAM WORK

"We greet the Self as we might greet a lover,
at the end of a long and costly war."
Julia Cameron

In this chapter, I am going to outline a method for working with your dreams using the *Inner Peace Treaty* model. Looking at your dream material is another way of understanding your personal archetypes and expanding your *Archetypal Fluency*. Each night, the psyche brings us new actors on the dream stage, who introduce a whole new set of archetypal energies. You can add them to your *Inner Cast of Characters*.

For many years I have devoted myself to recording and analyzing my dreams. Symbol association methods of dream work are a powerful way to connect the dots between your dream content and the unfolding patterns of your life. However, life is busy and most people find it hard to devote the time it takes to write down dreams, list personal and collective associations, and reflect on how this relates to their lives.

Learning about myths and the historical significance of symbols can yield some tantalizing associations; the danger in such an approach is to watch our dreams like a movie on the screen of our consciousness rather than to enter into the unfolding action. We can become fascinated spectators of our dreams, analyzing the symbols and marveling at their meaning but not integrating the life-changing energies they bring us.

The "aha" or "tingle pop" that Jeremy Taylor talks about indicates that we have found the gold of the dream. We still have to carry that gold into our lives. Good dream work creates the internal shift that moves the dreamer into a different way of living. Sometimes that means a major negotiation with our *Inner Cast of Characters*. This is where *Inner Round Table* work intersects with dream work.

People who do *Inner Peace Treaty Dream Work* become increasingly aware that dream work is not a cognitive exercise. Dream work is an experiential engagement with archetypal energies. Thinking about your psyche as having an *Inner Cast of Characters* will give you a whole new way of engaging your dream material. For those of you devoted to symbol associations, carry on! This approach to dream work will augment your current endeavors.

Archetypal Fluency

The body is like a tuning fork. It knows the resonance of particular archetypal energies. Working with the archetypal energies in *Inner Peace Treaty* work means that you are attending to the *felt sense* of these energies in your body. It is important for us to remember that *Archetypes* are not mere categories. They are systems of energy.

At the center of every dream symbol is an essential energy or resonance. This is the archetypal core. The image of a particular archetype will vary from person to person. For example, while everyone has a sense for the *Good Mother*, one person might picture her as the mother on a television show like *The Waltons*. Another person might picture the *Good Mother* as the mother of a childhood friend. Likewise, the same image might have a very different meaning for two people. Some women feel a warm affection for the 1950's mother, *June Cleaver*, while others can't stand her. We develop our personal reactions to certain archetypes based on our life experiences, but the collective archetype is present in everyone.

INNER PEACE TREATY DREAM WORK

Percolating Your Dreams

I often awake early, before anyone else in the house, and go downstairs to make some coffee. I may have written down a fragment of a dream in the middle of the night in the notebook I keep by the bed. I am often able to recreate an entire dream based on some scribbled notes I made in the night. It is important that I write something down, or the whole dream evaporates in the mists of the night, buried under subsequent dream adventures.

Because I work my dreams regularly, I am in the practice of staying attuned to the dream world as I begin to move into my day. As I stand in the kitchen waiting for the coffee to brew, I am reviewing my night-time journeys. What was the *felt sense* of my dreams? What were the images and how did they affect me?

Reality is different in the dream world. I am often amused when people say something like, "the person was my aunt, but also my boyfriend. How could that be?" or "It was a place like my high school, but also the moon." In the dream world, two things can be true at once, and realities morph. This is a lesson in life. Getting stuck in one perspective is a mistake. It also points to an even more mysterious truth. We are living in a quantum universe where two things can be true at the same time. So, in those early morning moments, I try to dwell in the space of the dream without trying to figure it out.

If I have the luxury of time, I pour a cup of coffee and go to my big white chair by the window. I write down a more detailed version of my dreams, wondering things like:

Exploration

- *What was the lingering feeling on awakening?*
- *Where was I? Was it a familiar or unfamiliar place? What was it like?*
- *Who did I encounter there? What were they like and what were my reactions to them?*
- *What was unusual about the dream or me in the dream?*

I know the dream world has brought me something important. It may be asking me to look at things differently. It may be suggesting a course of action. Perhaps I am out of balance or over-valuing something and need to reconsider my priorities.

If there is something that disturbs me, something unusual or wondrous, I sit with it. I try to resist the urge to put this dream into an established frame of reference. I know the dream is bringing me something new. I am sipping a brew created in the unconscious. Like water percolating through coffee, I am letting the dream infuse my world.

Scripts and Themes

As I sit with a dream, I begin to notice the scripts, themes and actors on the stage. Here is a list of things you might wonder about as you reflect on your dream experience:

- *What was the story line in this dream and how did it unfold?*
- *Who were the actors on stage? Have they appeared in other dreams I have had?*
- *What part did I play? Was I the main actor, supporting cast, or an invisible observer? Was I a hero, villain, victim, saint, etc.?*
- *At this point, I might name the archetypal energies I inhabited.*
- *What was important to me? What was I trying to accomplish?*
- *Is this typical for me or a different way of being?*

- *Where is the energy highest in the dream? What was happening here?*
- *Are there any highly unusual or humorous aspects to the dream?*

Shadow Work with Dreams

At this point, you can move to considering the energies in your dreams, particularly noticing if they were familiar or unfamiliar. What were the characteristics of the other actors on the dream stage? Describe their qualities. These may be energies seeking entry into your life. They may be very foreign to your values and behaviors. You might judge them in waking life. The further away they are from your core identity, the more they come from the shadow realm.

The psyche is very purposeful in picking dream images. They are here to bring you something that will move you forward on your journey. Here are some things to be curious about:

- *How would I describe the other figures in my dream? What were their qualities and characteristics?*
- *What archetypes might they represent?*
- *How do I feel about them? Was I attracted or repelled?*
- *How are these dream figures different from how I think about "me?"*
- *What disowned or shadow energy might they be carrying?*

Exploring the Tension of Opposites

In Jungian work, it is important to look at the opposites that appear in your dreams. Any time you move strongly to one end of a spectrum, it will constellate the opposite. Often the opposite remains in the shadows, but it is there nonetheless. Our dreams can show us this shadow activity. One way to identify shadow characters in your dreams is to notice who carries qualities that are most opposite those which you would claim for yourself.

You can follow the *Inner Peace Treaty* process with dream characters. *Name* them, get to *Know* them, and *Negotiate* with them. This will prevent you from acting these energies out unconsciously, or judging or idealizing them in others. *The more opposing energies you can stand between with equanimity, the clearer and less reactive you become.* So take a look at the opposites that appear in your dreams: young and old, rich and poor, good and evil, rigid and flexible, fragile and strong, etc. Learning to stand between opposites is a true spiritual practice and not an easy thing to do.

Expanding your Archetypal Fluency

This can be accomplished by engaging the familiar and unfamiliar energies that appear in your dreams, *Naming, Knowing* and *Negotiating* with them. People who can house and direct a lot of archetypal energies have a lot of personal power and creativity. Anyone can expand their *Archetypal Fluency*. Pick a symbol, a setting, or a person in your dream, *Name* them and get to *Know* them. You can imagine sitting across from the dream image and asking these questions or you can experiment with entering into the dream image and answering these questions from inside that perspective. You will notice that the answers and experience is very different.

Exploration

- *Tell me about yourself.*
- *What is important to you? What do you value?*
- *What do you want or need?*
- *Do you have a motto or philosophy?*
- *Where are you active in my life?*

— *How could you help me in my life?*
— *What would you like to say to me?*

Looking From the Inside Out

The most powerful way to engage any dream symbol or figure is to *enter into them and look from the inside out.* I have found that doing this has never occurred to many people. They have dialogued with figures imagining them sitting in front of them, but never actually entered into the experience of being that figure. Looking out of the eyes of a dream figure is a completely different experience. You can inhabit anything in your dream, including inanimate objects, buildings, rivers, environments, etc. I often have people explore and speak from inside dream figures during individual sessions.

You can work alone, writing about your experience in a journal. You can also work with a partner, switching back and forth, interviewing each other. People who enter into their dream figures report that the experience is quite surprising. The change in perspective can be significant. You will experience life, yourself and your situation in a totally different way through the eyes of "the others" in your dream. It can really expand your world.

If one of the dream figures happens to be a person in waking life, it is important to note that you are not actually entering into that person. You are entering into *your own projections* of who that person is. You are still in the realm of your own psyche.

If you are working alone, you need to heed the warnings we mentioned earlier in the book about moving into *Inner Characters.* This is a powerful method of inner exploration, and some people find it disorienting and hard to make their way back into a sense of "themselves." They may feel not quite back in their bodies. If you find that this happens to you, I recommend that you stop working in this way. I recommend that you work with a therapist or facilitator trained in Gestalt or Jungian methods.

For some people, any form of imaginative visualization is difficult. Not a problem. If you can't do it or are uncomfortable about it, just continue interviewing your dream figures as if you were sitting across from them. There is plenty of rich material to glean.

Symbol Association Work

You can include symbol association work at any point along the line if you wish to explore the dream through this lens. Certain associations will spring up naturally. Try to cycle back and forth between the *felt sense* of the dream and the vast array of meaning that symbols can hold. There are many excellent books and training programs related to symbol association. A list of resources can be found in the Appendix.

Dreams, Alchemy and Psychic "Heat"

When you touch into the archetypal energy of a dream symbol, the dream will heat up. The adage, "now we are cooking," is suitable here. Archetypal energy is alchemical. When you encounter something in the dream that begins to stir and bubble, stay with it. Wait and see what images and associations surface from this place in the psyche. These associations are very important. You may discover something about yourself that you never realized before.

Resolutions

It is always instructive to notice how the dream ends.

- *What was the lingering feeling?*
- *Did the ending feel resolved or unresolved?*
- *Was there a moral to this story?*
- *Did the dream pose a question to be pondered?*

– *Did the dream invite me to some sort of action in waking life?*
– *What new energies am I being called into relationship with?*
– *How might I be changed by this new relationship?*

Finally: How Is this Dream Informing My Life?

This moves us into the very important question of how we integrate the wisdom of our dreams into our waking lives. Remember that dream work is not a spectator sport. Ask yourself:

– *How is this dream related to what is going on in my life?*
– *Why has the Divine Director brought me these particular images now?*
– *How is my understanding of myself and my life being shifted in a new direction by my dream experience?*
– *Is this dream affirming or challenging what I am valuing or the direction I am going in my life?*
– *Does the dream suggest that I am out of balance?*
– *If I approached life from this perspective, what would I do differently?*
– *Is this dream offering me a new internal resource or a new approach to an old problem?*

Negotiating at the Inner Round Table

Any time we make changes in life, it creates anxiety and the system attempts to shift things back to the way they used to be. Dreams call us into a new way of being. When we are on the path of *Individuation,* we do not always make sense to the people around us. People close to us can be concerned or irritated by our changes, saying things like, "You are not yourself." Not being yourself may mean you are getting healthier or more on purpose, but we may still meet resistance from those around us. We need a lot of support to sustain certain changes. Dreams can provide us with inspiring, resonant images that support us in the process of change.

When change is on the horizon, dialoguing with *Inner Characters* that are anxious and might resist that change becomes an important part of moving forward. You can use all the same methods of dialoguing that we outlined in the Negotiation Chapter with any chosen dream figure or around any important change you want to make. Consider:

- *How might my life be different if I incorporated some aspects of certain dream figures?*
- *What other Inner Characters in my cast might not like this change and why?*
- *What are their fears and concerns?*
- *What kinds of assurances or treaties do I need to negotiate so that this change can move forward?*

Making a place for a dream member at your *Inner Round Table* is an effective way to negotiate the process of deep change in your life.

Create a Tincture

From the moment I heard Hal Stone describe this method of integration, I loved its simplicity and its power. He generally uses it as a way of integrating disowned energies or shadow material. For example, if you can't stand your mother-in-law because she is so self-absorbed and entitled, you may have moved too far into qualities of selflessness and humility, the opposite end of the archetypal spectrum. You may actually need to integrate just a little bit more of your mother-in-law's entitlement in order to do what you need to do in your life.

In a small dose, entitlement looks like self-confidence. This "poison" might be just the medicine you need. So imagine that you are boiling down your mother-in-law into a tincture and take a few drops of this energetic medicine (assured self-confidence) several times a day.

You can also use this imaginative method to increase particular energies you are attracted to and want more of. Perhaps you feel like a dull person who is not very creative. Then you have a dream in which you are a celebrated artist opening a new exhibit at a gallery. In the dream you are dressed in colorful, flamboyant clothing. You are vibrant and free spirited, filled with the fire of creativity. The psyche is bringing you your undeveloped creative energy here! In addition to wearing a colorful scarf the next day, you might want to create an imaginary tincture of creativity! Find a bottle and put some water in it and label it "creativity." Place it where you will see it and take a few drops daily, imagining that you are integrating this quality. Here are things to reflect on:

- *How would you think, act and feel with a bit more of that quality in your system?*
- *Would you interact with people differently?*
- *How would your world view be different?*
- *Would your priorities change?*
- *How would you spend your time?*
- *Who would you spend your time with?*
- *Would you dress differently, eat differently, spend your money differently?*
- *Would you pursue something you are currently not pursuing?*

Creative Expression

Taking your dream experiences into some form of artistic expression is a wonderful way to deepen your relationship with them and continue to plumb their depths. Here are some suggestions for creative things you can do with dream images:

- *Create some art.* Draw them. If you think of yourself as someone with no artistic talent, do a stick figure drawing, or something that looks like a little kid did it. Use clay, paper mache, or modeling compound to bring them into form. Study what you have created and notice what you see. What does it stir in you? Does it evoke any new associations?
- *Create a poster board collage* about a dream theme. Select a pile of images that calls to you and see what is stirring in your psyche.
- *Find some music* that represents the energy of the dream and add it to your music collection. Marion Woodman has been dancing her dreams for years. Try this sometime. Put some music on and imagine that you are inhabiting a dream image. Let your body move in whatever way it wants to move. Let the image move you. Notice how you feel. Notice how it progresses or changes. Notice if the image changes.
- *Write a poem* about a dream image or experience. Take a writing workshop with someone like Cathy Smith Bowers who teaches us how to take dream images into poetry.
- *Create a personal altar* somewhere in your home where you can place items that represent your inner process. I have a shelf in my bathroom where I put pictures, quotes, figurines, rocks, feathers, and mementos that are significant symbols for things I am honoring or in process with. I will change the content of my altar as my inner process moves from one focus to another. I like to be able to see this first thing in the morning and the last thing at night.
- *Play with your wardrobe*. A great way of exploring or integrating a new archetypal energy is to dress the part! Choose clothing, colors and jewelry that amplify a particular energy. Are you becoming more peaceful, bold, motherly, or ambitious? What clothing might you wear to express and amplify this energy? Do you even own these clothes?

Might you need to go shopping? Do you have clothes in your closet that need to be let go of because they represent *Retired Selves*? In terms of shopping, it is worthwhile to pay attention to *who is* selecting your clothes, artwork, furniture, car, house, career or even life partner!

- **Throw a party** in which everyone dresses as a dream or shadow character.

Embed the Dream in Your Body and Brain

Deep and lasting change occurs when an experience embeds itself in the physical body and creates new neural pathways in the brain. Both traumatic and ecstatic experiences rewire the brain. When we revisit a nourishing dream image over and over, we reroute old pathways created by painful experiences to new neural pathways of healing.

Dream Images to Help You Prepare for the Day

Let's say in the coming day you have a meeting with someone you often have difficulty communicating with. Perhaps in a recent dream you visited a beautiful place where you were filled with peace and well-being. Wouldn't it be nice to be able to pull up that feeling of peace before, even during your interaction with this difficult person? How might it change the way you interact if you could maintain that peaceful experience at your core. The dream brought you this experience. You can become adept at pulling it forward and using it.

Take a few moments to prepare yourself before you have the actual conversation with this person. Re-enter the space of the dream, your peaceful place. Immerse yourself in that experience as if it were a meditation; imagine the sights, sounds, tastes, smells, sensations. Now open your eyes and carry that *felt sense* with you as you meet with this "difficult" person. Imagine the backdrop of the room is the setting of the dream. Notice how shifting your own *inner* state reduces the reactivity in others. Cultivating your own *Calm Core* means you will increasingly reduce the drama generated by others. You will also be able to confront and address the things that you need to with courage and clarity.

Explore a New Course of Action

If a dream is calling you into a new course of action, you will have some *Negotiating* to do with your *Inner Cast of Characters*. *Inner Self Systems* do not like change. A good way to explore the wisdom of this possible change is to do some dialogue work to find out *who* in you supports this direction and *who* objects to it. *Who* in you is most drawn to this path and why? Call a *Round Table* meeting and let the players with something at stake talk. Don't forget to look behind them for *Inner Children* who may be secretly driving this agenda. Stay with what is getting stirred up in you while you consider this new course of action. Take all parts of yourself into account as you dialogue. Notice *who* is excluded and why. Consider what the potential consequences of this action might be, and how more vulnerable *Inner Selves* feel about this. Is this course of action leading you more deeply into your destiny or further away from it? Is this driven by an old *Ego Identity* or by the *Soul Print*? Explore this path through creativity. Observe your dream life to see if you are getting *Yes* or *No* dreams. What are your dreams telling you about what you haven't considered? Attend to *Synchronicities*.

Attending To Synchronicities

Synchronicities are those odd little happenings on the outside that seem to parallel what is going on inside. Note any interesting coincidences that surround your dreams. An example of this would be having a dream of someone you haven't seen since high school and then having that person call you in the next couple of days. You might dream about a historical event and then turn on the television with a documentary about that event. Ask yourself, *why is my psyche highlighting this at this time?*

Staying With One Dream for Awhile

There are times when it can be incredibly valuable to stay with one dream or one image for a few days or even weeks. I have a handful of dream images that I return to again and again. They have become very powerful symbols for me over the years. Staying with one dream or dream symbol can be a very profound and alchemical way to do dream work. You might work with other dreams as they come, but you keep returning to this particular focus for a while. You engage the dream in a number of creative ways and from a variety of directions letting it bubble and cook within you.

The Dream Series

Tracking your dreams over time will often show you an emergent process. You may have a recurrent dream or perhaps a series of dreams where there is a recurrent image or theme. What is the connection here? What is the psyche trying to tell you? Is it about healing? Are you stuck in some pattern or missing something important in your life? Are you being called in a new direction? Do you need to make a major life change?

When you notice a series of dreams that have a similar feel, setting, set of characters, theme, etc., take note. You might want to review your journals and gather other dreams that seem to be connected and just be with them. What do you see? Is there any obvious message or thematic emphasis? Over time you will begin to identify something of importance.

Dreams of the Past

Sometimes we find ourselves in scenes from the past, reliving an old relationship, sleeping in a childhood home, or working at a job from years ago. These dreams can be the psyche's way of underlining how much you have grown and changed. These dreams can also be the psyche's way of pulling forward something from the past that you need today. Remember that our *Inner Cast of Characters* changes over time. We retire characters from our cast and let them fall back into the mists of time. Why is the psyche bringing this particular *Cast Member* to you now? Are you ready to face and process some unfinished business? Do you need to bring forward some *Retired Character* from your past to help you where you are today? Is the psyche showing you how much you have grown and changed over the years? We tend to forget how we used to be when the change is gradual.

On Remembering Your Dreams

For those of you who only remember dreams on occasion, don't worry. Work with what you have. One good dream can keep unfolding its treasures for years and years. Here are a couple of things that help:

- The unconscious knows when you are paying attention to it. The mere act of wondering about your dreams and beginning to write them down will increase dream recall.
- When you awaken from a dream, remain still. Moving seems to disrupt the strands of memory. Sometimes you can return to the position you were sleeping in and recapture some of the threads. Collect as many images and feelings as you can before moving or getting up.
- Write your dreams down as quickly as possible. Dreams fade fast as your daily agenda comes to the forefront. A notebook by the bed is a great way to scribble down notes

in the night. Serious dream workers often transfer these scribbles into a more official journal where they work with the content.

- Finally, tell your inner *Consciousness Achiever* to relax. You don't have to remember everything. If it is important, the psyche will bring it to you again on another night. One resonant dream image can go a long way when using this method of dream work.

CHAPTER 16

DREAM WORK FOR BUSY PEOPLE—
One Luminous Pearl

"Bliss and joy come from moments when what we do
is consistent with our archetypal depths."
Jean Shinoda Bollen

People have busy lives. Unless you are devoted to dream work, you probably won't work your dreams every morning. If you worked through the entire *Inner Peace Treaty* process, it might have taken you a couple of hours. While taking an occasional morning to do inner work is an immensely fruitful endeavor, most people don't have many mornings in which to do this.

The time it takes to become a serious dream worker is intimidating to many people. So I have outlined some things you can do to tap into the wisdom of your dreams in the midst of your busy life. I do hope that periodically you will grant yourself the luxury of a little retreat, where you can delve deeper and fill your coffers full of the riches of inner work. In the meantime, here is how you can harvest *One Luminous Pearl* to carry into your day.

Harvesting a Luminous Pearl

I once had a dream in which:

I am underwater exploring a beautiful coral reef. All around the reef hundreds of brilliantly colored fish dart about in a beautiful display. I am captivated and delighted by the color and motion, and then I notice an enormous clam shell resting quietly at the

221

bottom of the ocean. I know in the dream that the shell is for me.
It slowly opens and inside is a large luminous pearl. As I gather
it in my hands, I hear a voice saying, "One Luminous Pearl."

The wisdom of this dream has come back to me again and again. In our fast-paced world, we tend to move quickly from one glittering thing to the next, never really going deep. Sometimes, we become overwhelmed by the bounty of what the unconscious offers thinking we must gather more and more. I am reminded of the movies in which the treasure hunters finally find the treasure and cannot possibly carry away all the riches before them. We can actually get a form of spiritual indigestion, trying to consume too much insight at once rather than taking the time to really digest an important truth.

Rather than greedily filling our hands with the glittering jewels of our dreams, sometimes it is better to gather, treasure, and integrate one *Luminous Pearl*, deeply appreciating its beauty and integrating it into our lives. This is the secret of dream work for busy people.

Even a brief period of time spent with your dreams can put you in touch with resonant images that can change your life. Gather one *Luminous Pearl* and work with it.

1. Keep a dream diary near your bed or in your bathroom and jot down some information about your dream. Try to capture the places where the energy was high. Notice if you are curious about a particular dream character or scenario.

2. As you are getting ready, or driving to work, wonder about:

   – *What are you being invited to consider?*
   – *Is this a dream providing a warning or guidance?*

- *Is the dream compensating for something you are missing in your life? Is this something you need to take more seriously?*
- *Is this a healing dream? What is being healed?*
- *Does any image resonate or stand out?*
- *What foreign or shadow energies are you being invited to become aware of and to integrate?*
- *Who at your Inner Round Table doesn't have a voice? What are they trying to tell you?*
- *Does this dream speak of an area of calling or growth?*
- *Does the dream indicate a course of action?*
- *How is this dream expanding your understanding of yourself, others and all of life?*
- *How is this dream deepening your connection with the Divine and with your Soul Print?*

3. Select one image, question, energy or insight as a *Dream Pearl* to carry into your day. You might choose a character who was carrying something that you wish to explore or amplify in yourself. Perhaps there is an image or a place in the dream that captures you or has a lot of resonance. You may have already had some sort of realization as you pondered the dream. Any of these can be *Dream Pearls*. Keep something around to remind you to revisit this resonant *Dream Image* throughout the day, a note on your mirror, a stone in your pocket or a pearl on your desk.

4. When you return to your *Dream Pearl*, spend a moment in the resonance of that image, energy, or realization. See how it feels and what emerges. Notice how doing this affects your attitude, judgments, perspectives and reactions to people.

5. Record any interesting synchronicities that seem to be reinforcing something in your dream.

6. If one dream figure or symbol is particularly powerful for you, you can stay with it! There is no rule that says you have to work with a new symbol or dream every day. If a certain "aha" or energy continues to resonate for you, deepen it through creative expression or more dialogue process. Consider adding a new character to your *Inner Round Table*.

7. There are several creative activities that do not take much time.

   – Create a designated altar space where you can place objects that represent your inner process. The altar can focus your intention or signify your openness to the unfolding mystery of life.
   – Keep old magazines around and find pictures that seem to carry the essence of a theme, question, character or energy you are working with. Clip them out and create a poster board collection or put them up where you can see them.
   – Collect music that matches your archetypal moods and *Inner Characters*.
   – Check out your wardrobe and see if it expresses the range of your *Inner Cast of Characters*. Does it express who you are becoming? Do you need to clean out some clothes bought by *Outdated Selves*.
   – Keep journaling and dialoguing. Learn to think in terms of *who* is activated in you.

Day Retreats

Periodically, give yourself the restorative gift of a day retreat. Some of the greatest productivity experts recommend this. Take time to reflect on your life. Review your dream journals. Review your life goals and see how your dreams are commenting on them. See if you notice any patterns or interesting developments.

- *What is emerging through your dreams and in your life that may not be part of your conscious planning?*
- *Are your dreams indicating that you are out of balance in some area or that you need to integrate something?*

One Luminous Pearl at a Time

Remember that the path of *Individuation* is not about stuffing your pockets with more treasure than you could ever carry. Opening to your deepest potential takes time. Attuning to and living in accordance with your *Soul Print* takes courage. Allow the unfolding. Let go of the familiar shore. Honor each treasure that you find on your journey. Take time to integrate your deep realizations, the luminous pearls. Hold them sacred, wonder about them, struggle with them, experiment, percolate and let them illuminate your life.

CHAPTER 17

INTEGRATION:
What People Need to be Whole

*"Each life is formed by a particular image,
an image that is the essence of that life and calls it
to a destiny, just as the mighty oak's destiny
is written in the tiny acorn."*
James Hillman

*"Each life contains the necessities and problems that set the terms of its
individual destiny as well as the possibilities of its integrity."*
Ira Progoff

What People Need To Be Whole

Much of our struggle in life comes from being over-identified with roles, scripts and stories that are too small for the vastness of our souls. We get scrunched down into tight little compartments, where we have to disown aspects of ourselves that are crucial to our well-being and the achievement of our full potential. The final step of *Negotiating the Inner Peace Treaty* is *Integration*. This means that we are bringing to the *Inner Round Table* that which has been disowned. We also begin to develop aspects of ourselves that lie uncultivated in our archetypal seedbed.

Jungian psychology teaches us that life is about the process of *Individuation*. *Individuation* is understood as the growth of the soul into its ultimate expression of wholeness. It is a process and not an endpoint. None of us get to a place where we can consider ourselves fully "individuated." There will always be new places in the psyche that need to be explored and new material to be integrated. What we can rely on is that mysterious central organizing principle of our lives, which I call the *Soul Print*.

The problem is that we live in a world that continually encourages us to be disconnected from our *Soul Print*. We are not taught to anchor in our depths, and so often we feel like ships adrift with no harbor to call home. We look to others to direct us and they are more than happy to tell us who we are and shape us for their own needs and purposes. It becomes hard to know what our true essence is. We are so thoroughly socialized and shaped by our early experiences, parents, teachers, society, and religion.

Life as an Artform

In *Writing For Your Life*, Deena Metzger describes the prohibition against traveling to the inner realm of ourselves. When we enter that world, we find ourselves outside the perimeter of conventional society. We are in a place where rules, regulations, traditions, and legislated ways of seeing and behaving do not apply. In this place, we are connected to our unique personal essence. At the same time we are participating in the communal world that Jung called the *Collective Unconscious*. The *Collective Unconscious* can be viewed as a sea of eternal values, images, cultural memories, and experiences. These find their way into our inner life through dreams, synchronicities and creative work.

Depth psychologist Ira Progoff talked about how the primary characteristic of creative persons is that they experience their lives as an unfolding of multiple mini-processes within rather than a series of events or static contents. Thus, their lives become an art form, and the contents of their lives become the raw material by which their achievements are brought about. Otto Rank, another transpersonal psychologist believed that the essence of the soul is creativity, and the ultimate creative work of a person's life is life itself.

When you begin to explore your *Inner Cast of Characters*, you begin to understand what has brought you to where you are today, why you think, feel and react the way you do. You become aware that you are more than your roles, relationships, traits, achievements, health, or history. You are developing an *Observing Self*, integrating shadow material and dream characters. Your experience of "who you are" is continually expanding. You know that even today's understanding is limited. Tomorrow you will change and grow. You are directing your *Inner Cast* and rewriting the unconscious scripts of your life. You are also participating in the mystery of life, as your "destiny" meets you through unexpected encounters and events.

Missing Persons

One of the things that becomes evident to people as they work through the *Negotiating the Inner Peace Treaty* process is that we all have *Missing Persons* at our *Inner Round Tables*. There are certain crucial *Inner Characters* that would help us tremendously if they were present in our lives. We all have missing pieces in our development. I know of very few people who were adequately prepared for adult life. Our foundations give way because they were never built adequately to begin with. We harbor a lot of unnecessary shame and hide these weaknesses rather than rehabilitate them.

In the chapter on *Shadow Work*, we talked about how we lose parts of ourselves to the shadow realm whenever we disown that which is upsetting or displeasing to people. Any time we amputate a part of ourselves, we are selling our souls for safety. When parts of us are banished into the shadow realm, we can no longer direct them or work with their energy. We also lose the gifts they bring. Every aspect of us holds an important piece of the puzzle.

When my son was young, he used to like to build things from kits. Often times he would discover that a piece that belonged in an earlier stage of the assembly had not been put in place. Overwhelmed by the prospect of having to go back, deconstruct and reconstruct the project, he would insist that it didn't matter. The piece may have been small, but the toy or the engine would not work quite right until we went back and got that piece in place. Life is like that. Every piece and part of you is important and without all of it, you will never live the life you were born to live.

Building Structural Integrity

None of us had perfect childhoods. Even the best parents could not provide perfect nurture, support or protection. We have all been wounded in some way that creates weakness in our interior structure. So we find it difficult to hang onto our center. We collapse in times of stress. In Jungian terms, we all have our *complexes.*

People often construct their lives to avoid their complexes. This is like having a house and saying, "In this room dwells my painful past. I just never go into that room." The problem is that you also keep your art supplies in there. In spite of our efforts to avoid distressing people and situations, we encounter them anyway. To build a lasting inner peace, we need to have confidence that we can face what life brings us. Our boat needs to be a seaworthy vessel. It has to have structural integrity.

Integrity means much more than "good behavior" or adhering to a set of moral principles. People who have integrity are living in alignment with their essential *Soul Print,* their deepest most sacred personhood. When they suffer the vagaries of life, their center holds.

When we heal the wounds of childhood, we reclaim what was lost in shadow or we develop parts of us that were never encouraged to grow. We are building structural integrity. Then we will have the *Cast of Characters* that we need to meet the challenges of life, and to live purposefully and meaningfully. This is the ultimate outcome of what *Integration* work is about.

If you have been working through the exercises in this book, raising things to consciousness, exploring the shadow realm and engaging your dream material, you are doing *Integration Work*. You are exploring the undiscovered country of your psyche and expanding the scope of archetypal energies you can own and direct.

Sharon and Her Brother

Let's return to Sharon, from Chapter One, and see how *Integrating* the energy of a dream character helped her. If you recall, she went home for the holidays and was reduced to a stammering twelve-year-old in the presence of her arrogant, disdainful brother. Sharon was preparing to return home for another holiday dinner the following year. She was filled with anger and anxiety about the upcoming visit. She was struggling with how to maintain her sense of self with her family. How did she need to shift internally and what did she need to integrate, so that she could be ok? Sharon's answer came to her in a dream which introduced her to a different way of being.

Sharon's Dream

> *I am a Powerful, Ruling Queen. There are treacherous men in my kingdom who are continually trying to overthrow me. I have searched them out and gathered them before me. My advisor stands on my right and suggests that the best course of action is to put them all to death. On my left stands a beautiful woman whose face is shining with a soft, heavenly light. She is a Wise Woman, filled with compassion, who can see into the hearts of all. She is soft, but has an amazing strength, and is completely unafraid of the cold, cruel men who stand before us. She looks past their hard exteriors and sees frightened, hungry children trapped inside, orphans, all of them. I begin to look at them through her*

231

eyes. Suddenly I am filled with compassion. The stony exteriors
of the men melt away and the children trapped inside begin to
run to me. I kneel down and embrace them assuring them that
they will be loved and protected from this time forward. The men
fall to their knees and vow to serve me for the remainder of their
days. Love has won out. The Wise Woman of Compassion and
I have merged and become one. I am now the Wise, Benevolent
Queen. As one of the kneeling men lifts his head, I see the face
of my brother.

This dream changed Sharon's life. She realized that in dealing
with her brother, her *Warrior Self* had taken center stage, gearing
up to go to battle with him. As we dialogued with her *Warrior
Self,* we learned that she came into being to protect and support
Sharon, who always felt silenced and overlooked as a child. The
Warrior had helped her get through law school and become a
successful, competent attorney. The *Warrior* wanted Sharon to
have the respect she deserved.

Sharon's dream brought a new energy to the table. The *Wise,
Benevolent Queen* presented another solution that did not involve
battle. This *Queen* held a different kind of power. She was not the
slightest bit threatened by her brother's dismissive arrogance. She
saw through his persona into the vulnerability that drove it. She
saw how her brother was still trying to win his father's approval
and respect, and a Thanksgiving Dinner battle would have no real
winners. She had compassion for him and decided that she could
shift the dynamic and de-escalate the war.

Infused with the energy of the *Wise and Benevolent Queen,*
Sharon travelled to her family gathering. She was centered, calm
and confident, keeping her *Vulnerable Twelve-year-old* tucked
under the protection of the *Queen.* During the visit, she held her
Calm Core and skillfully redirected every contentious conversation
towards a childhood memory where she and her brother had
shared moments of connection, laughter and camaraderie. Her

brother began to relax. When Sharon and her brother parted, he gave her a hug and commented with genuine warmth on how good it was to see her. Sharon's *Inner Twelve Year Old* smiled back and agreed.

Sharon continued to cultivate a relationship with her *Wise, Benevolent Queen* who had both strength and compassion. This was a new combination for Sharon. She began a meditation practice of entering into the compassionate energy of the *Wise, Benevolent Queen* and looking at various people in her life through the *Queen's* eyes. As she pictured each one, particularly those with whom she had difficulty, she visualized herself sending them compassionate energy, generating from her heart. The *Queen* and the *Warrior* began an ongoing negotiation about where to draw the line between compassion and taking a strong stand.

As Sharon continued to integrate the energy of the *Wise, Benevolent Queen* into her life, she began to relate to people differently and noticed that she was evoking a different reaction from them. While retaining her strong, intelligent presence, she became more approachable. Sharon had to *Negotiate* with the *Voices of Warning* that told her that being connected to her heart would ruin her career. What she noticed instead was that the *Wise Queen's* compassion was able to see beyond the surface appearance of things in a way the *Warrior* never could. The *Warrior* was always ready to battle and evoked defensiveness in others. The *Queen* could see into the needs and potentials of people and could evoke cooperation and compromise.

As Sharon continued to learn how to integrate heart and mind, balancing the *Warrior* and *Wise Queen*, she met a man who shared her values and interests. They began a relationship. She believed that their deep, vibrant connection was made possible because she had integrated the intuitive, heart-oriented energy of the *Wise and Benevolent Queen* at her *Inner Round Table*.

Integration Examples

Over the course of this book, you have heard the stories and struggles of many people who identified and came to understand the *Inner Cast* of *Characters* that played out some dilemma of their lives. Each of them needed to heal or re-direct *Inner Cast* members, or integrate something, or add "someone" to their *Inner Round Table*.

You met Patricia, who got control of her night time binging by developing an *Inner Comforter*, who could re-direct her sad, scared *Wallflower* towards non-caloric ways of self-soothing. You met Dominic, who needed to reclaim the creative, life-celebrating *Chef* he had left behind, and negotiate a new way of being a *Good Son* to his father. Judith rediscovered and developed the *Artist* she had left behind, when she became entirely invested in being a *Good Wife* and *Devoted Mother*.

Devin reconnected with the *Young Lover* in him through a dream that gave him the courage to be open and vulnerable with his wife. They re-established their deep connection and he faded out his online *Sex Junkie*. Sandra reclaimed her capacity to be joyfully embodied as she brought *Damaged Goods* out of the shadows, healing the lingering shame, and finding that she could experience a loving connection with her partner.

Lorraine freed herself from the domination of her *Responsible Perfectionist*. She developed a relationship with her *Inner Peasant* and began to relax and enjoy life. Carla was shielded and held by a *Protective God*. Her *Vigilant Child* learned that she was lovable, and that there are people and places in this life where she can be safe and protected.

Each of the stories in this book is ultimately about courage: the courage to engage the *Inner Cast*, to change and integrate new aspects of *Self*. Each person recalibrated the *Inner Self System*, moving certain *Inner Characters* into a less dominant role, creating new internal committees to accomplish the work at hand, welcoming new archetypal energies to their *Inner Round Table*.

Living Into a Bigger Story — Possible Selves

As a social worker, I acknowledge that many people encounter very challenging life circumstances. There are injustices and realities that severely limit people's options, but self-limiting scripts compound the problem. Even when resources and opportunities appear, many people are unable to take advantage of them, because they are mired in the wounds of the past, limited by internal ceilings, unable to move out of the archetype of the *Victim*, the *Oppressed,* the *Outsider.*

We all have gifts and strengths that can lead us out of adversity, but we sometimes cannot conceive of any other story than the one we have always lived. This is why we must surface our unconscious scripts and begin to rewrite them. We need to expand *who* we think we are, house new archetypal energies, and walk through the doors that open to us. Regardless of life's obstructions, the *Soul Print* is ever inviting us to transcend our history and live into a bigger story.

Round Table Work — Discovering "who" is needed

Often, what is needed to resolve a conflict or move forward on an important goal is revealed in the dialogues between *Inner Characters.* Unresolved conflict usually indicates some imbalance in the *Inner Self System.* Some people are strong on protecting, but weak on connecting. Some are naturally attuned to spiritual things, but can barely manage their daily lives. Some people are incredibly intelligent, but unable to establish a meaningful personal relationship.

We are sometimes missing crucial *Inner Characters* because we have never met anyone who carried this energy in a way that could be modeled. This does not mean that it cannot be developed. If we do not house a particular archetypal energy, it does not negate the existence of its potential. The fact that severely abused children can grow up to become great mothers speaks to the reality of an archetypal seedbed. Within us are the seeds of all potential. We have only to cultivate them and grow them into fullness. Certain places in the psyche feel like foreign countries. We don't speak the language or understand the customs, but we can travel there and learn.

Over the years, I have developed a list of what people need to be whole human beings.

If you do not have at least one *Inner Character* in each of these categories, your well-being sits on a precarious foundation. We need:

- *Functional Selves* that think, plan, problem solve, and manage our lives
- *Relational Selves* that know how to connect with others and navigate emotions
- *Inner Nurturers* that help us identify our needs and take care of ourselves
- *Inner Protectors* that can assess danger and help us set limits and boundaries
- *Power Selves* that help us assert ourselves and go after what we need and want
- *Inner Children* who help us to be creative, enjoy life and access joy and wonder
- *Sensual Selves* who help us to enjoy our senses and take care of the body
- *Spiritual Selves* that connect us to deep wisdom and transcendent meaning

The Archetypal Spectrum

As you read the list above you can see that you easily inhabit some of these energies. Others seem foreign or dangerous. They are all part of the archetypal spectrum. Sometimes we avoid colors of the archetypal spectrum because we don't understand them, or were never taught the skills to navigate them. All of these archetypal energies dwell in you and can be developed and integrated into your *Inner Cast.*

Anyone who is over-identified with one end of an archetypal spectrum will struggle with the opposite end of that spectrum. This is why very "sensitive, giving, loving" people are often hurt by people who are "selfish and uncaring" (take care of their own needs first). Very responsible people often judge or resent those who are "irresponsible" (fun loving and free spirited). "Spontaneous, innovative or creative" people tend to dislike "conservative protectors of the status quo."

We avoid our opposites and at the same time are strangely drawn to them. Sometimes we even marry them! This is because there is something in the psyche that is always seeking the "center point." Whenever we have moved too far to one end of an archetypal field, we draw in the opposite somewhere in our lives. This energetic opposite may appear in the form of people and situations in our lives, or on the stage of our night time dreams. It is the internal corollary to Newton's law of physics, "for every action there is an equal and opposite reaction."

Your Integration Work

- *What do you need to integrate to live into a greater wholeness?*
- *What in you has yet to be developed? What is calling you to you?*
- *What are your roads not taken?*
- *Who do you need to add to your Inner Round Table?*

EXPANDING YOUR INNER CAST: DEVELOPING NEW POTENTIAL

Using Dreams

Remember that one of the key functions of dreaming is to rebalance the psyche towards the center. Dreams can also be reparative, when they bring us an experience that provides exactly what we needed in life, but didn't get. Dreams can heal current hurts and distant wounds, bringing us deep experiences of nurture, protection, courage, belonging, acceptance, etc. Dreams also expand our archetypal spectrum, bringing us the energies we need to move us forward.

Role Models for Living — What Would Margot Do?

Twenty five years ago, I wanted to be more confident in making decisions. My problem was that I had a whole chorus of *Inner Voices of Doubt and Warning* that cautioned me, if I considered doing something without checking first with someone who was in charge. I often paralyzed myself in the process. I had a very confident, capable friend named Margot, and she could really get things done. She rarely asked permission. One of her "rules" was that it was easier to ask for forgiveness. Margot had good instincts and rarely got herself into trouble! I found her amazing. So, when I found myself mired in paralysis by analysis, I began to ask myself, "What would Margot do?" Then, I would do just that. Things worked out well, and I came to trust my instincts more. Occasionally, I got myself into trouble, but I also got better at working things out. This was one of my first experiences in studying and integrating aspects of other people who do something well. My *Inner Margot* became a member of my *Inner Round Table*.

Your Turn — Cultivating New Potentials

What *Missing Persons* have you discovered in yourself? Let's do some cultivation work.

Think for a moment of someone in the world who carries a particular energy or quality that you lack, someone you might employ as a role model. It might be someone you know personally, a character in a book or movie, or a person in history. Pick someone that captures the archetypal energy you want to integrate.

- *Does this energy live anywhere in you?*
- *Have you had any dreams that bring this energy into your world?*
- *Who do you know that carries this energy?*
- *Take a few moments and immerse yourself in this energy. Imagine being he or she for a minute. How does it feel?*
- *Look at your life from this place. What do you see?*
- *If you integrated more of this energy, how would your life be different? What might you say or do?*
- *Imagine naming and claiming this energy as a member of your Inner Round Table.*
- *If you are contemplating a problem or decision, what would they do?*
- *What words of wisdom would they offer to you?*

Changes Inside Evoke Changes Outside

As you integrate new energies into your life, your relationships with others will shift. When you are different in the world, people will respond to you differently. Sometimes this is wonderful. Long-standing problems will clear up as if by magic. Sometimes it is hard. Other people will not always be happy when your changes do not suit their wants and needs. They may try to get you to return to your old way of being. Even if you are changing for the better, it is disruptive to the people around you, so you are likely going to negotiating in your outer life as well. If you use the same process outlined in the *Negotiation* chapter, you will have some effective tools for this relationship challenge. Remember that everyone has an *Inner Round Table*. Discover *who* it is in another person that is disturbed by your changes. What are their needs and wants? Begin your negotiations there.

To sustain certain changes, you will need outer support. Your *Not So Supporting Cast* will kick in, your *Inner Critic* and the *Voices of Warning* will tell you that you are ruining your life. It is wise to have at least one trusted person to evaluate a new course of action. In uncharted waters, this trusted person can help you discern whether you are on a positive path or wandering into the *Shadow Lands*. You always want to check to see who in your *Inner Cast* is driving an agenda, and if other *Round Table* members have been consulted. When you blunder, have mercy on yourself. Pull forward your *Inner Comforter* and *Encouragers*. Know that you are learning. Everything is valuable when viewed through the lens of *Individuation*.

Watch for images in your dreams that will guide, energize and encourage you in times of uncertainty. Seek out friends who are also on the journey of *Individuation*. If you can't find friends or a support group, consider enlisting the help of a therapist or spiritual director. You need companions on the way, who can uphold you as you make crucial changes in your life and become the person you were born to be.

CHAPTER 18

CONCLUDING THOUGHTS:
The Soul Print

"The treasure we seek is never far away.
We need not go looking for it in distant lands,
for it lies buried in the most secret recesses of our own house;
in other words, of our own being."
Heinrich Zimmer

The greatest loneliness a person can experience is to be separated from themselves. The *Inner Peace Treaty Process* helps us to center ourselves in our inherent strengths, wisdom, and capacities. When we live from that inner center, we are better equipped to face the storms of life. This four-fold process can be used in every area of your life, from the most basic decision making to the most complex challenges.

As you engage the process of *Naming, Knowing, Negotiating and Integrating*, you will continue to explore your potential and expand the archetypal realms you can inhabit. Your *Inner Cast of Characters* will continue to change and grow. This journey does not end with resolving your current conflicts, or making peace with your past. As you peel away the many layers of "who you thought you were," you will discover our own unique essence, your *Soul Print*. When you begin to let the *Soul Print* guide you, it opens you to a whole new realm of existence.

Throughout this book you have seen how the experience of your truest *Self* can be obscured by the limiting ways in which you define yourself. We are required to clean out the basements, attics and closets of our lives, to separate the junk from the hidden treasures. When we reclaim those lost treasures, we can bring them back to the light of day, and put them to use for everyone's greater good. When you begin to live from your *Soul Print*, your life begins to change in interesting ways. Situations shift. As you live from a deeper place, you will develop a sense of security that transcends circumstance, a core sense of peace amidst the changing tides of life.

Discovering the person you were born to be is an ongoing process. As you learn to cooperate with this process, you begin to relax, and not cling so tightly to what is familiar. New chapters will open and you will continue to define the meaning of your life in ever deepening ways. Doors will close; others will open. People will leave your life and new people will come in. Cycles of birth and death, conflict and resolution are an innate part of life. They are archetypal patterns. Where we get into trouble is when we cling to something that has ended: a job we have outgrown, a relationship that no longer has meaning, a lifestyle that no longer fits our deeper purpose.

As in the classic fairy tales, the path of *Individuation* sometimes takes us through a dark forest. Our story unravels, and we feel a sense of despair. But we can slow down and note that we are in that liminal place between what has been and what is about to be. We can watch life reweave itself into a beautiful new tapestry beyond what we could ever have imagined. There is a concept in Jungian psychology called the *Felix Culpa* or "fortunate catastrophe." This means that sometimes when life falls apart, something new becomes possible that would never have taken place otherwise. When we are open to the unfolding, we see that there is a grand orchestration taking place.

The realm of the *Soul Print* includes the vast sea of the *Collective Unconscious* where all archetypal possibilities exist. Being connected to and operating from your *Soul Print* puts you on a spiritual path. Our *Soul Print* is continually inviting us to integrate new dimensions from this archetypal realm. It speaks to us through our dreams and synchronicities, through the longings of our heart, through unexpected happenings in our lives, through the healing of our wounds and the transcendence of our struggles.

There will always be a struggle between the *Ego Identity* and the *Soul Print*. When you feel threatened or vulnerable, you will be more likely to rely on what is most familiar: roles, achievements, relationships, places where you can feel validated or powerful. But once you begin to experience the richness of the soul, the pull to attune your life to this more subtle resonance becomes stronger. For many people the struggle to decide which guiding force to follow goes on for a long time. Then, there is finally a tipping point where enough trust is gained to allow the *Soul* to be the guiding force of life. At this point the channel opens and all of the resources of this realm begin to flow in: wisdom, intuition, compassion, joy, mystical and quantum experiences, deep healing, creativity, and a sense of deep peace, "the peace that passeth understanding."

Deep Resources become Available as the SoulPrint becomes the Guiding Force of the Life

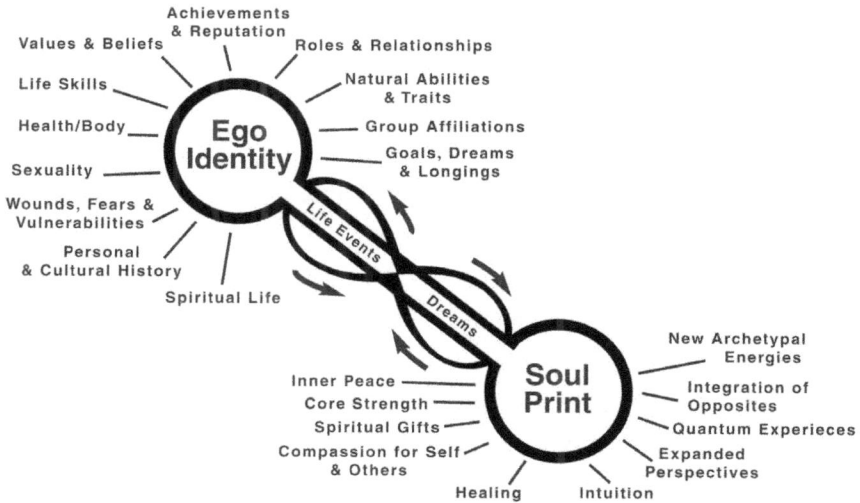

Changing the Archetype Shifts the Experience

Every thought, feeling, point of view, attraction, and reaction that we have in life is generated from our *Inner Cast of Characters. Individuation* is the great work of building an interior theatre large enough to house all that we are, all that we have been, and all that we will be.

As you become more adept at directing your *Inner Cast*, you will develop *Archetypal Fluency,* the capacity to speak many archetypal languages and travel from one interior country to another. You will be able to inhabit many archetypal energies and do your life work from different places in the psyche. Any shift in your archetypal perspective will instantly change the meaning of your life.

There is an old story about the three men cutting stones for a cathedral in the middle ages. When asked what they were doing, the first replied that he was cutting stone (archetype of the *Worker*). The second replied that he was making a living to provide for his family (archetype of the *Provider*). The third replied that he was building a cathedral to the glory of God, (the *Visionary and Spiritual Servant*). Three stone cutters, each working from a different archetypal perspective.

The same can be true for us. Andrew is a teacher. So is Tisha. For Andew, teaching is a job with tasks to be completed. He shows up, disseminates information, assigns homework, and gives tests. For Tisha, teaching is about transformation. She seeks to awaken her students to their innate gifts and to enlighten them to the idea that education can open doors into new worlds. Both of them are teachers, but they are working from two very different archetypal orientations. If you feel stuck in your life, experiment with moving into a different archetypal perspective. Some of your problems will simply vanish when viewed through the eyes of a different *Inner Character.*

Likewise, if you are having problems in a relationship, experiment with viewing the problem from the eyes of a different

Inner Character. You can experiment with communicating and relating from a different archetypal energy and see what that evokes in those around you. Often times it's not what you say to people that is the problem, but "who" is saying it. We will evoke different responses from people based on which *Inner Character* is speaking.

Recognizing Triggers and Getting Back to the Calm Core

The more you work this process, the more awareness you will have about situations and people that trigger you. It is always wise to wonder *who* in you is pushing a strong agenda and why it is so important to them.

You will get better at catching yourself before you get swept away into an unconscious reaction, hijacked by an *Inner Character* who has just stormed the stage. You will learn that any time you have a really strong reaction to something, positive or negative, it's time to *STOP, LOOK, LISTEN and DIRECT.*

STOP—Learn to recognize the warning signs of when your *Observing Self* has gone off line. Notice that you are no longer operating from your *Calm Core.* Check in with your body. Has it become suddenly numb, tense or electrified? Tune in. You've just gotten triggered and are experiencing shock, upset, enchantment, etc. Begin to breathe and ground yourself in your body and in the here and now.

LOOK—Ask yourself *what* just happened and *who* has gotten activated in you.

LISTEN—See if any of those inner voices sound familiar. Do you know this *Inner Character*? Have you done previous dialogue work with him or her? If so, you are familiar with what they usually say and urge you to do.

DIRECT—When you stop, look and listen, you will have gotten your *Observing Self* back on line. Now you have some insight, and a better chance of directing your actions with consciousness and wisdom.

The Observing Self

When we separate out from our emotional reactivity, and develop the consciousness of the *Observing Self,* we can take a step back, breathe, and center ourselves in our *Calm Core.* We hear the inner dialogue and can identify *who* is at play in us, *how* they have gotten activated, and *what* they want. We can identify the vulnerability that caused our *Inner Children* to become needy or upset and address the needs before they take over the show. We don't have to shut down in fear or go ricocheting into the defenses of a *Power Self,* who will now make things worse. We can regain our balance more quickly.

Before developing an *Observing Self* and an *Inner Director,* many people judge themselves very harshly. They make mistakes and feel horrible, concluding that they are hopeless or worthless. When you begin to do *Inner Round Table* work, you see that it is often one or two *Inner Characters* that are causing your biggest problems. The more you do this work, the more skillful you will become at directing yourself in times of distress.

When we operate from our center, we do not need to abandon one realm of experience in favor of another. We can hold dynamic tensions, waiting for the emergence of solutions we haven't even imagined yet. We can work out dilemmas such as how to be a reclusive mystic as well as an involved mother, or a serious corporate executive as well as a free-spirited rock and roll guitarist.

Your sense of trust in the process increases as life and relationships become more meaningful. You have the sense of "coming home." Your interior world becomes a safe harbor into which you can sail to regroup and re-provision yourself for new adventures.

The following creed was written in summary of the ideas in this book. It echoes the Assagioli creed[6], which I have loved for so many years, that begins, "I have a body, but I am not my body . . . I have emotions, but I am not my emotions . . . I have desires, but I am not my desires . . . I have an intellect, but I am not my intellect . . ." I decided to create my own creed by which I seek to live. You might consider doing the same.

The Inner Peace Treaty Creed

- *I have a history and life experiences. They have shaped me, but they do not define me. I am more than my history.*
- *I have a life script, but I can rewrite that script at any time.*
- *I have roles and responsibilities, but I can change them, retire them or expand them.*
- *I can live my life from a variety of archetypal perspectives. I can make mistakes and recover. I do not have to be perfect. I can learn and grow.*
- *I am a thinking person with values and beliefs. I have the capacity to evaluate things and make choices. I can re-evaluate my life as my understanding evolves.*
- *I am a member of a family, and I can also create a family of choice.*
- *I participate in various community, work, social, recreational, political and religious groups. I can define what kind of time, energy and resources I want to devote to these according to my unfolding life purpose.*
- *I have personality traits and various gifts and talents. I can use them in a variety of ways. I can choose not to. I can develop new traits and gifts. I can live creatively.*

---

[6]   Reference Pg. 103-106 in Psychosynthesis: A Collection of Basic Writings by Roberto Assagioli, MD

- *I have achievements, but I am not defined by them. My reputation may rise and fall. My sense of self is not dependent on what others think of me. I can value my accomplishments and involvements even if others do not. I can spend my time and energy on what is most deeply meaningful to me.*
- *I live in a body but I am more than my body. I can enjoy the realm of the senses and care for my body, but I am not defined by my appearance or my state of health.*
- *I can love whoever my heart and soul lead me to love, even if others do not understand.*
- *I have a spiritual life and I can continue to seek truth and worship in the ways that are most meaningful to my soul. I am not limited to the religion of my childhood.*
- *I can seek quiet times away from others to replenish myself and reflect on my life.*
- *I can balance my Individuation process with my commitments to others. I can adjust those commitments in alignment with my deepest truth and life purpose.*
- *I can allow others to do the same.*

The Inner Theatre of Our Lives

When we begin to think of ourselves as the theatre in which life takes place, we can approach life as an art form. We can be curious and creative rather than self-judging and fearful. We can work with the raw material of our lives, reconfiguring the *Inner Cast,* open to the mystery as we live into new ways of being. We will encounter the experiences we need to awaken us. Life shapes us, and we embrace new understandings. We recover what was lost and build new interior structure. We heal and become whole.

Every human potential lies within your archetypal seedbed. The inner world really is the vast, undiscovered country. It does not require an airline ticket or a passport. It does require time, courage, and the willingness to let go of previous notions about who you thought you were.

When we listen to the intuitive leading of our *Soul Print* and trust the unfolding of life, we are cooperating with a mysterious process that is working in us and through us. We begin to experience a deep peace amidst change, to know our purpose, to actualize our vast potential and to live into the life we were born to live.

BIBLIOGRAPHY

Assagioli, Roberto (1965-2000) *Psychosynthesis: A Collection of Basic Writings*. Amherst, Mass: The Synthesis Center Inc.

Bradshaw, John (1988, revised 2005) *Healing the Shame that Binds You*. Deerfield, Beach, FLA: Health Communications.

Campell, Joseph (editor) (1971) *The Portable Jung*. New York: Penguin Books.
_____ (1991) *A Joseph Campbell Companion: Reflections on the Art of Living*. New York: Harper Collins.

Campbell, Julia (1992) *The Artist's Way: A Spiritual Path to Higher Creativity*. New York: Tarcher/Putnam.

Combs, Gene & Freedman, Jill (1996) *Narrative Therapy: The Social Construction of Preferred Realities*. New York: Norton & Co.

Deikman, Arthur (1982) *The Observing Self: Mysticism and Psychotherapy*. Beacon Press, Boston.

Dyak, Miriam (1999) *The Voice Dialogue Facilitator's Handbook, Part 1*. Seattle: L.I.F.E. Energy Press.

Edinger, Edward (1972) *Ego and Archetype*. Baltimore: Penguin Books.

Goulding, Mary and Robert (1979) *Changing Lives Through Redecision Therapy*. New York: Grove Press.

Hall, James (1983) *Jungian Dream Interpretation*. Toronto, Canada: Inner City Books.

Hillman, James (1996) *The Soul's Code: In Search of Character and Calling*. New York: Random House.
_____ (1979) *The Dream and the Underworld*. New York: Harper & Row.

Hollis, James (2007) *Why Good People Do Bad Things: Understanding Our Darker Selves*. New York: Gotham Books.
_____ (2000) *Archetypal Imagination*. College Station, Texas: Texas A&M University Press.

Hopcke, Robert (1999) *A Guided Tour of the Collected Works of C.G. Jung*. Boston: Shambhala.

Hoss, Robert J. (2005) *Dream Language: Self Understanding through Imagery and Color*. Ashland, OR: Innersource.

Hudson, Joyce Rockwood *Natural Spirituality: Recovering the Wisdom Tradition in Christianity*. Danielsville, Georgia: JRH Publications.

Illsley Clark, J., Dawson, C. (1998) *Growing Up Again: Parenting Ourselves, Parenting Our Children*. Minnesota: Hazeldon.

Jacobi, Jolande (1953) *Complex/Archetype/Symbol in the Psychology of CG Jung*. Princeton University Press.
_____ (1965) *The Way of Individuation*. New York: New American Library.

Johnson, Robert (1986) *Inner Work: Using Dreams and Active Imagination for Personal Growth*. Harper San-Francisco.

_____ (1991) *Owning Your Own Shadow: Understanding the Dark Side of the Psyche*. Harper San Francisco.

Jung, Carl G (1978) *Aion: Researches into the Phenomenology of the Self*—Collected Works of C.G. Jung Vol. 9, Part 2. Princeton University Press.
_____ (1981) *The Archetypes and the Collective Unconscious*—Collected Works of C.G. Jung Vol.9, Part 1. Princeton University Press.
_____ (1974) *Dreams*. Translated and Edited by R.F.C. Hull, gathered from the Collected Works—Volumes 4,8,12,16. Princeton University Press.
_____ (1971) *The Portable Jung*. Translated by Hull, edited by Joseph Campbell. NY: Penguin Books.
_____ (2009) *The Red Book*. Sonu Shamdasani (editor, translator). Norton & Co
_____ (2010-New in paperback) *Synchronicity: An Acausal Connecting Priniciple*. From Collected Works of C.G. Jung Vol. 8. Switzerland: Bollingen.

Kaplan-Williams, Strephon (1980) *The Jungian-Senoi Dreamwork Manual*. Berkely, CA: Journey Press.

Metzger, Deena (1992) *Writing for your Life: Discovering the Story of Your Life's Journey*. San Francisco: Harper.

Ogden, Gina (2006) *The Heart and Soul of Sex: Making the ISIS Connection*. Boston: Trumpeter.

Pearson, Carol (1986, 1998) *The Hero Within: Six Archetypes We Live By*. Harper San Francisco.
_____ (1991) *Awakening the Heroes Within: Twelve Archetypes to Help Us Find Ourselves and Transform Our World*. Harper San Francisco.

Progoff, Ira (1975,1992) *At a Journal Workshop: Writing to Access the Power of the Unconscious and Evoke Creative Ability*. New York: Tarcher/Putnam.

Rainer, Tristine (1978) *The New Diary: How to Use a Journal for Self Guidance and Expanded Creativity*. Los Angeles: Tarcher, Inc.

Satir, Virginia (1983) *Conjoint Family Therapy: Your Many Faces*. Palo Alto, CA: Science and Behavior

Stewart, Ian & Joines, Vann (1987) *TA Today: A New Introduction to Transactional Analysis*. Chapel Hill: Lifespace Publishing. (This book has excellent information about script formation and exercises for rewriting the one you have.)

Stone, Hal & Sidra. (1989) *Embracing Our Selves: The Voice Dialogue Manual*. Novato, CA: New World Library.
_____ (1993) *Embracing Your Inner Critic: Turning Self-Criticism into a Creative Asset*. San Francisco: Harper Collins.
_____ (1997, 2000) *The Shadow King: The Invisible Force That Holds Women Back*. Authors Guild BackinPrint.

Taylor, Jeremy (1992) *Where People Fly and Water Runs Uphill: Using Dreams to Tap the Wisdom of the Unconscious*. New York: Warner Books.
_____ (1983) *Dream Work: Techniques for Discovering the Creative Power in Dreams*. New York: Paulist Press.

Van Eenwyk, John (1997) *Archetypes and Strange Attractors: The Chaotic World of Symbols*. Toronto: Inner City Books.

Whitmont, Edward (1969) *The Symbolic Quest: Basic Concepts of Analytical Psychology*. Princeton University Press.

Zweig, Connie & Abrams, Jeremiah (1991) *Meeting the Shadow: The Hidden Power of the Dark Side of Human Nature.* NY: Tarcher/Putnam.

Zweig, C. & Work, S. (1997) *Romancing the Shadow: Illuminating the Dark Side of the Soul.* New York: Ballentine Books.

More Recommended Readings

Adams, Kathleen (1990) *Journal to the Self: 22 Paths to Personal Growth.* New York: Warner Books.

Allione, Tsultrim (2008) *Feeding Your Demons: Ancient Wisdom for Resolving Inner Conflict* New York: Little Brown and Co.

Au, W. & Cannon, N (1995) *Urgings of the Heart: A Spirituality of Integration.* New York: Paulist Press.

Booker, Christopher (2004) *The Seven Basic Plots: Why We Tell Stories.* London: Continuum.

Bolen, Jean S. (1984) *Goddesses in Everywoman: A New Psychology of Women.* New York: Harper and Rowe.
_____ (1989) *Gods in Everyman: A New Psychology of Men's Lives and Loves.* New York: Harper & Rowe.
_____ (2002) *Goddesses in Older Women: Archetypes of Women Over Fifty.* New York: Harper & Rowe.

Brennan, A. Brewi, J. (1999) *Passion for Life: Lifelong Psychological and Spiritual Growth.* New York: Continuum.
_____ (1988,1999) *Mid-Life Spirituality and Jungian Archetypes.* York Beach, Maine: Nicolas-Hays.

Field, Joanna. (1981) *A Life of One's Own*. Los Angeles: JP Tarcher.

Ford, Debbie (1998) *The Dark Side of the Light Chasers: Reclaiming Your Power, Creativity, Brilliance, and Dreams*. New York: Riverhead Books.

Gould, Joan (2005) *Spinning Straw into Gold: What Fairy Tales Reveal About the Transformations in a Woman's Life*. New York: Random House.

Gongloff, Robert (2006) *Dream Exploration: A New Approach*. Woodbury, Minn: Llewellyn Publications.

Grant, Toni (1988) *Being A Woman: Fulfilling Your Femininity and Finding Love*. New York: Random House.

Haden, Robert (2010) *Unopened Letters from God* Flatrock, NC, Haden Institute Publishing.

Joy, Brugh (1990) *Avalance: Heretical Reflections on the Dark and the Light*. New York: Ballentine Books.

Leonard, Linda (1985) *The Wounded Woman: Healing the Father-Daughter Relationship*. Boston: Shambhala.

Levoy, Gregg (1997) *Callings: Finding and Following an Authentic Life*. New York: Three Rivers Press.

Mellick, Jill (1996) *The Art of Dreaming: Tools for Creative Dream Work*. Berkley: Conari Press.

Molton, M. & Sikes, L. (2011) *Four Eternal Women: Toni Wolff Revisited* Carmel CA: Fisherking Press.

Moore, Thomas (2004) *Dark Nights of the Soul: A Guide to Finding Your Way through Life's Ordeals*. New York: Gotham Books.

Moore, Robert (1990) *King, Warrior, Magician, Lover: Rediscovering the Archetypes of the Mature Masculine*. New York: Harper Collins.

Myss, Caroline (2002) *Sacred Contracts: Awakening Your Divine Potential*. New York: Three Rivers Press.

Parker, G. Keith (2006) *Seven Cherokee Myths*. Jefferson, NC: McFarland&Co.

Richo, David (1991) *How to be an Adult: A Handbook on Psychological and Spiritual Integration*. New York: Paulist Press.

Savary, Louis, Berne, Patricia, & Kaplan Williams, Strephon (1984) *Dreams and Spiritual Growth: A Judeo-Christian Way of Dreamwork*. Mahwah: Paulist Press.

Schwartz, Richard C. (1995) *Internal Family Systems Therapy*. London: Guilford Press. (Colleagues of mine have introduced me to his work, commenting that his ideas and methods sounded similar to Hal and Sidra Stone's Voice Dialogue and my Negotiating the Inner Peace Treaty. Internal Family Systems appears to be a blend of Jungian theory and Family Systems theory. The book contains valuable additional perspectives, clear methodology and good case histories.)

Small, Jacquelyn (2001) *Psyche's Seeds: The 12 Sacred Principles of Soul-Based Psychology*. New York: Tarcher/Putnam.

ACKNOWLEDGMENTS

This work is the culmination of thirty five years of life, reading, graduate education, post-graduate training programs, individual therapy, workshops and many conversations. It is impossible to sift out the source of every phrase and metaphor that I have collected over the years, but I have done my best to acknowledge the pivotal sources that I know. They are listed without initials behind their names, as I wish to acknowledge them as people rather than as educations. I want to thank the many clients and workshop attendees that have taught me so much as I have watched them utilize this material in ever more creative ways. I thank them for the honor of walking with them as they have done their soul work.

The work and writings of Carl Jung are primary to this work. I have also learned from the pioneers of the therapeutic journaling movement, in particular Ira Progoff, early on from Tristine Rainer, and later, Deena Metzger. I wish to acknowledge Carol Pearson for her foundational ideas about the Innocent and the Orphan. Hal and Sidra Stone have been important teachers and supporters in my life and work. Their Voice Dialogue method caused my journaling process to jump off the page into a living work. Their Psychology of the Selves gave my work a theoretical underpinning and their understanding of working with archetypes as energies instead of mere cognitive processes transformed my work and my life.

Gratitude to Bob Haden, who has given me a wonderful platform since 2000, from which to teach, express and develop. Also to my fellow staff members at the Haden Institute, who have supported the long gestation and birthing of this book in a variety of important ways, especially Cathy Smith Bowers, Jeremy Taylor, Joyce Rockwood Hudson, Jerry Wright and Bob Hoss.

Great appreciation to Pam White, who teaches so profoundly from her heart and soul about the theory and practice of psychotherapy. Also to Al Pesso, for his teaching on healing trauma, early childhood wounds and for the profoundly helpful insights into how we get caught in Omnipotent Inflations. Gratitude and respect to Keith Parker, brilliant Jungian analyst and soul friend. Special thanks to Gina Ogden, pioneer, soul sister and supporter, who read early chapters and assured me I could and must write this book. Deep gratitude to Susan Sims Smith, soul sister, who linked me to Hal and Sidra Stone and has upheld me and dialogued me through some swampy places along the way. Love, hugs, and big hoorays to my treasured Circle of Friends who have embraced my Inner Cast and encouraged and loved me through this long delivery: Carmon McGee, Sara Nafziger-Shelly, Layne and Ken Racht, Shirley Nicholson, Paul Feldman, Tim Evans, Cindy Jordon, Leanna Graves, Luanne Fulbright, Laura Chapman and my awesome sis, Ruthie Harper.

Tom Wakefield, in addition to all the things you are to me, you have been such an encouraging and patient editor to my occasional *Madwoman Author.* Gratitude to my soulful son, Tommy, joy of my life, who birthed the archetype of the *Mother* in me and grounds me in the goodness of daily life. To Myra, my mother, who taught me to be merciful and loving and protected the *Sensitive Mystic* and *Creative Artist* in me. To Darwin, my father, who taught me to be bold and courageous, encouraged my *Innovator* and birthed the *Rebel Daughter* in me. They have all been important members of my *Inner Team.*

APPENDIX

THE FOUR STEP PROCESS

NAMING: "Who" is in your *Inner Cast of Characters?* Identify the "Voices in your Head", look at your primary ego identifications, your history, your values, needs, hopes and dreams, script, the roles you play, the energies you carry and give them names. Who is in the background behind the *Main Players*? Who are your *Inner Children,* the *Kids Behind the Curtain?* Who is your *Not So Supporting Cast*? Who have you *Retired* or *Disowned*? Identify and name *Shadow Characters* and *Dream Figures* as they present themselves.

KNOWING: Interview and get to know your *Inner Cast,* their history, needs, perspectives, values, role models and agendas. Discover what makes them tick?

NEGOTIATING: Inevitable conflicts will arise between your different *Inner Characters*. Gather the parties with a vested interest at an imaginary *Inner Round Table,* surface unconscious material and begin to address needs and discover where cooperation can occur, conflicts can be resolved, opposing energies can both be honored, and new resources can be brought to the table.

INTEGRATING: In the process of *Individuation*, we are continually integrating new material from our depths, expanding our archetypal realm and our understanding of life. Life brings us opportunities for growth and redefining ourselves. Dreams bring us new material each night. Integrating opposites and working with our shadow aspects is a big part of this process.

LIST OF EXPLORATORY EXERCISES

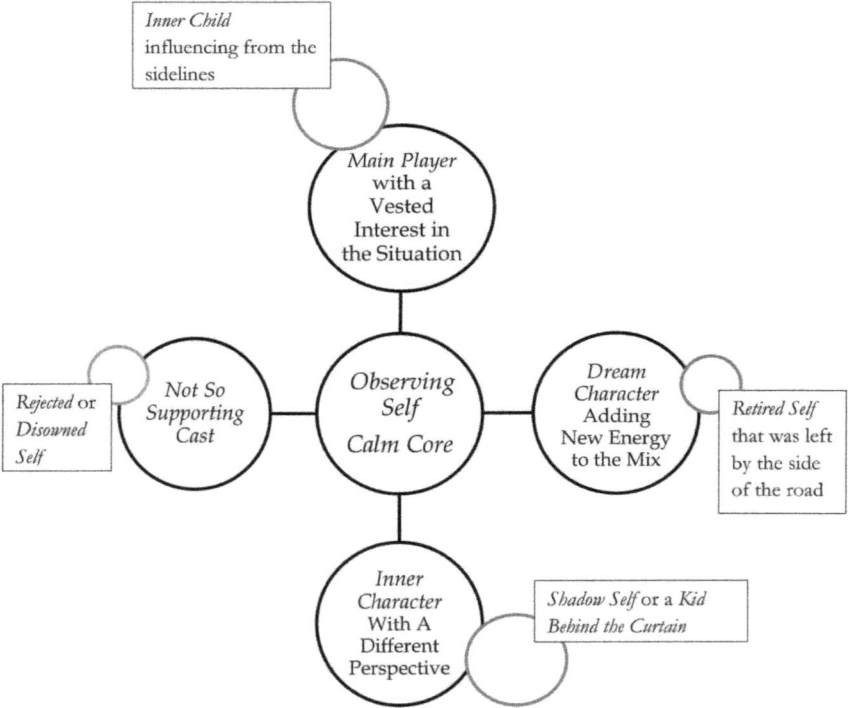

Inner Child
influencing from the
sidelines

Main Player
with a
Vested
Interest in
the Situation

Not So
Supporting
Cast

Rejected or
Disowned
Self

Observing
Self
Calm Core

Dream
Character
Adding
New Energy
to the Mix

Retired Self
that was left
by the side
of the road

Inner
Character
With A
Different
Perspective

Shadow Self or a *Kid*
Behind the Curtain

Characters Seated At My Inner Round Table

The number of circles here is just a suggestion. You can have as many or few as you want. You can group them in a variety of ways, make them different sizes, experiment with changing positions to see how it shifts the dynamics. You can add new characters that carry what you are missing, or characters that present themselves in your dreams. Remember to act as an Inner Moderator, so that everyone has a voice.

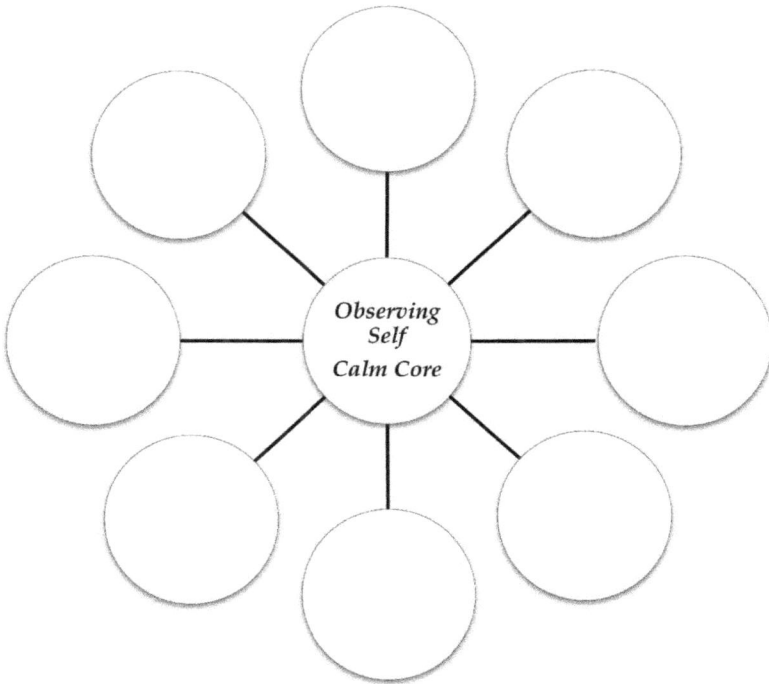

Observing Self
Calm Core

CHECKLIST FOR CONSCIOUS LIVING

- ☐ Am I developing my *Observing Self?*
- ☐ Am I cultivating my capacity to live from my *Calm Core?*
- ☐ Have I learned to separate out from the processes going on inside me in order to *Name, Know and Negotiate* with "who" is operating in me?
- ☐ Am I familiar with the *Inner Characters* that cause me the most trouble in my life?
- ☐ Am I attending to my vulnerability and taking care of my *Inner Children?*
- ☐ Do I know how to take care of their needs and direct them constructively?
- ☐ Am I aware of where I bounce between polarized extremes? Am I learning to live in the midst of dynamic tension and find creative ways to honor each side?
- ☐ Am I doing my *Shadow Work,* observing my judgments, reactions and attractions, and the foreign or dark characters in my dreams?
- ☐ Am I gathering *Dream Pearls* and allowing them to enrich my life?
- ☐ Do I welcome that which is seeking entry into my life as an invitation to expand my archetypal spectrum?
- ☐ Am I grounded in my body, aware of how it is speaking to me?
- ☐ Have I negotiated among heart, mind, body and soul about the important things in my life?
- ☐ Am I growing in compassion for myself and for others?
- ☐ Am I developing soul friends to share with and support me on my journey?
- ☐ Have I opened the channels to the realm of *Soul?* Am I listening?
- ☐ Am I learning to trust in the mystery of life?

A POSSIBLE ENTRANCE MEDITATION

Sit upright in a chair, with your feet flat on the floor and your hands resting in your lap. Close your eyes and begin to take deep, slow breaths. Imagine you are breathing into every part of your body, all the way down to your toes and into your fingers. Try breathing in through your nostrils and blowing the air gently out of your mouth. Allow the air to move below the chest area, deeply into your lungs, so that your belly moves in and out as you breathe and your shoulders stay still.

Locate your feet on the floor and imagine breathing into them and then exhaling any tension, discomfort, or numbness there. Now imagine breathing into your legs and releasing anything you are holding there. Feel yourself sitting on the chair and notice the pressure of the chair against your bottom. Move a bit to unlock your pelvis and lower back and notice how your upper body is resting on this foundation. Breathe into and release any tension or holding in your pelvis or groin area. Now move through your torso, breathing and releasing tension in your stomach, solar plexus, and heart area. Notice any emotions that rise up in you as you are breathing into these areas and see if you can relax into them rather than resisting them. Imagine breathing into the place where you feel them most strongly and release them as you exhale.

Now move up to your shoulders. Make a few circles backward and forward with your shoulders, loosening this area. Notice the weight of your arms hanging from your shoulders. Follow your arms down into your hands and imagine breathing down to the tips of your fingers and out. Move your neck around and lift your head. Notice how the weight of your head is balanced on your shoulders. Find a comfortable place to center your head over your body. Take a moment to again breathe back down throughout your entire body. Now focus on your head and face. Notice any tension in your forehead, frowning, or holding around the eyes, ears and mouth. Move your face and let it go. Is your jaw relaxed? Breathe into and release any tension or holding. Move up and be aware of the location of the top of your head.

Imagine now that you are breathing in a soft, loving light that comes through the top of your head and moves down through your entire body. Breathe it into your heart, your belly, and all the way down to your toes. Notice how your body feels at this moment. Notice any thoughts or emotions and let them go. Breathe deeply and release any remaining tension or holding. Do this several more times, following the breath in and out. When you are ready, open your eyes and look around the room taking in what you see. Notice how you feel.

OTHER DREAM WORKERS

Robert Hoss and the Six Magic Questions

Robert Hoss, MA, is the former President of the International Association for the Study of Dreams and author of *Dream Language: Self-Understanding through Imagery and Color.* In addition to his very intriguing work on the meaning of color in dreams, he has developed a method of dream work that incorporates Gestalt methods and has come to be known as *The Six Magic Questions.*

I enjoy Bob's method because it encourages relationship and conversation with dream characters and symbols. At a recent conference, he told me that he was going to add one of my questions to his six original. I have included it below.

Begin by picking a dream image to explore. It can be anything in the dream: a person, animal, symbol, animate or inanimate. Then interview the Dream Image as if it were sitting in a chair in front of you by asking the following questions:

1) Who or **what are you**?
   If the dream character is someone you know: describe the personality; describe how you are like them or different from them.
2) What is your **purpose or function** (what do you do)?
3) What do you **like** about being this dream element?
4) What do you **dislike** about being this dream element?
5) What do you **fear most** as this dream element?
6) What do you **desire** most as this dream element?

My additional question would be "Is there anything you would like to say to me?"

Bob then moves into what he calls the *Image Activation Method*, which parallels my method of *Inner Peace Treaty Dream Work*. In this approach, you imagine entering into and inhabiting one of the dream images. Looking out of the eyes of this dream figure, then revisit these questions. Thus, "Who are you?" shifts to "I am . . . ."

1. I am . . .
2. My purpose or function is . . .
3. What I like about myself and what I do is . . .
4. What I dislike about myself and what I do is . . .
5. What I fear most is . . .
6. What I desire most is . . .

After you have interviewed your dream image and then inhabited it, you return to your original ego orientation. Then you look to see how the answers you gathered address a situation in your life. Another application of this method is to re-rewrite the dream substituting the answers to the *Six Magic Questions* in place of each dream symbol. This technique can bring tremendous insight. For more information on these techniques and a deep exploration into the realm of color in dreams, refer to Bob's book, *Dream Language*.

Dream Themes

Robert Gongloff has written a great book called *Dream Exploration*, which focuses on the thematic content in dreams. The jumping-off point for his book is another excellent resource book called *Dreams and Spiritual Growth* by Louis Savary, Patricia Berne and Strephon Kaplan Williams. This group is the originator of the *Title, Theme, Affect, Question* approach to dream work and is a great way to quickly harvest some insight from your dreams. In this method you would:

1. Give the dream a *title*
2. Determine its *theme*
3. Note the *affect* or emotion of the dream
4. Notice what kind of *question* the dream leaves us with.

In building on the *Title, Theme, Affect, Question* method, Robert Gongloff found that the most difficult part for most people was identifying the theme. His book is devoted to exploring and unpacking some major underlying themes in your dreams. I highly recommend this book as it will augment your understanding of the underlying scripts held by your *Inner Cast of Characters.*

SUGGESTIONS FOR FACILITATING
ANOTHER PERSON

The most important thing about facilitating another person is to simply be present and allow them to be wherever they are. If you are interviewing an *Inner Character*, have them move their chair over a bit to differentiate between their primary *Ego Identification* and the *Inner Character* they will be speaking from. They might also move out of the chair onto the floor or around the room, if space permits.

As your partner responds, just acknowledge what is being said. Don't try to comfort, fix, enlighten, convince, reframe, or add your "two cents worth." Adding anything, trying to get them to see things differently, or suggesting "solutions" indicates that there are "right, wrong or better" ways of being or seeing things. It interferes with the process of exploration, takes them out of the flow of the energy, and sends them into their head to consider what you are saying. Your solutions that may not fit for this person. Simply ask the questions, and acknowledge whatever answer your partner provides. You want them to feel safe to express themselves fully and explore the perspective of that particular part of their psyche without judgment or interference.

As you move through the process, see if you can match the type of energy that your partner is in. If they are upbeat, allow your energy to brighten up. If they are sad, then slow down and become more subdued. Sometimes people take notes as their partner is answering and give the notes to the partner when they are done. When your partner is finished responding, thank them and have them move their chair back over into their original position to indicate that they are moving back into a place of centered awareness, and out of the part of the psyche you have been interacting with. Make sure that the person gets fully anchored back into their body and into present time. Miriam Dyak's has written an excellent Voice Dialogue Facilitator's Manual (see bibliography).

INTEGRATING OPPOSITES

Here are some key OPPOSITES that present themselves in our lives that warrant *Integration* work. Take a look at this list and see if you can find some polarized opposites of your own.

Arrogant/Humble
Being/Doing
Civilized/Primitive, Instinctual
Contracting/Expanding
Detached/Engaged
Direct/Indirect
Entitled/Disenfranchised
Hopeful/Cynical
Independent/Dependent
Individual/Group Collective
Innocent/Worldly
Logical/Emotional
Manipulative/Straightforward
Mind/Heart, Soul, Instinct
Nice/Mean
Open/Secretive
Perfectionist/Careless
Personal/Impersonal

Pleaser/Selfish
Positive/Negative
Power/Vulnerability
Protector/Violator
Pusher/Laid Back
Rebel/Rule Follower
Responsible/Irresponsible
Saint/Sinner
Selfish/Selfless
Special/Ordinary
Spirit/Body, Mind
Spiritual/Material
Structured/Unstructured
Victim /Persecutor, Abuser,
Exploiter
Visionary/Practical
Warrior/Philosopher

Twelve Dangerous Don'ts

Based on the list originated by the Gouldings, I have included some of the things that people have said to me in the midst of *Voice Dialogue* sessions:

1. ***Don't Be Close.*** People can't be trusted. Don't let people get to know you, they might betray you. Don't reveal yourself, they may ridicule you. Don't let people in, they may hurt you. Your true self is un-loveable.

2. ***Don't Be A Child***. Take care of others. Don't have fun, don't play, don't experience or seek pleasure. Work hard, be strong, responsible and successful. Don't ever look foolish or stupid. If you feel weak, needy, sad or scared, don't let anyone know. Don't waste time or spend money on frivolous things.

3. ***Don't Be Important***. Don't draw attention to yourself. Don't expect too much. Don't show off. Don't speak up. Keep your head down. Don't assert yourself. Don't make demands. Be thankful for what you get. Don't ask for more. Don't have needs.

4. ***Don't Make It***. Don't be more successful than your parents. Don't show people up. Don't succeed, people only demand more.

5. ***Don't Grow Up***. Don't marry or form attachments to a potential life partner. Your loyalties and obligations are to your parents. Don't leave home or pursue your own life, we need you here.

6. ***Don't Be You***. Be who we expect you to be. We hoped you'd be a boy (or girl), now you have to make up for it. Don't develop the talents or interests we don't support or approve of. Chose the career we want for you. Marry the person we approve of.

7. ***Don't Be Well (Sane)***. We will only respond to you or give you attention when you are sick, in trouble or creating problems. We are dysfunctional, you should be too! Don't set limits on unhealthy demands. Don't develop boundaries for abusive, intrusive behavior.

8. ***Don't Belong***. We are better, holier, smarter or meaner, more alternative, eccentric, or "hip" than others. Don't associate with those who are not like us. Don't fit in or find a place in life. Don't join. Don't bond. Be odd. Feel like an outsider.

9. ***Don't Think.*** Don't figure things out. Think like we think. If it doesn't make sense, don't question, do it anyway. Be confused.

10. ***Don't Feel.*** Feel nothing, be numb. Feel what we feel. In this family, certain emotions (this varies with the family) are not allowed: fear, vulnerability, weakness, pride, sadness, anger, sexuality, happiness, joy, etc. People who feel those things are weak, bad or unlovable.

11. ***Don't Be (Exist).*** This theme runs in the underbelly of people who were not wanted at birth. They go to great lengths to justify their right to exist or engage in self-destructive behaviors.

12. ***Don't Do Anything.*** Everything in life is pointless or dangerous. Don't take risks, don't make an effort. Don't try, you might fail or make a fool of yourself. Don't hope, and don't dream, you will only be disappointed.

Multiple Personality and Dissociative Identity Disorder

Occasionally in my workshops and trainings someone will express humor or concern about how this work makes people sound like they have a "Split" personality or a Multiple Personality Disorder. To clarify the difference, I usually talk about how even normal people have "splits" in their personalities. We have all been raised with confusing messages, and we have all have strong emotions and unresolved inner conflicts that can cause us to act in ways where we are "not ourselves."

A Multiple Personality Disorder and other Dissociative Disorders are quite a bit further along the continuum. This diagnosis describes what happens when a protective function of the psyche creates strongly isolated compartments to contain experiences that were too traumatic to bear. Sometimes people deal with traumatic experiences by "leaving their bodies". This is called dissociation, and helps a person survive intolerable situations and overwhelming emotions that they are unable to handle at the time. The problem is that life stress and triggering reminders of these experiences can open up these compartments, overwhelming a person with the same internal chaos that originated from an experience that was never processed or healed. People with the serious clinical diagnosis of Dissociative Identity Disorder or Multiple Personality Disorder have a very difficult time establishing or maintaining an Observing Self, or a stable, "core" personality. They often have very self-hating, self-destructive Inner Characters that run away with them. There is no Inner Director to help them manage overwhelming emotions. They can suffer from amnesia, "waking up" in one personality, to find they cannot remember things that they have done in another. They often feel "unreal", as if they are floating outside of themselves. Staying in the body and in present time becomes difficult as strong emotions are stirred up.

276

If you have been diagnosed or suspect that you suffer from Dissociation, Multiple Personality Disorder, a Psychotic Disorder or Borderline Personality Disorder, the work in this book may open up too much material for you to process. As a therapist, the exercises contained here have been a significant cornerstone of healing for people with traumatic histories, but if you have this history or diagnosis, you should ***only undertake them if you are under the care of a qualified psychological professional.*** They can help keep you safe, in your body, and processing any traumatic memories and intense emotional states that may arise.

Archetypal Possibilities at our
Inner Round Tables or in the Shadows

Here is a list of possible characters that you may find within you. You can name them in your own creative way, but this gives you a starting place. In addition to this list, you may find that aspects of self are better described by animals, things in the natural world, or characters found in fairy tales, movies, books, mythology, and holy writings.

Jungian analyst, Toni Wolff, outlined four primary archetypes that women inhabit: Mother, Hetaira (Lover/Inspiritrice), Amazon, and Medial Woman (Wise Woman, Mystic, Saint). Jungian analyst Robert Moore has done a lot of work on Male Archetypes: King, Warrior, Lover and Sage/Magician. Also worth referencing are Jean Shinoda Bolen's wonderful work and typologies for both women and men based on the Greek Gods and Goddesses. Carol Pearson has identified 12 archetypes that appear to be central in most people's lives. Carolyn Myss has outlined an entire Gallery of Archetypes in Sacred Contracts.

Accountant	Avenger	Career Person
Achiever	Awkward Person	Caregiver
Activist	Beach Bum	Charmer
Actress	Benefactor	Cheater
Addict	Bitch	Child
Adulteress	Bitter one	-Frightened
Adventurer	Black Sheep	-Gullible
Advocate	Boring person	-Lost
Alcoholic	Bossy person	-Needy
Angel	Buddy	-Playful
Angry Person	Builder	-Sacred
Artist	Builder/Founder	-Sad
Ascetic	Bully/Bulldozer	-Shy
Authority	Brooding One	-Spoiled

Clinging Vine
Clown
Co-dependent
Companion
Compassionate one
Competent one
Competitor
Complainer
Condescending One
Conflict Avoider
Conservative
Controller
Counselor
Couch Potato
Courtesan
Crazy One
Creator
Critic
Crusader
Cynic
Daddy's Girl
Dancer
Daughter
-Rebel
-Adoring
-Daddy's Girl
-Dependent
-Dutiful
-Father's
-Good
-Mommy's Girl
-Obedient
-Princess

-Special
Dramatic One
Deceiver
Defender
Demanding One
Denier
Dependent One
Destroyer
Detached One
Detective
Diplomat
Doer
Doormat
Doubter
Dreamer
Earthy One
Eldress
Empath
Enchantress
Entitled One
Envious One
Executive
Facilitator
Fanatic
Father
-Abusive
-Cold
-God
-Loving
-Protector
-Provider
-Critical
Feeler

Femme Fatale
Flake
Flighty
Flirt
Fool
Forgiving One
Fragile One
Free spirit
Friend
Gardener
Gifted one
Giver
Gold digger
Gossip
Gracious one
Guide
Gullible one
Has Been
Healer
Healthy One
Helpless one
Helpmate
Heretic
Hermit
Heroine
Hippy
Homemaker
Hostess
Huntress
Hypocrite
Ice Princess
Idealist
Improviser

Inhibited One	Manipulator	Nun
Initiator	Martyr	Nurse
Innocent	Materialist	Nurturer
Innovator	Matriarch	Obsessive One
Insensitive Person	Mediator	Optimist
Inspiratrice	Mentor	Ordinary One
Intellectual	Mercenary	Organizer
Intercessor	Mercy shower	Orphan
Intimidator	Midwife	Outcast
Intruder	Miser	Outsider
Intuitive	Missionary	Partner
Jealous one	Misfit	Passed over one
Judgmental person	Mistress	Passive one
Keeper of the	Mother	Patriarch
hearth	-Abusive	Patron Saint
King	-Controlling	Peacemaker
-Wicked, Despot	-Critical	Perfectionist
-Wise, Benevolent	-Devoted	Persecutor
Klutz	-Devouring	Persuader
Know It All	-Good	Pessimist
Lady	-Nurturing	Philanthropist
Lazy one	-Rebel	Pilgrim
Leader	-Smothering	Pioneer
Liar	Mystic	Plain one
Liberator	Nag	Planner
Logical one	Narcissist	Pleaser
Lonely one	Nature Lover	Poet
Long Suffering One	Neat-nick	Politician
Lover	Needy one	Pouter
Madonna	Negotiator	Pragmatist
Maid	Networker	Predator
Magician	Nice person	Procrastinator
Manager	Non-conformist	Professor

Priest	Seeker	Stoic
Priestess	Seer	Secret Keeper
Princess	Selfish One	Strategizer
Problem Solver	Sensual One	Striver
Professional	Servant	Strong One
Promoter	-humble	Student
Proper One	-suffering	Stupid person
Prophet	Shopaholic	Supporter
Protector/Defender	Show off	Survivor
Prude	Shy person	Taker
Psychic	Sinner	Take charge
Pushover	Siren	Teacher
Queen	Sister	Tell it like it is
-Dark, wicked	Skeptic	Thinker
-Good, Benevolent	Slave	Tradition Keeper
Rage-aholic	Slob	Transformer
Rational one	Slouch	Translator
Realist	Sneak	Tyrant
Rebel	Snake	Victim
Rescuer	Social climber	Virgin
Responsible one	Soldier	Wanderer
Righteous One	Son	Warrior
Rude person	-Good Boy	Well Behaved One
Rule Maker	-Favored	Whiner
Rule Follower	-Heir	Whore
Ruthless One	-Loyal	Wicked Stepmother
Saboteur	-Prodigal	Widow
Sage	-Rebel	Wife
Saint	-Responsible	-Devoted
Scholar	Special One	-Dutiful
Score keeper	Spiritual person	-Long Suffering
Secretary	Spy	-Loving
Seductress/Seducer	Star	-Bride

-Schrew

-Nagging

-Betrayed

Winner

Wise Man

Witch

Woman:

-Behind the Man

-Emotional

-Feminist

-Jealous

-Liberated

-Old

-Proper

-Scorned

-Wild

-Wise

Worry Wart

Workhorse

RESOURCES

Chelsea Wakefield www.chelseawakefield.com
Emotional Freedom Technique www.eftuniverse.com
Gina Ogden www.ginaogden.com
Haden Institute www.HadenInstitute.com
International Association for the Study of Dreams www.asdreams.org
Jeremy Taylor www.jeremytaylor.com
Pesso Boyden Psychomotor www.pbsp.com
Robert Hoss www.dreamscience.org
Seedwork www.seedwork.org
The Somatic Experiencing Trauma Institute www.traumahealing.com
The Southeast Institute for Group and Family Therapy
    www.seinstitute.com
Voice Dialogue International www.delos-inc.com

INDEX

ABOUT THE AUTHOR

Chelsea Wakefield, Ph.D. (c), LCSW is psychotherapist, and dream worker who works with individuals, couples and groups. She has a master's degree in clinical Social Work, with additional training in Jungian psychology, dream work and several other innovative methods of psychotherapy. She is currently completing her Ph.D. with a dissertation researching archetypal aspects of sexuality.

In addition to her workshop, *Negotiating the Inner Peace Treaty™*, she is also the originator of *The Luminous Woman® Weekend*, a retreat in which women learn about *Archetypes of the Feminine* and *A Woman's Journey of Individuation*. Throughout the weekend, women explore their *Inner Cast of Characters* and return to their lives having embodied more of their deep wisdom, unique beauty and archetypal power.

When she is not working as a therapist, teaching, or facilitating workshops, she enjoys sharing family life with her husband and son. She loves reading, cooking, films, gathering friends for food and soul-sharing, and walking beaches and forests, contemplating the mystery of life and the beauty of creation.

Chelsea travels and is available for retreats, workshops and pilgrimages. To learn more about her and various program offerings, visit her website www.chelseawakefield.com, or email her at chelsea@chelseawakefield.com.

Milton Keynes UK
Ingram Content Group UK Ltd.
UKHW011417110424
440997UK00041B/269